THEOLOGY

and

SACRED SCRIPTURE

THEOLOGY
and
SACRED SCRIPTURE

Carol J. Dempsey
William P. Loewe

Editors

THE ANNUAL PUBLICATION
OF THE COLLEGE THEOLOGY SOCIETY
2001
VOLUME 47

ORBIS BOOKS

Maryknoll, New York 10545

Founded in 1970, Orbis Books endeavors to publish works that enlighten the mind, nourish the spirit, and challenge the conscience. The publishing arm of the Maryknoll Fathers & Brothers, Orbis seeks to explore the global dimensions of the Christian faith and mission, to invite dialogue with diverse cultures and religious traditions, and to serve the cause of reconciliation and peace. The books published reflect the views of their authors and do not represent the official position of the Maryknoll Society. To learn more about Maryknoll and Orbis Books, please visit our website at www.maryknoll.org.

Copyright © 2002 by the College Theology Society

Queries regarding rights and permissions should be addressed to: Orbis Books, P. O. Box 308, Maryknoll, New York 10545-0308.

Co-published by the College Theology Society and Orbis Books, Maryknoll, NY 10545-0308

Manufactured in the United States of America

Library of Congress Cataloging-in-Publication Data

Theology and sacred scripture / Carol J. Dempsey and William P. Loewe, editors.
    p. cm. — (The annual publication of the College Theology Society ; v. 47)
  ISBN 1-57075-411-X
  1. Bible—Evidences, authority, etc.   2. Theology, Doctrinal. 3. Bible—Theology.   I. Dempsey, Carol J. II. Loewe, William P., 1941-III. Series.
  BT89 .T47 2002
  230'.041–dc21

                        2002002873

Contents

BROADENING HORIZONS: SCRIPTURE
AND COMPARATIVE THEOLOGY

Acknowledgments

This volume would not have been possible without the efforts of many colleagues from the College Theology Society who have contributed so generously of their time and effort, gifts and talents. We, the editors of the 47th annual CTS volume, would like to express our appreciation to the 2001 CTS conference plenary speakers Francis X. Clooney, Diana L. Hayes, Amy-Jill Levine, and Kathleen M. O'Connor, and to Russell A. Butkus, Patricia McDonald, Maria Pascuzzi, Daniel Van Slyke, John Topel, Jason Bourgeois, Terrence W. Tilley, Regina A. Boisclair, and James M. Donohue, whose contributions appear in this volume. We would also like to acknowledge the University of Portland for the gracious hospitality of its administration, faculty, students, and staff.

We also must thank those CTS members who refereed the many excellent article submissions: William H. Bellinger, Jr. (CTS-NABPR, Baylor University), Joseph Capizzi (The Catholic University of America), Dennis Doyle (University of Dayton), Barbara Green (Dominican School of Philosophy and Theology at Berkeley), Frank Holland (St. John's University, New York), Alice L. Laffey (College of the Holy Cross), Patricia McDonald (Mount Saint Mary's College, Emmitsburg), Barbara Miller (Edgewood College), J. Edward Owens (St. John's Seminary, California), Peter Phan (The Catholic University of America), and Raymond Studzinski (The Catholic University of America).

We would be remiss if we did not thank Susan Perry, editor of Orbis Books, for her wonderful enthusiasm, her dedication, astute attention to detail, her superb expertise, and her robust patience and unflinching good humor that she offered throughout the entire project. Because of Sue's energy and persistence, we were able to complete this volume in a timely manner, with joy and delight.

Introduction

Carol J. Dempsey, OP and William P. Loewe

In its early years of conception and gradual maturity, sacred scripture was part of a larger discipline, theology, and part of a much larger agenda, theological studies. Then, slowly, it began to emerge as a discipline in its own right and became known as biblical studies—a multidimensional and interdisciplinary field that focused on and was informed by history, archaeology, the social sciences, and, most recently, literary, multi-cultural, and cross-gender studies, to name a few. Central to the study of the Bible is the rich dialogue that continues to take place among Jewish and Christian scholars within their respective traditions and across the traditions, which attests to a myriad of ways for approaching, appropriating, and listening to the biblical text, a text that was and continues to be a living text, a living tradition.

As sacred scripture began to take on a life of its own as a *bona fide* discipline and as theology as a sacred science began to move in its own various directions, the relationship of Bible to theology and theology to Bible became more distant and less defined, especially as Bible began to pursue its own theological agenda within an ancient historical context, and as theology sought to pursue its own necessary agenda, often in a more contemporary contextual setting.

With recent advances being made in the area of hermeneutics in both biblical studies and theology, and with both disciplines now bringing significant contributions to the table, it is time for the two disciplines to engage in a mutual dialogue that represents Bible being informed by theology and theology informed by Bible, with both disciplines making a joint contribution to the fields of liturgical-pastoral theology, spirituality, and finally, comparative theology.

This volume, entitled *Theology and Sacred Scripture*, attempts to bring together two scholarly fields in a way that shows the rich dialectic that exists between the two fields. It also tries to capture the thought and conversation of biblical scholars and theologians who can see and articulate the relationship of Bible to theology and vice versa, and the challenges that now face this new dynamic relationship.

Divided into six sections, the volume opens with three different perspectives on "The Particularity of Interpretation." In her essay entitled "Surviving the Storm in a Multi-Cultural World," Kathleen O'Connor offers, from a Christian perspective, a new reading of Acts 27, the account of Paul's shipwreck. She uses this narrative as a backdrop to place biblical studies and theology "in the same boat rather than in competition with one another." O'Connor raises a number of powerful and challenging questions that she addresses to biblical scholars and theologians alike. Embedded in her discussion and questions are elements capable of initiating a deep transformation in both fields, which, in turn, could have a life-giving and sustaining effect on all people.

In her essay, "A Particular Problem: Jewish Perspectives on Christian Bible Study," Amy-Jill Levine brings to the fore the relationship of Christianity and Judaism, which she asserts is "increasingly absent from scriptural and theological academic radar." Levine concludes that "theology informed by scripture and done in light of interfaith relations need not be a search for common ground. It may instead be an attempt to determine how we can, each on our own territory and with our own idiom, be good neighbors."

In response to biblical scholars O'Connor and Levine, systematic theologian Diana Hayes reflects on the ideas already presented and takes them a step further in her essay, "The Art of Interpretation: Contexts, Challenges, and Interconnections." Written from the perspective of a black Catholic theologian, Hayes notes that the points made by O'Connor and Levine are critical not only to "interfaith dialogue" but also to "*intra*faith dialogue." In her concluding comments, she asserts that "it is the theologian's task to be always conscious of the contextually foundational basis of scripture in her/his efforts to bring light, life, and hope to all by his/her God-talk; our God-talk tells not only of the God of Abraham, Isaac, and Jacob, but also of the God of Jesus who is the Christ."

These three essays set the stage for the contributions that follow and, in a sense, become the guiding light for the volume as a whole.

The second section of this volume, which focuses on "Scripture and Biblical Theology," features three essays. The first, "Creation-in-Crisis: Biblical Creation Theology and the Disclosure of God" by theologian Russell Butkus, examines various biblical texts from the Old Testament wisdom tradition and their relation to biblical creation theology. Butkus argues that biblical creation theology should be the starting place for theology, questioning the more traditional paradigm that places salvation history as the primary locus for beginning the biblical-theological conversation. Butkus's contribution challenges theologians to revisit the theme of revelation in light of this new biblical paradigm, which can have profound implications for theology, one's sacramental consciousness, and one's understanding of justice from a social and ecological perspective.

Following the thought of Butkus, in her essay, "From Malachi to Matthew: A Gift of the Tradition," biblical scholar Patricia McDonald examines the last part of the Old Testament and the first part of the New Testament. Her analysis leads her to conclude that "the world is sacramental," and, thus, revelation is broader than the biblical text and broader than the life of Jesus as attested to by the biblical text.

New Testament scholar Maria Pascuzzi moves readers further into New Testament literature. Her essay, "Paul the Enforcer: Using Rhetoric to Deconstruct an Image and to Reconstruct Theology," focuses in large part on 1 Corinthians 5. With this as a primary text, she argues that one can recover from scripture "valuable theological insights" that may have relevance for today and that community has a primary role within the enterprise of theology.

Building on the rich foundation of scripture and biblical theology, the third section of the volume focuses on "Scripture in Tradition." In his essay, "Is the End of the Empire the End of the World? Exegetical Traditions," Daniel Van Slyke draws us into the postbiblical world of Quodvultdeus, a fifth-century bishop of Carthage. In a chaotic age of civil wars and collapsing empire Quodvultdeus found meaning in apocalyptic. Van Slyke demonstrates how Quodvultdeus used two exegetical traditions originating in the pre-Constantinian church to wrest meaning from his situation for the church he led.

The fourth section of the volume considers "Scripture and Systematic Theology." The first essay by biblical scholar and theologian John

Topel addresses directly the relationship between Bible and systematic theology. It is aptly titled, "What Does Systematic Theology Say to New Testament Interpretation?" After focusing on the contributions that Bernard Lonergan has made to the conversation of theology, Topel uses Lonergan's thought and method as a starting point to demonstrate how one might do a systematic reading and interpretation of Paul's Letter to the Romans, with its focus on justification.

Jason Bourgeois deftly explicates the biblical hermeneutics of Hans Urs von Balthasar. In his essay on "Balthasar's Theodramatic Hermeneutics," Bourgeois demonstrates how, for Balthasar, modern historical-critical methods fall short of grasping *Die Sache* with which the biblical text is concerned. Scripture grasps us first of all through the imagination, so hermeneutics takes on an inescapably aesthetic dimension. It is only the religiously transformed imagination, animated by the Spirit's gift of the love of God, that is capable of discerning in scripture faith's witness to Christ as God's Word of self-revelation.

In his essay, " 'O Caesarea Philippi': On Starting Christology in the Right Place," Terrence Tilley questions the appropriate starting point for christology through his reflection on the Caesarea Philippi story in the Gospel of Mark (8:27 ff.). Tilley argues that while Peter may have used the correct title for Jesus in answering the question, "Who do you say that I am?," he misconstrued the nature of Christian discipleship. Tilley concludes that christology and discipleship are dialectically entwined: discipleship grasps christology, while christology narrates discipleship. Hence, Tilley joins Topel and Bourgeois in identifying the Christian imagination, tutored and shaped by the praxis of discipleship, as the ground from which christologies spring.

Moving from the conversation between scripture and systematic theology, the fifth section of the volume looks at the link between "Scripture and Liturgical-Pastoral Theology." Here, two essays are represented: the first by Regina Boisclair, "Conflicting Messages? The Sunday Lectionaries and Official Church Teachings," and the second by James Donohue, "The Choice and Function of Biblical Texts in the Post-Conciliar Rites for the Commendation of the Dying."

Boisclair's study acknowledges how "biblical scholarship has enriched every theological discipline for the past half-century," and notes how important it is "to consider how the scriptures are incorporated in Sunday worship." Substantiating the claim made by some scholars, namely, that contemporary three-year lectionaries include passages "that convey premises that have marked and marred Christian history with a teaching of contempt for Jews and Judaism," Boisclair examines what the Roman and revised common lectionaries have to say about the Pharisees in the Gospel of Matthew "in order to establish beyond question that there really is a problem."

Liturgical reform has proven a minefield of ecclesiastical conflict, and yet it is in liturgy that scripture is uniquely actualized. In his essay, "The Choice and Function of Biblical Texts in the Post-Conciliar Rites for the Commendation of the Dying," James M. Donohue traces the choice and function of biblical texts used in those rites, highlighting one key shift. Whereas the rite provided in the 1614 *Rituale Romanum* sought to alleviate the fear of judgment and damnation, post-conciliar versions focus instead on the fear of dying. Donohue also notes how exchanging modern biblical texts for the Vulgate have, in some instances, had unforeseen and not always positive consequences. His essay provides another reminder of the contextual character of both theology and liturgy.

Globalization frames the context for the reflection on Paul's experience of shipwreck with which this volume begins and it frames the concluding essay as well. The last section, "Broadening Horizons: Scripture and Comparative Theology," includes an essay by Francis X. Clooney that launches considerations of theology and sacred scripture on a new voyage. Once Christians come to regard their "other," the practitioners of the other world religions, as neighbor, a new horizon opens up. In "Theology and Sacred Scripture Reconsidered in Light of a Hindu Text," Clooney focuses on a Tamil sacred poem, which, in a process analogous to that operative in Christianity, has been received as canonical and has in turn engendered line-by-line commentaries as well as a more systematic body of theological literature. Clooney's meditative presentation unleashes the religious power of the poem and, through a series of cross readings with strategically chosen Christian texts, illustrates the potential of interreligious encounter to unleash new meaning.

THE PARTICULARITY
OF INTERPRETATION:
THREE PERSPECTIVES

Surviving the Storm
in a Multi-Cultural World

Kathleen M. O'Connor

Toward the end of the Acts of the Apostles (chapter 27), a shipwreck almost prevents Paul from arriving in Rome. Whatever the role of the journey in the book of the Acts, the account of the shipwreck serves as a symbolic narrative that both evokes our present global, multi-cultural contexts and challenges the common work of theology and biblical studies in the United States today. The text poses the problems of survival among groups with competing interests and loyalties and of how to negotiate interaction remaining firmly in possession of cultural and religious identity.

New Testament scholarship has often overlooked and underplayed the chapter. Some see it as merely a link in Paul's missionary journey to Rome, where he will fulfill the Lukan goal that the gospel be preached to the whole world. The dangerous voyage shows that nothing can hinder God's plan, but the journey itself matters primarily as a way to get Paul to the center of world power.[1] Or, in addition, the journey reveals that God declares Paul innocent of earlier charges against him because he survives it.[2]

Yet another view of the text is possible. My interpretation is influenced by Robert Tannehill's narrative study of Luke Acts[3] and by my location as a Euro-American and Roman Catholic. This essay has three parts: the story retold, reflections on survival, and questions for theology and biblical studies.

The Story Retold: The Shipwreck (Acts 27)

The narrative reason for Paul's journey to Rome is Paul's own demand, in relation to charges against him, for a hearing before the emperor's tribunal because he is a Roman citizen (Acts 26:32, 25:10).

On board the ship headed for Rome is an international cast of characters. They are multi-ethnic, multi-religious, and drawn from different classes within the Roman Empire.

They include Paul and some other prisoners, perhaps Jewish and Jewish Christian—the "we" who narrate the story. They are placed in the custody of a Roman centurion named Julius. They all embark upon a ship in Adramyttium, probably occupied by sailors and passengers from around the Mediterranean. With Julius are soldiers of the Augustan cohort, from Rome and probably the provinces. A Macedonian named Aristarchus also accompanies them. At Myra, they change to an Alexandrian ship (27:6), presumably crewed by sailors from Egypt and other African parts and perhaps from various Mediterranean ports. The story's characters represent the whole Roman world.

A storm, almost a character itself, propels events in the narrative. Shortly after the voyage begins, Julius the centurion treats the prisoner Paul kindly, even allowing Paul to visit friends at one of their ports of call (Sidon). This relationship will be crucial for the story. As the global party sets sail, they have difficulty with the wind "because the winds were against us" (27:4). They sail safely under the lee of Crete but with increasing difficulty and come to Fair Havens. Sailing is now dangerous because of the time of the year.

Paul advises his shipmates: "I can see the voyage will be with danger and much heavy loss, not only of cargo and ship but of our lives" (27:10). The centurion, however, does not listen to Paul but pays more attention to the views of his peers, the ship's pilot, and owner (27:11). And, it turns out, Fair Havens is not actually a fair haven, so they put out to sea again on the chance they might somehow reach Phoenix.

As they set sail past Crete, a moderate south wind soon becomes a violent northeaster, and they can barely keep the boat under control. To try to maintain control, they undergird the ship and, fearing to run aground, lower the sea anchor (a device that enables steering). The storm drives them onward. The narrator reports, "We were being pounded by the storm so violently that on the next day they began to throw cargo overboard" (27:18), and on the third day they cast off the ship's tackle. The tackle is not fishing equipment but anything used to run the ship that is not nailed down. Neither sun nor stars appeared for days. A great tempest raged. "All hope of our being saved was at last abandoned" (v. 20).

In the midst of despair, Paul stands up and says in effect, "I told you so," but then he revises his own prediction and his short speech foreshadows the ship's fate.

> "I urge you now to keep up your courage, for there will be no loss of life among you but only of the ship. For last night there stood by me an angel of the God to whom I belong and whom I worship, and he said, 'Do not be afraid, Paul, you must stand before the emperor; and, indeed, God has granted safety to all those who are sailing with you.' So keep up your courage, men, for I have faith in God that it will be exactly as I have been told. But we will have to run aground on some island." (27:22-26)

There is no response to Paul's speech. On the fourteenth night, the ship drifts, sailors take soundings and fear rocks. During the night, under a pretext of putting out anchors, the sailors try to escape the ship, but Paul notices and warns Julius and the soldiers, "Unless these men stay in the ship, you cannot be saved" (27:31). The soldiers cut the ropes and manage to keep the sailors on board.

The people on board the imperiled ship have been without food for fourteen days. At dawn Paul urges them to eat to help them survive. "He took bread; and giving thanks to God in the presence of all, he broke it and began to eat. Then all of them were encouraged and took food for themselves" (27:35). Then they throw the remaining wheat into the sea.

In the morning they see land and plan to run the ship ashore. Instead, they strike a reef, run aground, as violent, pounding waves begin to break up the ship. At this point, the soldiers plan to kill the prisoners so none will swim away and escape. But Julius wants to save Paul. He orders those who can to swim ashore and others to follow on planks and pieces of the ship. "And so it was that all were brought safely to land" (27:44b).

Reflections on Survival

Rather than reflecting on how biblical studies and theology interact with each other, as the title of the book—*Theology and Sacred
Scripture*—suggests, I want to focus on how the two disciplines together look toward the crises of our world. I place theology and biblical studies in the same boat rather than in competition with one another in relation to our present multi-cultural and multi-religious
situation. I am interested in how we look together toward the world
rather than in our internal disputes. The shipwreck in Acts conjures up
elements of our situation and possible responses to it, and it challenges
assumptions of our common work.

Representatives of the whole known world are on board a ship about
to perish. I declare the ship to be a metaphor of our world, our culture,
our religious institutions, and of theological and biblical studies at the
beginning of the millennium.

Imperilment of the Ship

The situation is grave and both the ship and all on board are in
danger of perishing. The storm builds slowly, becoming increasingly
violent and death-dealing, but the greater threats to the ship come from
within. These include:

— the inability of Julius, the one in power, to hear the warning
   voice and wisdom of the prisoner; his preference is for his natural allies of pilot and owner who want to make money;
— the self-serving actions of the sailors who want to save themselves alone;
— the limited vision of the soldiers who want to kill the prisoners
   in an act of duty to the empire;
— and the despair that takes hold of those on board ship.

Responses to the Crisis

The passengers on board ship survive because of a number of life-
giving actions. They have the courage to throw overboard even things
they think they need to survive. Some among them have a vision of
the common good. Some among them form relationships across group
lines that enable them to lead others to work together for the good of

all. Finally, Paul draws upon his own cultural identity and religious experience to find strength to support his vision of the common good.

Relinquishment. For survival to occur, the passengers must throw things overboard: the cargo, the ship's tackle, the remaining wheat. By pitching over the cargo, they abandon the rich profits awaiting them in Rome. By casting off the tackle, they abandon all elements of the ship's structure that can be unlashed from the decks. By throwing over the wheat, they relinquish future nourishment. Finally, they must abandon even the ship itself. To survive, they must relinquish everything upon which survival normally depends.

A Vision of Solidarity. Besides relinquishing goods, nourishment, and the seeming safety of the ship, survival requires a vision of the good of the whole, a vision held only by the prisoner Paul and later by Julius. But circumstances force all the occupants of the ship to work together, even if unwillingly, for the sake of their survival. No group can survive without the other. For survival to occur, everyone must work for the good of all. For survival to occur, people must recognize the networks of relationships that connect their fates. For survival to occur, people need the capacity to listen to other voices and to form alliances across divides of various kinds.

Embracing One's Identity. Yet in this story, the relinquishment of old structures and goods and the possession of a vision of solidarity for the sake of survival, does not mean the relinquishment of one's cultural and religious identity. In this story Paul is not on the way to Rome merely to *preach* the gospel to the whole world. Instead, he *enacts* the Lukan theme that the gospel will be spread to the whole world, and he does so in a manner different from his previous characterization in Acts. He does not carry on in long speeches. He does not demand from his hearers assent to or acceptance of his God and his message. He changes from being a proclaimer of the gospel in Acts to becoming a quieter observer, commentator, and encourager. In the story of the shipwreck, he *enacts* more than he speaks the gospel.

Paul is a prisoner here, not a figure of power, though he still enjoys class privilege by virtue of his Roman citizenship. He even changes his mind from his first dire prediction of death, learning as events unfold. When he speaks the second time, he is certain of his position gained from his own experience. When he tells his shipmates that they should have listened to him, he at first seems arrogant, but instead, he is "drinking deeply from his own well," to adapt a phrase from Gutiérrez.[4]

Paul's authority in this story arises from his personal revelatory experience and from the depths of his own cultural and religious identity. From that identity alone, he is able to motivate and lead others on the ship. He demands no affirmation or agreement from them and receives none. When all seems utterly hopeless, he quietly practices Eucharist. Conzelmann,[5] Dibelius,[6] and Talbert[7] deny that the meal is a Eucharist because it does not seem to be communal and the participants are not believers. But anyone who has read Luke-Acts straight through[8] or is Roman Catholic recognizes the language as clearly eucharistic (Lk 9:16; 24:30). "He took bread, and giving thanks [eucharistesen] to God in the presence of all, he broke it and began to eat it" (27:35).

Paul encourages the others and urges them to eat, and they take nourishment. Is it the same food? Are they eating from the same table? Are they participating in Eucharist? Exact components of the meal are not clear, but the meal marks a turning point in the story and, for the first time, hope counters despair. But Paul's steadfast loyalty to his cultural identity, his faith, his own tradition, and his God becomes the resource from which hope emerges and out of which the story moves forward.

Forming Friendships. Paul forms links across the divide between Jewish prisoner and Roman captor, between the colonized and the colonizer. He befriends or at least gains the respect of Julius, the Roman centurion, and that alliance, undoubtedly based on bonds of class and citizenship, will be the salvation of all. Paul does not rescue the ship; "Christianity" does not rescue the ship. Salvation of the whole world on board the ship does not depend on accepting Jesus Christ.

Cooperation alone, after multiple miscommunications, struggles, and conflicts, enables all on board to come "safely to land" (27:44). In this narrative Paul is not trying to convert the others but to join them, to save them, and to save himself. The story of the sinking ship "becomes a sign in miniature of God's promise of salvation for all flesh,"[9] but the terms of that salvation do not require conversion to Paul's belief. Paul's God plans to save everyone on board ship.

Questions for Biblical Studies and Theology

The shipwreck story is a suggestive symbolic narrative that enacts Lukan goals to preach the gospel to all nations and signifies God's plan to save all peoples, whether they are believers or not. At issue is the survival of the world. In our world where 80 percent of the people around the globe and some within the United States live immensely onerous lives and some barely subsist, the context of our work suggests we are on board an imperiled ship. The September 11 attacks upon the World Trade Center and the Pentagon, upon civilians on our own shores, add to this impression. Our world is becoming one, but differences of faith, of culture and, above all, of economic resources, rather than enriching human life for all, imperil everyone.

I belong, though in complex ways, within the dominant Euro-American culture of the United States. I believe that theologians working in this context might first read the story of the shipwreck, not by identifying with Paul, the colonized, the prisoner, and the disrupter of empire, but with the colonizing empire in its fractiousness, self-serving actions, and violent destructiveness.

To save life, to save ourselves, and for all the people to be saved, what must we throw overboard? As theologians, must we lose the cargo, the tackle, and the ship as well that all may survive? Can we relinquish the trappings of privilege, the profit motive, the self-centered maneuverings, and the violence of this culture in relation to the poor nations of the two-thirds world and the poor among us, the racial and cultural other, to immigrants and refugees? Can we critique injustices more passionately, more convincingly? Can we create public theologies that seek more than our own class and national well-being—that instead seek the salvation of the world?

Can we relinquish Euro-centered male theologies that too often encode and support our present world, either by leaving too much out or by implicitly affirming violence, individualism, and arrogance? Can we make more room for theological re-visioning that seeks the well-being of all, that draws upon the resources and voices of all, that respects the cultural and religious identity of all? Can we teach in such a way that we stop reproducing students who assume privilege, power, and the truth as their birthright?

The story of the shipwreck offers a dynamic of survival from the side of the empire. The dynamic is simple. Julius befriends Paul. The Roman centurion cares for and collaborates with the Jew; the colonizer learns from the colonized. The relationship is asymmetrical, as relationships always are in cross-cultural and cross-religious conversations,[10] but the powerful one eventually learns from the one with no power, except for the life-saving power of his truth, his tradition, his culture, his experience, and his faith. The centurion changes; he is finally able to hear Paul and accept his analysis of the situation. Julius's change of heart, his friendship with Paul, and his actions save the ship.

Can we in the dominant culture hear the voices of the other, the outsider, the powerless, the different? Can we hear and receive their analyses of our collective situation? We need their voices not merely for political advantage or for the sake of inclusion; we need them for the salvation of the planet and for our own humanity. Can we seek mutual relationships, form friendships, and engage in strong colleagueship with cultural and religious others? Perhaps, the "others" need our friendship but we most surely need theirs. We need them for their fidelity, their courage, and for their suffering to which we contribute and from which we benefit in complex ways. We need them for their faith and for the power of their cultural traditions. We need them because we live side by side with them. We need them because they call us to conversion, because they bring us truth, and because they give us hope.

Canadian theologian Douglas John Hall proposes that "covert" despair characterizes North American culture.[11] Our despair is hidden, anesthetized by our wealth, power, and frenzy, and it is to be distinguished from the conditions of the poor and afflicted who acknowledge the desperation in which they may find themselves. Can we face our own corporate despair? Our despair endangers the world for it fuels destructive, self-serving behavior.

If, like those on board the Lukan ship, despair threatens us, then theology must address it and feed our broken spirits. Can we offer our students what Dorothee Soelle calls a "hermeneutics of hunger" to accompany our hermeneutics of suspicion?[12] Can we face ourselves first so that we can mobilize our passions for the works of justice or praise?

Finally, we Christians are, of course, direct inheritors of Paul's legacy. Identifying with him calls us into a world of new relationships of multiplicity and diversity. He relates to others on board with uncharacteristic restraint. He is respectful and non-coercive. He lives out of his own unfolding identity. He forms alliances. One of the dangers in cross-cultural and inter-religious relationships is to abandon one's identity either from guilt—usually a paralyzing response—or from the profound attraction of other cultural worlds in comparison to one's own. When that happens, no one benefits. Paul's courage comes from possession of his own experience, his own culture, his own God.

Paul rejoices in his difference, celebrates his eucharistic ritual, encourages his shipmates from his own experience but in this story, at least, he does not demand that others become like him. His concern is the salvation of the world, not the promotion of his newly growing movement, his religious rituals, or his institutions. Can we teach in such a way that our students learn to hold fast to their cultural identities, their experiences, their faith, their tradition, and their God, and in the process be open to the voices and lives of the others for the sake of all on board ship? Friends and resources for the task are all around us.

Notes

[1]Hans Conzelmann, *Acts of the Apostles*, Hermeneia (Philadelphia: Fortress Press, 1987), 213-21.

[2]Charles H. Talbert, *Reading Acts: A Literary and Theological Commentary on the Acts of the Apostles* (New York: Crossroad, 1997), 215-25.

[3]Robert C. Tannehill, *The Narrative Unity of Luke-Acts: A Literary Interpretation*, vol. 2 (Minneapolis: Fortress Press, 1990), 330-43.

[4]Gustavo Gutiérrez, *We Drink from Our Own Wells* (Maryknoll: Orbis Books, 1983).

[5]Conzelmann, *Acts of the Apostles*, 220.

[6]Martin Dibelius, *Studies in the Acts of the Apostles* (London: SCM Press, 1956), 205.

[7]Talbert, *Reading Acts*, 219.

[8]Tannehill, *The Narrative Unity of Luke-Acts*, 335.

[9]Ibid., 337.

[10]Carlos F. Cardoza Orlandi, "Walking the Tightrope," in *Mission: An Essential Guide* (Nashville: Abingdon Press, forthcoming).

[11]Douglas John Hall, "Despair as Pervasive Ailment," in *Hope for the World: Mission in a Global Context*, ed. Walter Brueggemann (Louisville: Westminster/John Knox, 2001), 83-93.

[12]Dorothee Soelle, *The Silent Cry: Mysticism and Resistance* (Minneapolis: Fortress Press, 2001), 45-49.

A Particular Problem:
Jewish Perspectives on Christian Bible Study

Amy-Jill Levine

The past several decades have witnessed numerous new claimants for the attention of Christian academic, cleric, and lay communities. As the foci of theology, history, liturgy, pastoral care, ethics, and biblical interpretation all expand beyond white, Western, elitist, heterosexist, masculinist . . . paradigms, the myopia of hegemonic models is corrected, and this is all to the good. The occasional speck of identity politics may briefly cloud hermeneutical vision, but whatever tears (pronounced as you will) it brings can themselves serve to sharpen sight.

However, one priority does, and should, remain at least for this particular gathering, the College Theology Society[1]: that is the priority of Christianity—defined as you will—itself. The question becomes then how the Christian theologian maintains this priority without sinking either into an insidious triumphalism on the one hand or a watered-down relativism on the other. I am particularly interested in delineating models of Christian theology grounded in scripture (increasingly rare though these may be) that stand together with competing truth claims rather than dismissing or disparaging them. That is, I believe that the Christian *kerygma* can stand on its own without an attendant need to show how it is "better" than or the "fulfillment of" the proclamations of other traditions. My own concern is one that, perhaps especially given the globalization of Christian discourse, is increasingly absent from scriptural and theological academic radar: the relationship of Christianity to Judaism.

Anti-Judaism continues to appear in meditation guides, homilies, Christian feminist biblical interpretation, liberation theologies, etc.[2] The problem, as I see it, centers less in the biblical text itself (although in my view it bears some culpability; I do not go as far as my self-proclaimed post-modern friends who would locate the source of meaning only with the reader[3]); it lies with editors and presses that continue to print this drivel and with consumers, especially those of us in the academy—i.e., those of us who should know better—who remain silent or, worse, recommend the material to students and congregants and then fail to comment on the problems.

Tragic as well: many of us don't know better. Like sexism, anti-Judaism is often ideologically hard-wired into Christian culture. Most scholars of Christian origins or Christian theology lack expertise in Jewish sources. Too few have read the Mishnah let alone selections from the Gemarah or the Midrashim. Too few took courses on, or even had the opportunity to take courses on, first-century Judaisms (let alone on any of the Judaisms since then). Too few have ever met, let alone worked with, a Jew. While in today's New Testament and theology classrooms, readings by women and by non-Western writers are expected, students rarely note whether there are Jewish sources, or sources by Jews (save for the one Pharisee from whom we have any writing: Paul). Judaism thus threatens to become in students' perceptions a combination of stereotype and negativity: Levitical legalism and Pharisaic hypocrisy. Some historical house-cleaning is in order.

Now, there are those in the guilds, both biblical and theological, who view history as a fully blighted discipline; there are even those who would claim that historical-critical approaches—approaches that in fact broke the ecclesial stranglehold on biblical interpretation (this is, by the way, an historical observation)—are only, *only*, problems to be overcome. Without some history, the anti-Jewish miasma of Christian teaching will only spread farther. Further, I doubt good, sustainable, comprehensible theology or theological instruction can be based on bad history, or on no history at all.

Coupled with questions of history are questions of perspective. Matters look different, given differing social locations, and a minor point for one group may be major to another. Many liberal Baptists dismissed the comment, made over a decade ago, by the erstwhile president of the Southern Baptist Convention, Bailey Smith, that "G-d does not hear the prayers of the Jews." They saw it as hyperbole for which Smith was known and, since they thought it ridiculous, did not comment. Yet we Jews remember; the statement for many of us remains an open wound.[4] For a more recent example: during Pope John Paul II's visit to his country this year, Syrian President Assad publicly insisted that not only did the Jews kill Jesus, they also—here adding to Islamic tradition—threatened the life of Mohammed. For many American Jews, the problem here was less what Assad said than what John Paul II did not say. I do understand that the pope does not depart from prepared remarks and that, as Philip Cunningham reminded me, he had already on this trip to the Middle East urged leaders in the area to be responsible for promoting interreligious respect (a petition Assad obviously failed to heed). There were also some pertinent remarks in the papal "Regina Coeli" prayer about a week later. The Vatican's position would seem to be that Dr. Assad is not a credible spokesperson for Christian teaching.

Yes, we in the West have heard the pope make numerous, heartfelt pleas concerning positive relations between church and synagogue. But has the Muslim world heard these comments, or will too many in Assad's audience have their own prejudices concerning Jewish violence confirmed by the pope's silence. Indeed, have Roman Catholics throughout the Middle East heard the pope's statements about Judaism proclaimed? Then again, given the setting of Assad's remarks, what would John Paul II say, when, and to whom? I can easily name the problem; locating the solution in this case is infinitely more difficult.

We all have failed to act or to speak out when we should have, and we all carry terrible baggage. We Jews, for example, have not been as proactive as we should when Catholic-bashing occurs, and it does occur. Moreover, as a Jew, I am repelled by my scriptures that command genocide and appalled by those fundamentalists who would appeal to those scriptures in the attempt to extend the borders of Israel. I condemn those who, claiming "sanctification of the Name," enjoin murder, from Rabin, to the worshipers in the Hebron mosque, to the most recent atrocities in the Middle East of which no group—Jewish, Christian, or Muslim—can wash its hands and proclaim itself innocent and in which, for each case, scripture becomes yet another rock to be thrown.

But, back to the question of anti-Judaism in Christian proclamation: I am not desiring of or even interested in Christians today "apologizing" for the problems prompted by New Testament texts or for the sins of their forebears, either by commission or omission. Instead, I am interested in encouraging new views of scripture and theology that recognize both what church and synagogue share and that do not hesitate to honor the differences.

Jewish-Christian relations are getting better, but there's much left for us all to do. On the encouraging side: in September 2000, over two hundred and fifty rabbis (notice that the term is not "Jewish" rabbi—that would be a tautology, like hot-water heater) and Jewish professors including myself signed a statement called *Dabru Emet* (Speak Truth), in which we expressed the extent of the rapprochement synagogue and church overall have obtained. Even better: the major reason we were able to make such an overture is because of the good will and understanding expressed toward us by numerous Christian groups—the Vatican being at the forefront.

Nevertheless, these are several areas where more theological attention is needed for the purposes of avoiding both triumphalism and dilution and of aiding mutual understanding. Here are three that I, from the perspective of biblical studies, find among the most pressing:

- I suggest we all pay more attention to the distinctions between the canons of church and synagogue, and reconsider the terminology we use for those texts. *Dabru Emet* noted that Jews and Christians seek authority from the same book. Although I signed the statement because its benefits outweighed my concerns, this is one point to which I do not subscribe: I do not think we are reading the same scripture.
- I suggest we be more critical when we appeal to history to contextualize the problematic material in the New Testament. Too often we explain away those potentially anti-Jewish materials, or ignore them entirely, or fail to note how they might sound to non-Christian ears, rather than confront them.
- I suggest we be more precise when we speak of Jesus the Jew. And thus, I suggest churches stop celebrating Jewish holidays such as Passover and Hannukah to recover their connection to Jesus. Let Christians be Christians and Jews—like Jesus—be Jews.

Canonical Distinctions

There's been a move in interfaith circles to speak not of the "Old Testament" but of the "Hebrew Scriptures" or "First Testament" or even "Jewish Scriptures." For a while, I was on the "Hebrew Scriptures" bandwagon; I found "Old Testament" marginalizing at best, and often demeaning.[5] I've since changed my mind:

"Hebrew Scriptures" is wrong for several reasons:

- The canons of some churches are based on the LXX, not the Hebrew.
- The majority of us in the United States and Canada are reading not the Hebrew, but English translations (as well as, given the role of globalization, numerous other translations). Students on more than one campus have been flummoxed by catalogues listing "Hebrew Bible," since they presume that foreign-language fluency is requisite.
- If the point is interfaith sensitivity, "Hebrew" does not mean "Jewish."[6]
- We also don't use the linguistic equivalent—Greek Scriptures—for the New Testament.
- The analogous term, "Christian Scriptures," eliminates the first part of the church's canon and so gives Marcion a belated victory.
- The term "Hebrew Scriptures" may even smack of Protestant imperialism: Catholic and Orthodox traditions also include the Deuterocanonical (Old Testament Apocryphal) materials in their list of pre-New Testament Scripture, and these texts are preserved in and translated from the Greek.
- As for "First Testament," the term presupposes that there's a second, and perhaps a third. This does Jews no good, and it winds up selling short most of Christianity (save for those who hold the Book of Mormon as another testament). The central scripture of the church is the story of Jesus; it may come second in what is called salvation history, but it is primary for the church.
- And as for "Jewish Scriptures": this makes the material sound as if it belongs only to the synagogue and not to the church. It also, implicitly, equates Judaism and the scripture, such that naïve hearers gain the impression that Judaism stops at Leviticus. Furthermore, "Jewish Scriptures" sometimes plays directly into the conceits of those who seek negatively to categorize Judaism. In biblical studies one frequently reads about "Jewish purity rules" and then finds citations to Leviticus, but never have I seen references to the "Jewish ten commandments." Too often, the "Jewish" part of the "Jewish Scriptures" winds up being everything the gentile church dismissed.

If we want to talk about the Bible of Judaism, we should use the term Jews use, the Tanach. In other words, the church should not sacrifice its own theology on the altar of interfaith dialogue. For the church, the earlier material is the "Old Testament"—but what is old can certainly be treasured. Frankly, little Christian children do not begin catechetical education thinking that the "Old Testament" is somehow worth less than the New: it's the Old that has most of the stories found in children's Bibles: the elephants and kanga-roosies, roosies going onto the ark two by twosies, Joseph and the Amazing Technicolor Dream Coat, the "Prince of Egypt" (even if the title never actually appears in the text). In many churches, during the reading of the "Old Testament" one mercifully (from the perspective of numerous children and, I suspect, quite a few adults) gets to remain seated. Disparaging the "Old Testament" is something one learns; the problem arises not because of the term "old" but because of the treatment the material receives in lectionaries, homilies, liturgical practice, and even some theologies.

Distinct terms also acknowledge that we are not telling the same story. The Christian narrative's first part ends with Malachi's prediction of Elijah's return. Part two picks up with John the Baptist and Jesus. Thus, the Old finds its fulfillment in the New. In turn, the New tells us how to read the Old: Adam finds his correction in the Christ (Romans 5), Jesus fulfills prophesy, those who persevere regain Eden (Revelation 2-3).[7]

This is not Judaism's canonical story. The Tanach (not just in present-day editions but according to a *Baraita* in *B. Bat.* 14b) ends not with Malachi, but—at least in modern versions—with 2 Chronicles 36: "In fulfillment of the word of the Lord spoken by Jeremiah, the Lord stirred up the spirit of King Cyrus of Persia, so that he sent a herald throughout all his kingdom, and also declared in a written edict: '. . . the Lord, the G-d of heaven, has given me all the kingdoms of the earth, and he has charged me to build him a house at Jerusalem, which is in Judah. Whoever is among you of all his people, may the Lord his G-d be with him! Let him go up.' " Our story's *telos* is to make *aliyah*, to come home. In the Tiberian manuscript tradition dating from the turn of the first millennium (on the Christian calendar, of course), Leningradensis and Aleppensis end with Nehemiah 13:31b: "Remember me, O my G-d, for the good." The repetition of the terms *Elo[k]im* and *tov* echo Genesis—for the canon insists through this frame that all creation is good, and all creation is watched over by a caring G-d of remembrance. The two endings complement each other—and neither needs a new story in order for the text to be complete.[8]

Explaining Anti-Judaism

Jesus was a Jew and his words, spoken to Second-Temple Galilean and Judean Jews in their own idiom, resonate with prophetic voice: demands for repentance, calls for social justice and a renewed attitude toward worship, historical urgency coupled with the conviction of divine righteousness. But his legacy has been preserved by the church, and his words are placed in a Christian canon. Our problem is less the legacy itself than what the heirs have done with it as they proclaimed to "the Jews" (*Ioudaioi*): "You are from your father the devil, and you choose to do your father's desires" (John 8:44), and described "the Jews" and those "who killed both the Lord Jesus and the prophets and drove us out; they displease G-d and oppose everyone . . . they have constantly been filling up the measure of their sins; but G-d's wrath has overtaken them at last" (1 Thess 2:14b-16). *If* we read these words to our classes (a big "if"—some professors ignore them; some prefer not to raise problems; some don't see them as problems), and there is no reaction from the students, something is wrong. It is wrong with the students, the text, and with us.

These texts should be studied, and for the sake of Jewish-Christian relations they should be studied by Jews and Christians together: Christians need to recognize the impact that these verses have on Jews as well as on their own attitude toward Jews. In turn, Jews should be aware that most Christians do not consciously read the texts anti-Jewishly. And academics should not be so quick to appeal to history to explain problematic biblical passages.[9]

We have claimed that because the gospels are Jewish documents or examples of in-house polemic, they cannot be anti-Jewish. The argument is slippery: we do not know the communities to which the texts were written, although we do know that those communities, even if not originally gentile, became gentile very quickly.

We have insisted that the gospels' depictions of Jewish characters are not specific; Jews rather serve as representatives of everyone. However, Buddhists and Bahais, Mexicans and Kenyans, have not been persecuted for killing Jesus.

We have noted it conventional to imprecate one's enemies and asserted that Matthew and John's harsh language is no different from that of Amos or Isaiah. The comparison is false: Isaiah wrote to and his words were preserved by Jews; Matthew and John write to groups unknown but with some gentile component, and their words were preserved by the church. Moreover, Isaiah is prophecy, but Matthew and John are narratives in which the narrator as well as the main character condemn those who don't follow the Christian model, and in which the Jews are depicted as killing the main character.

As for Paul's language: we scholars have argued that it is an interpolation. While the point is not without some merit, it should not be used to suggest that the verse is no longer problematic. Whether by Paul or written in his name, it is in the canon.

We also need to consider who makes the judgment as to whether a text is anti-Jewish. Even the formulation of the question is ultimately unhelpful. Both those who see it as anti-Jewish and those who do not are right. The same text, read through different eyes, can be seen as liberating or constraining, and that is why we need to read together.

And we need to look at all texts, not just the obvious candidates. Even passages typically hailed as liberating can have a negative resonance.

For example, there is the well-known Galatians 3:28. Many among Paul's gentile audience may have welcomed news of the elimination of ethnic distinctions. I, however, am not a Galatian gentile eagerly anticipating circumcision. I am a post-*Shoah* Jew, and in this verse I hear an erasing of my religion and ethnic identity. To put this as provocatively as possible—Hitler and Galatians 3:28 have a great deal in common: they both seek to erase Jews as Jews.

Second is the so-called model of interfaith theology, Romans 11. Yes, we could celebrate Paul's point that "if you [gentiles] have been cut from what is by nature a wild olive tree and grafted, contrary to nature, into a cultivated olive tree, how much more will these natural branches [the Jews] be grafted back . . ."(11:24). But it is faint praise to be called "enemies of G-d for your sake" (11:28) or to be seen as temporarily cut off from true Israel, especially since this pruning has now lasted for two thousand years.

Finally, an example that surfaced this past Thanksgiving. My rabbi called to ask if I had any concerns about a gospel reading proposed by a clergy colleague for an interfaith celebration. The reading was

Matthew 6:25 and following. "Therefore, I tell you: do not worry about your life, what you will eat or what you will drink, or about your body, what you will wear. . . ." When Jesus said this to fellow Jews— and I suspect he did say it—he made perfect sense. His audience saw his fringes; they knew he kept the dietary regulations, so they were able to focus on the underlying point. But what happens when the same words are proclaimed by a Christian minister in an interfaith gathering, where there are Jews with *kippot* and *tzitzit*, Jews who observe Kashrut, Jews who do care about what we wear and what we eat?

Jesus the Jew and the Celebration of Particularism

This observation about Jesus' religious praxis leads to the final point: precision in speaking of Jesus the Jew. Christians sensitive to interfaith issues emphasize that Jesus was a Jew, and this is a good thing. The problem arises when that identification remains unexplored, because congregants—and far too many clergy and academics—have little idea what this label entails.

If we want to give the term "Jew" content, we might look at what Jesus and his followers do *as Jews*: keep the Sabbath; worship in the Temple in Jerusalem and participate in the activities of local synagogues; keep their bodies holy and their focus continually on the *Mitzvot* through special clothing, dietary regulations, and ritual immersions. The center of their lives, theologically and communally, was love of G-d and love of neighbor—as Deuteronomy and Leviticus already note.

However, diversity within Judaism, over time as well as within a single setting, also needs to be acknowledged. Thus, Jesus should be contextualized within a quite heterogeneous setting rather than seen as docetically unique amid a monolithic culture. Moreover, looking at diversity within Judaism diachronically as well as synchronically, I find generally unhelpful those theological moves that see the crucified Jesus as suffering with his Jewish brothers and sisters at Auschwitz or those curricula moves in liberal seminaries and divinity schools that regard the study of the *Shoah* as fulfilling a "Judaica" or "non-Christian religion" or "interfaith dialogue" diversity requirement. The association of "Judaism" primarily with Auschwitz ignores Jewish cultural and religious identification in favor of a reified ethnic one (i.e., the model is Hitler's, not Judaism's). The image of Jews conveyed to students and congregants should not be one of victimization.

I have frequently remarked that in the attempt to eliminate anti-Jewish attitudes among my divinity students, I bring my son to class; he's now eleven, and he studies at Nashville's Orthodox Day School. I place this adorable little boy, in *kippah* and *tzitzit*, before the class, and say: "Whenever you speak of 'Jews' or 'Pharisees,' picture this kid in the front pew. Don't say anything that would hurt this child, and don't say anything that would cause a member of your congregation to hurt this child." It's theatrical; it's manipulative; it works. It is also, in my view, preferable to showing photos of concentration camp victims in the effort to warn against Christian anti-Judaism.[10] As *Dabru Emet* states, National Socialism was not a Christian phenomenon (although church teachings and church members often abetted it). I'd like to respect the victims: to use their corpses as an educational tool is quite possibly obscene. Finally, I want to stress what my students can do, not what others did.

Nor are recent evocations of the canonized Sister Teresa Benedicta of the Cross, otherwise known as Edith Stein, of much help in the understanding of Judaism or of fostering Jewish-Christian relations. Like Jesus, Edith Stein has two contextualizations: the former is both Galilean Jew and the second person of the Trinity; the latter is both Jewish daughter and Carmelite sister. Rather than erase the distinctions, perhaps interfaith relations would progress if we acknowledged them instead.

It is Jesus who is Jewish, not the divine Christ, a point theological development promulgated in terms of interfaith relations sometimes unfortunately ignores. For example, some theological circles stress that in eucharistic celebrations, the church incorporates a Jewish body and so shows its connection to Judaism. The effort is well intentioned, but erroneous: the eucharistic body is no more Jewish than it is male, Middle Eastern, or Aramaic-speaking. Particularity has its limits.

This plea for particularism extends to liturgical activities. It has become quite the thing in Protestant churches and of increasing interest to Roman Catholic laity to celebrate the Seder, the ritual meal commemorating the Exodus—usually on Thursday of Holy Week. This too is a well-intentioned but misguided effort. The Passover as celebrated today is a post-Second Temple tradition. Jesus would not have read a Haggadah, cited the Tannaim, or eaten matzah ball soup. Nor would Jesus' Seder, or any Seder, have gentile participants; the meal was restricted to the covenant community (as today, in many churches the "Supper of the Lord" is a closed table). Those who did participate would have obtained the lamb from the Jerusalem Temple, not the local butcher. To complicate the wishes of the modern Christian celebrant further, it is not even clear the Last Supper was a Passover meal—no account mentions matzah, bitter herbs, or even the lamb. There is no evidence women and children were at the Last Supper, as they would have been at Passover. John, who does not make the Last Supper a Seder, may even be the most historically accurate on the question of dating.

The theological problem is even weightier: for the church, the Seder is replaced by the Eucharist, as some traditions intimate when they speak of "Jesus our Passover" or Jesus as the "Lamb of G-d." We are what we eat, as the saying goes; in this case, let the meals signal even as they celebrate our differences. We do not need to share the same food in order to share the same earth, or the same desire for Shalom.

Put another way, theology informed by scripture and done in light of interfaith relations need not be a search for common ground. It may instead be an attempt to determine how we can, each on our own territory and with our own idiom, be good neighbors.

Notes

[1]According to its website, the College Theology Society "is a professional association of college and university professors. Founded in 1953 as a Roman Catholic organization of lay and religious teachers of undergraduate theology. . . . While maintaining its roots in the Roman Catholic tradition, the Society is increasingly ecumenical in its membership and concerns." I take "ecumenical" (as opposed to "inter-faith") to be the *oikos* of the Christian communions. This connotation is implied by the website's listing of "Theological Resources": "The emphasis in this guide is to list resources for research in Christian theology, and more specifically in Catholic theology. Some more general resources and resources for other religious traditions are listed as well."

[2]See my "Lilies of the Field and Wandering Jews: Biblical Scholarship, Women's Roles, and Social Location," in I. R. Kitzberger, ed., *Transformative Encounters: Jesus and Women Re-viewed* (Leiden: E. J. Brill, 1999). The model of making Jesus look progressive on women's issues by denigrating his Second Temple context (i.e., if one can't make Jesus look proactively good, make Judaism look bad) is still popular. For documentations of the problem in recent popular, theological, liturgical, and liberationist contexts, see Mary C. Boys, *Has G-d Only One*

Blessing? Judaism as a Source of Christian Self-Understanding (New York/ Mahwah, N.J.: Paulist Press, 2000), esp. 78-82.

[3]I am quite sympathetic to the models of interpretation lucidly delineated by Mark Allan Powell's theologically informed *Chasing the Eastern Star: Adventures in Biblical Reader-Response Criticism* (Louisville: Westminster/John Knox, 2001).

[4]The College Theology Society sometimes meets with the National Association of Baptist Professors of Religion; thus this example seemed particularly apt.

[5]Much of this section is informed by the essays in *Hebrew Bible or Old Testament? Studying the Bible in Judaism and Christianity*, ed. Roger Brooks and John J. Collins (Notre Dame: University of Notre Dame Press, 1990) and, in particular, the contribution to the subject there and elsewhere by Jon D. Levenson.

[6]My own institution's catalogue presents as the first sentence under the heading "Commitments" the following: "The Divinity School is committed to the faith that brought the church into being, and it believes that one comes more authentically to grasp that faith by a critical and open examination of the Hebraic and Christian traditions" (*The Bulletin of Vanderbilt University 2001/2002: Divinity School* 101/2 [July 2001], 9). If the wording just spoke of "Christian" traditions, that would be fine. "Hebraic" seems inappropriate: surely much of the "Old Testament" represents not "Hebraic" traditions but rather Israelite, Judahite, and Jewish ones. Then again, as with the Pope's visit to Syria, locating the problem is much easier than locating the solution.

[7]On the move from Malachi to Matthew, and on the general matter of canonical order, see most recently Patricia McDonald's "From Malachi to Matthew: A Gift of the Tradition," pages 53-68 below.

[8]Points David Noel Freedman developed following a lecture I gave at the University of California-San Diego, in May 2001.

[9]See discussion in my "Anti-Judaism and the Gospel of Matthew," in William Farmer. ed., *Anti-Judaism and the Gospels* (Valley Forge, Penn.: Trinity Press International, 1999).

[10]See the article by Joseph M. Webb and my response in *Quarterly Review* (Fall, 2000): 297-304.

The Art of Interpretation:
Contexts, Challenges, and Interconnections

Diana L. Hayes

Kathleen O'Connor and Amy-Jill Levine have given us excellent examples of how our understanding and interpretation of scripture can and do impact our theologizing. They present radical interpretations of the connections between scripture and theology, radical in the historical sense of being deeply rooted in a particular historical and cultural experience; for O'Connor, that of a Western Euro-American Christianity and for Levine, that of Judaism. Obviously we are all, in various ways not always recognized or acknowledged, impacted by our particular contexts, myself included.

I am the descendant of a people brought against their will to this country to serve as the unpaid and dehumanized labor force for those who had, from the perspective of the indigenous peoples, invaded and devastated their homeland and their lives. My context is that of a minority within a minority within a minority. Thus, I found aspects of both presentations both challenging to my own faith-understanding yet also affirming of much that I have come to believe about my faith and my active participation in it.

First, let me be more specific. My context is that of an African American Catholic woman, a minority within the predominantly Protestant African American Christian community. I find myself speaking as a lay Black Catholic theologian (of whom there are only six) within the predominantly Euro-American U.S. Catholic Church (although this is rapidly changing). This church is itself a minority within the predominantly Protestant Christian United States. My "way of being in the world" has been undeniably shaped and influenced as well by being a life-long member of another over-looked community, that of the Two-Thirds World (a term I prefer as more descriptive of the reality than Third World) that is to be found in the United States and which, at a time of recent unparalleled economic growth, yet finds itself growing poorer, more under/miseducated, and increasingly underskilled. This is the world of African, Latino/a, and Native Americans as well as of many women, regardless of race or ethnicity, who are poor.

Kathleen O'Connor's reading of Acts 27 is of particular interest to me. I admit that I am one of those who have read the chapter innumerable times without probing it deeply. Her reflections are quite on target in terms of the symbolic narrative that the shipwreck story presents. She states starkly: "At issue is the survival of the world," a world that, for too long, has been divided between "us" and "them." Who has occupied these roles over the years has often shifted, but increasingly today it is "those who have" (the "One-Third World") and "those who have not" (the "Two-Thirds World"). The latter, including those in the very heart of this country, form the greater majority.

On the flight to Portland, Oregon, from Washington, D.C., I watched the film *Thirteen Days*, a highly fictionalized depiction of the Cuban Missile Crisis of 1962. The story, obviously, is told from the perspective of the United States rather than Cuba and purports to show how close we came to the brink of nuclear destruction. We learn little about the feelings and concerns of the Russian people themselves or of the Cubans or even the average American citizen, or of the impact these thirteen days of "brinkmanship" had on any of them.

I see a parallel between the film and the shipwreck story from Acts, for both offer "a dynamic of survival from the side of the empire," as Kathleen has noted. Ironically in the film, Kenny O'Donnell, the outsider, is an Irish Catholic like the Kennedys, but from a family that lacks the Kennedy wealth, upbringing, and innate assumption of privilege and superiority. Yet, it is through his eyes that we catch at least a glimpse of another perspective, for his is the only family group that we see, the only interaction of people, the only mounting tension between husband and wife. The Kennedys apparently have no families about which they are concerned!

But even O'Donnell still has the trappings, as a white male, of invisible privilege. It requires an almost violent re-orientation of our minds and hearts to even begin to acknowledge there might be an "other" perspective. I am reminded of the first time that I read an article, "Cowboys and Canaanites,"[1] that critiqued liberation theology's interpretation, perhaps even co-optation, of the Exodus story as liberating for all, not just the Jews. Is this a liberating narrative for Native Americans? Most certainly not, yet my realization of that came only after the raising of the question by Native Americans themselves. They see in the Exodus story not liberation but invasion and annihilation of their cultural heritage and identity as well as a plan for genocide, a story that parallels what happened to them when the colonists first arrived in North America to establish a New Jerusalem.

Similarly, the questions raised by *Thirteen Days*, as in the narrative of the shipwreck, are of critical importance for us today, but only if we acknowledge the legitimacy of the person(s) raising them and how they differ from those usually privileged to both raise and answer the questions. Can we hear the voice of the "Other"? Are we capable of recognizing the legitimacy of voices that challenge and critique our accepted understandings? Having heard these voices, do we really attempt to understand them or do we merely tolerate them? Finally, having done so, are we then actually willing not just to learn from the "Other" but to act upon what we have learned, action that may require significant, often painful, changes in our beliefs, behaviors, and our very lives?

Again, my experience serves as my context for understanding Acts 27. Paul is an outsider, a Jewish-Christian on his way to be tried in Rome for his teaching in the name of Jesus Christ. The very language of the text sets him apart from his fellow Jews who are simply and negatively lumped together as the "Jews." At the same time, he has aspects of "insiderness" because as a Roman citizen he is privileged and can demand to be tried in Rome by the emperor rather than by the local tribunal. This role of being both on the inside and the outside can be positive in that it enables Paul to change the site of his trial; it is also negative in that if Paul had not laid claim to his status as a Roman citizen, he would have, as King Agrippa notes, most likely been set free, thereby forgoing the ordeal by water that was to come.

As an educated Black woman in the United States, I too have been privileged in many ways that often make living out my understanding of Jesus the Christ as Liberator and my stance as a critical and irritating "thorn" in the side of both my church and my society difficult to maintain. I occupy the position of an "outsider-within" as Patricia Hill Collins defines it,[2] one precariously balanced in two worlds, that of academia, an often elite world with its own often deliberately obscurative language and accepted modes of behavior and thought patterns, and that of the Black American community, which is often radically different, much more diverse, and increasingly internally at war with itself. Standing comfortably in neither world as a result, yet unwilling to leave one for the other, I, like Paul, perhaps, seek to carve out a space of my own as a womanist from within which I can interact not only with other marginalized groups but with those in the so-called normative society, while exerting a constant effort to challenge and critique but also to learn.

Such a stance requires collegiality, the forming of relationships that may seem odd to others looking on, a willingness not just to listen but to truly hear and act on that hearing, to humble myself when necessary and enable others to speak and to prophesy, all the while recognizing and affirming the uniqueness of my own particularity while being open to that of others.

This brings me to Amy-Jill Levine's paper. She raises questions that sting my Christian complacency as the Native American narrative did, for hers is the voice of an "Other" made even more "other" because it is not and has no desire to become Christian. Her focused critique challenges us to rethink our self-understanding as Christians, our interpretations and even naming of Scripture, our liturgical rituals, our very language.

We are stung because what she says is grounded in the truth of her experience. I know my own efforts to more fully grasp the tenets of Judaism as a religion in and of itself, independent of its relationship to Christianity, began only when I was challenged by Jewish students in my "Introduction to Theology" course. They questioned the texts that I used for their inadequate and too often inaccurate depiction of the Jewish faith. I realized that I knew little or nothing about Judaism other than as I had learned about it through the lens of Euro-American and African American Christianity.

I grew up knowing, for example, that African Americans considered themselves an Old Testament people who also saw themselves as the new Chosen People of God in the United States because of their treatment and sufferings. I never questioned the possibly invalid appropriation of another people's history and heritage without so much as a "by your leave," while, at the same time, I harshly critiqued the Puritans of the Massachusetts Bay Colony for their audacity and myopia in proclaiming their colony as the new Promised Land. For if they were guilty, then perhaps so too are African Americans, for our understanding of the Old Testament and our assumed role as the new Hebrew children arose from a co-optation of scripture that narrowly focuses on those aspects that support our quest for a liberation affirmed by God; it overlooks or ignores those sections that contradict our interpretation.

It is similar to an Afrocentric emphasis on the Blackness and primacy of Ancient Egypt that overlooks the issues that emerge as a result. If the Egyptians were arguably Black and most certainly African, then the children of Abraham were not enslaved by some figurative pharaoh but a Black and African one! Can we, as descendants of Africa, be both enslaver and enslaved, oppressor and oppressed? This is certainly a provocative question, which, to my knowledge, has not been fully addressed by any Black intellectual, secular or religious.

These questions must and should be raised or we are living a lie. Levine is correct in stating that "even passages of Scripture typically hailed as liberating can have a negative resonance." Who makes the judgment? Who is the interpreter? What is his/her context, purpose, *telos*? All of this is critical not only when reading scripture but more importantly when attempting to lift particular meaning from it.

We recognize that all of theology is historically rooted in specific contexts upon which it builds a model for speaking about God. At issue, however, is the tendency for one or a limited few models based mainly in the contextualized readings of scripture of one allegedly normative group to silence and suppress any and all other contexts and perspectives. Thus, the turn to the "Other" today is, in fact, a rejection of the contextualized hegemony of white European and Euro-American theologies in an effort to uncover, discover, and recover voices and contexts that are equally legitimate.

As Patricia Hill Collins states:

> I place black women's experience and ideas at the center of analysis. . . . I have deliberately chosen not to begin with feminist tenets developed from the experience of white, middle-class,

Western women and then insert the ideas and experiences of African American women. Oppressed groups are frequently placed in the situation of being listened to only if we frame our ideas in the language that is familiar to and comfortable for a dominant group. This requirement often changes the meaning of our ideas and works to elevate the ideas of dominant groups.[3]

As Levine correctly notes, this has too often led to a misappropriation of the Tanach and its message solely as a context for the prefiguring of the coming of the Messiah. This misappropriation also results, as I noted earlier, in the assumption that everyone reading the texts will receive the same message. Yet for Native Americans, whose historical experience differs not only from that of African Americans but even more from that of Euro-Americans, the liberating message of Jesus the Christ is "tainted," if you will, by our denial of the entire story of the Exodus: liberation from slavery, yes, but also the suppression and annihilation of a people, the Canaanites.

"The same text," Levine notes, "read though different eyes, can be seen as liberating or constraining, and that is why we need to read together." The example of Galatians 3:28, used by Christians as a sign of Christian solidarity, is an apt one. I must admit I was startled by her critique of this verse as the "erasing of my religion and ethnic identity" but I then thought of a term often bandied about by liberals and conservatives alike in U.S. society today, the desire for a "color-blind" society. Although this is not itself a scriptural term, Galatians 3:28 is often used as the context and support for such a perspective. Quite frankly, I, as a person of color, find the term insulting and demeaning. To be color-blind is not a viable option for me, nor does it present an image of a perfect society, for it erases what is distinctive about me. It purports to put a negative or neutral value on skin color as a means of erasing "colorism" and its accompanying racism, but, in actuality, it simply, once again, lifts up "whiteness" or the lack of color as normative, thereby nullifying the legitimacy of my and every other person of color's existence. To be told that "I don't see you as Black or African American" nullifies my very existence; my Blackness is a critical and foundational aspect of my very being.

These questions are critical to our ongoing interfaith dialogue, but they are also critical to our intrafaith dialogue. How do we identify with and celebrate the Jewishness of Jesus without illegitimately appropriating Judaism into Christianity? How do we deepen our understanding of the Christos, the Messiah, while retaining our links to the Jesus of history in ways that do not concretize and universalize a particular historical context? For, after all, we do not limit ordination to male Jews from Galilee who speak Aramaic, yet only such a one truly images the historical Jesus of Nazareth. It is the Christ of faith upon which the church is founded, and that understanding is and can only be catholic if we are to remain faithful to the mandate given us, to teach all nations the gospel message that is always new and transformed by those with whom it comes into contact.

Yet, I must admit that I am somewhat troubled by the assertion of Levine: "Let Christians be Christians and Jews be Jews." For again, Jesus was a Jew, an historical Jew who lived and walked this earth for a brief period of time, but whose life, death, and resurrection have certainly made a lasting impact upon human history. How do we who are Christian honor Jesus' Jewishness and therefore his Jewish faith without stepping on toes? To be sure, this is a question for interfaith dialogue. Perhaps a seder meal is inappropriate if practiced as an historically correct reenactment of the Passover meal because we as Christians are not a part of the community who experienced the first Passover. But are there other ways to look at this burgeoning interfaith movement that brings together people of two faiths who have for too long a time seen themselves as adversaries rather than friends? Most of my first-year students don't even realize that Jesus was never a Christian or that the roots of Christianity are Jewish. How do we help them to see our interconnections while also being alert to the pitfalls in our path?

Dr. Levine's critique of the silence of Christians in response to the Southern Baptist's blasphemous assertions is one of these pitfalls, for it reminds me of the silence of Pastor Niemoller in Germany. As the accusations and attacks against not just Judaism but all religions, forms of Christianity other than Southern Baptist included, mount, we must respond critically and vigorously because soon there will be no one left to protest these distorted interpretations of God's message that are being spread.

Both O'Connor and Levine warn of the dangers of triumphalism and a narrow global perspective. As we move into the twenty-first century, it is even more important than ever in our rapidly shrinking world that we pay heed to the voices of those unlike ourselves, not just the poor and outcast or the marginalized and invisible but those of other religious beliefs who legitimately share this "brave new world" with us. Critical attention to the particularity of our faith stances must be paid while avoiding the temptations of a passive relativism that reduces us all into mere reflections of each other.

The challenge to us as teachers is to enable our students not simply to claim but to voice their "cultural identities, their faith, and their God" while remaining open to the cultural traditions, experiences, and faith expressions of others. It is to interpret without co-optation, without appropriation—a difficult balancing act to be sure, but a necessary one.

For me, Gustavo Gutiérrez's understanding of theology speaks to the critical interconnection of scripture and theology. He defines theology as critical reflection on praxis in light of one's faith and as guided by the Word of God. It is the theologian's task to be always conscious of the contextually foundational basis of scripture in her/his efforts to bring light, life, and hope to all by his/her God-talk; our God-talk tells not only of the God of Abraham, Isaac, and Jacob, but also of the God of Jesus who is the Christ.

Notes

[1]James Treat, ed., *Native and Christian: Indigenous Voices on Religious Identity in the United States and Canada* (New York: Routledge, 1995).

[2]Patricia Hill Collins, *Black Feminist Thought: Knowledge, Consciousness, and the Politics of Empowerment* (New York: Routledge, 1990), 11-13.

[3]Ibid., xii.

SCRIPTURE AND
BIBLICAL THEOLOGY

Creation-in-Crisis:
Biblical Creation Theology
and the Disclosure of God

Russell A. Butkus

Well over thirty years ago humanity began to recognize the signs of its destructive ecological footprint on the planet. During these years of disclosure and response some progress has been achieved in ameliorating environmental problems. Nevertheless, most ecological indicators vigorously suggest that serious environmental destruction continues unabated. In fact, humanity has been forced to recognize that the present ecological distress is truly a global phenomenon. Fortunately the dire effects of unchecked ecological degradation have not gone unnoticed by many in the Christian biblical-theological community and the churches they represent. This awareness has been punctuated by significant developments in the last thirty years that—in a time of ecological crisis—make for interesting possibilities in hermeneutical and theological reflection.

Around the same time that environmentalism broke into human consciousness, significant changes were occurring in biblical interpretation and theology. Until the late 1960s and early 1970s the overarching focus and domain of Old Testament interpretation and theology was driven by ancient Israel's theology of historical redemption. Because of the primacy of historical redemption in Old Testament interpretation, biblical creation theology was virtually ignored and even considered irrelevant for biblical scholarship. According to some Old Testament scholars such as Hans Heinrich Schmid, and Rolf Knierim, the major reason for ignoring Israel's creation faith was that it was considered a later theological development within the Old Testament and interpreted as secondary to Israel's soteriology of historical redemption.

This view, championed by Gerhard von Rad, remained the dominant model for Old Testament theology for more than forty years until 1971 when Claus Westermann mounted a serious challenge to its presuppositions.[1] He argued that the Old Testament contained two major theological poles: salvation history (soteriology) and creation (blessing), and that both were necessary for an understanding of the Israelite experience of God. Westermann claimed that creation was the ground of history and that history and creation functioned in a dialectical relationship that provided the foundation for understanding Old Testament theology in its entirety. Schmid, Knierim, James Barr and others continued in this vein of biblical scholarship signaling the denouement of *Heilsgeschichte* and the emergence of a new paradigm of biblical interpretation that accepts creation as the primary horizon of biblical theology.[2]

The significance of the paradigm shift from salvation history to creation in biblical theology seems apparent in a time of ecological crisis. The hermeneusis of creation as the axis for understanding biblical faith is pivotal for providing a theological interpretation of the present era.[3] Walter Brueggemann asserts that the creation model might create new possibilities for exchange between science and theology, a necessary partnership if humanity is to prevail in the twenty-first century. Moreover he states:

> The recovery of creation as the horizon of biblical theology encourages us to contribute to the resolution of the ecological crisis. New investigations in creation faith and its complement, wisdom theology, suggest that the environment is to be understood as a delicate, fragile system of interrelated parts that is maintained and enhanced by the recognition of limits and givens and by the judicious exercise of choices.[4]

Regardless of its particular method, the task of theology is to take stock of the signs of the times and, in dialectical fashion, to reflect and interpret the meaning of these events in light of Christian faith. This is precisely what ecologically minded theology seeks to accomplish. It is the modest aim of this article to contribute to this on-going enterprise. The central thesis contained herein is the claim that the hermeneusis of biblical creation theology is the primary lens through which the ecological crisis must be interpreted, and as such, creation must be considered a universal and unique revelatory event in earth history. This view will unfold through an analysis of selected biblical texts—from Wisdom literature, particularly the Psalms—which affirm the revelatory encounter with God in creation. The implications of this examination will then be drawn to give focus to the theological interpretation of the earth's ecological crisis as the self-disclosure of God, which may be construed as an advance toward a creation-eco-logical model of revelation. The treatment of these issues proceeds on the assumption that creation is a primary, though not exclusive, datum for God's self-revelation.

Biblical Creation Theology and the Meaning of Revelation

Revelation as a formal theological term and concept does not appear in the Bible; nevertheless, it has been developed as a dominant theme in biblical creation theology, particularly in the New Testament with respect to Jesus Christ. The focus in this section is on the revelatory encounter of God through creation as that experience is represented in certain Old Testament creation texts. This article recognizes that in the Bible, and especially in the Old Testament, God discloses God's self through divine speech. It is a vital, active word that addresses humanity in an experiential manner and requires response. This revelation of God occurs in manifold channels and creation is a primary medium for God's self-communication.

Creation Theology and the Wisdom Tradition

A major source of creation theology and, likewise, the notion of God's disclosure through creation is found in the Wisdom tradition of Israel. It is now generally accepted among Old Testament scholars that Wisdom literature is predominantly grounded in creation theology. It is interesting to note that von Rad, who championed the historical paradigm of biblical theology, contributed to the rediscovery of Wisdom literature in his last work, *Wisdom in Israel*.[5] In the chapter "The Self-Revelation of Creation," von Rad examines the three great didactic poems found in Proverbs 8, Job 28, and Sirach 24. Representative of this poetic genre is Sirach 24:1-7:

Wisdom praises herself,
    and tells of her glory in the midst of her people.
In the assembly of the Most High she opens her mouth,
    and in the presence of his hosts she tells of her glory:
"I came forth from the mouth of the Most High,
    and covered the earth like a mist.
I dwelt in the highest heavens,
    and my throne was in a pillar of cloud.
Alone I compassed the vault of heaven
    and traversed the depths of the abyss.
Over waves of the sea, over all the earth,
    and over every people and nation I have held sway.
Among all these I sought a resting place;
    in whose territory should I abide?" (NRSV)

In his analysis of these texts, von Rad understands wisdom as a "personified entity" and the primal world order immanent in the natural world that speaks, instructs, and addresses humanity from the depths of creation. He surmises that these three wisdom-creation poems indicate a significant development of wisdom, moving from the older concept of practical wisdom to what von Rad calls the "doctrine of the self-revelation of creation." He claims this marks a qualitatively "new" leap in Israel's understanding of revelation over the notion of God's self-disclosure through salvation history. He states that this new

phenomenon in our texts is that a bearer of revelation intervenes in the dialogue between Yahweh and Israel. . . . His speech proceeds in a highly elevated first-person style; but he is much more than the greatest of the prophets, he is, indeed, the mystery inherent in the creation of the world. In the opinion of the teachers, Yahweh had at his service a quite different means, besides priests and prophets, whereby he could reach men, namely the voice of primal order, a voice which came from creation, and this means of revelation was of particular interest to the wise men.[6]

Based on his assumption that this novel view of revelation is a later development in Israel's theology, von Rad's analysis clearly bears the stamp of the salvation history bias. Nevertheless, this interpretation of Wisdom literature is free of his earlier and more pejorative evaluations of the material. He summarizes his reflections on the self-revelation of creation with the assertion that the sages of Israel's sapiential tradition discovered a notion of revelation that was "fundamentally different from that which was elsewhere understood by 'revelation' in Israel."[7] He states that "the main difference consists in the fact that there is developed the doctrine of a revelatory experience which happens to men not through a specific, irreversible sign of salvation in history, but which, rather, emanates from the power of order which is held to be self-sufficient."[8]

The contribution of von Rad should not be underestimated. His work in Wisdom provided a baseline for interpretation that has been taken up by subsequent Old Testament scholars motivated by the newer creation model of biblical interpretation. A notable example is Leo Perdue. Perdue's *Wisdom and Creation: The Theology of Wisdom Literature* is perhaps the most extensive treatment of wisdom-creation theology to date.[9] His examination of Old Testament Wisdom is solidly grounded in the conviction that Israel's creation theology is the foundation of the sapiential tradition. For Perdue, Wisdom is the feminine Wisdom of God and is appropriately addressed as "Woman Wisdom." She is described as a personified divine attribute and, while Perdue does not use the language, his interpretation strongly suggests that Woman Wisdom is a divine hypostasis of God. In Perdue's analysis, Wisdom portrays a number of essential characteristics:

1. Woman wisdom is of divine origin. She existed before creation and was God's primary instrument of creation.

2. Woman Wisdom is God's imperishable spirit who is immanently present in creation.

3. Woman Wisdom is vital and active. She is poured forth; she calls, speaks, teaches, rebukes, and instructs in the ways of justice and righteousness.

4. Woman Wisdom is the principal means whereby creation and the support structures of life are ordered, sustained, and maintained.

5. Woman Wisdom is rational. She represents "constructive reason" ordering the physical (cosmological) and moral (anthropological) aspects of creation.

6. Woman Wisdom is also one of the primary means through which God is revealed.

That Wisdom reveals God is developed in many texts of the Wisdom corpus but especially illustrative is the magnificent "Hymn of Praise to the God of Creation" (Sir 42:15-43:33). The entire poem magnifies and extols the beauty, goodness, and purpose of creation. The sage-poet is filled with awe at the divine presence infused in the manifold works of creation and marvels at the gracious creativity and providence of God. The opening strophe, vv. 15-17, is quite distinctive in its revelatory nature:

> I will now call to mind the works of the Lord,
>> and will declare what I have seen.
>
> By the word of the Lord, his works are made;
>> and all his creatures do his will.
>
> The sun looks down on everything with its light,
>> and the work of the Lord is full of his glory.
>
> The Lord has not empowered even his holy ones
>> to recount all his marvelous works,
>
> which the Lord the Almighty has established
>> so that the universe may stand firm in his glory.

The poem begins with the sage remembering God's deeds that reflect the providential work of God in sustaining and governing creation. The key metaphor representing God's providence is "the utterance of his word." According to Perdue, "the dominant metaphor for divine providence throughout this poem is the word of the creator, which sustains life and establishes justice by means of divine decree."[10] In v. 16 the poet links the "work" of God with the "glory" of the Lord. This linkage is a direct reference to the "manifestation" of God's presence in a revelatory manner. Perdue claims that "while this way of speaking about divine manifestation connotes mystery and otherness, it also indicates that the purpose of theophany is revelation: God manifests himself in order to issue divine teaching."[11] This manner of poetic speech is an appeal to the imagination that declares the revelatory nature of creation and points, in Perdue's words, "to the power, majesty, and benevolence of God."[12] Perdue concludes his interpretation of this passage with the observation that

the glory of the Lord points to revelation: Creation testifies to the majesty and sovereignty of the creator. Yet at the same time, this creation that manifests the Lord is the avenue of divine instruction. Creation not only reveals the creator, but also becomes the instrument of his teaching given to those who seek wisdom.[13]

Creation, Revelation and the Psalms

The Psalms are another source of creation theology that clearly signals the experience of creation as the self-disclosure of God. Classified as Wisdom literature, many psalms contain parallels to other Wisdom poetry of creation in both theological content—the centrality of creation as a source of divine manifestation—and mood—the awe-inspiring consciousness that enthusiastically breaks into poetry and song. Psalms 8 and 19 are of special interest. Both psalms share creation theology as a common point of reference and are, to varying degrees, hymnic songs of praise extolling the creator God and the magnificence of God's handiwork. In Psalm 8:1-4 one reads:

> O LORD, our Sovereign,
>   how majestic is your name in all the earth!
>
> You have set your glory above the heavens.
>   Out of the mouth of babes and infants
> you have founded a bulwark because of our foes,
>   to silence the enemy and the avenger.
>
> When I look at your heavens, the work of your fingers,
>   the moon and the stars that you have established;
> what are human beings that you are mindful of them,
>   mortals that you care for them? (NRSV)

This psalm is obviously a hymn of praise responding to the resplendent beauty of creation and the disclosure of God contained therein. Artur Weiser remarks that Psalm 8 "combines a fine sense of feeling responsive to the sublime beauty of Nature and a profound understanding of the revelation of God expressed and yet hidden in Nature."[14] Given the tone and timbre of the song, its setting is most likely the cultic celebration of Israel. The reference to the glorious name of God in the opening verse suggests this and may be interpreted, as Weiser suggests, as the congregation's response "to the revelation of God as Creator that takes place in the festival cult when Yahweh manifests his 'name' and his nature."[15] Central to verse 1 is the linkage between God's name, glory, and the earth. This is reminiscent of the creation hymn of Sirach 42:15-17 examined above. In both texts a similar dynamic is at work in the hymnic praise of God's self-revelation of divine glory that fills the earth. Verses 3-4 of Psalm 8 link the cosmological (the heavens) with the anthropological (humanity's place in creation) dimension of creation. The psalmist, moved by the majesty of God's heavenly work, is forced to consider the meaning of human existence and the role of humanity within the magnitude of creation. Weiser's commentary on these verses is worthy of note. He writes:

> It is the impression made by God's revelation which enables man in the first instance to attain the right understanding of his own self. In the Bible the revelation of God and man's understanding of his own existence are intimately bound up with each other . . . there is no revelation of God except it also throws at the same time a special light on the nature of man; and, conversely, a true understanding of man cannot be achieved if God is disregarded.[16]

The point to consider regarding Psalm 8 is that God's self-disclosure, which is necessary for humanity's self-understanding, occurs within the context of God's revelation in creation and not in history. The question and meaning of human existence, at least in this psalm, is raised in relation to the glory of God's name revealed in creation. The psalmist answers the question by appealing to the royal model of stewardship (see vv. 5-9), whereby humanity is given dominion over creation.

Even more stunning in the depiction of creation as revelatory of God is Psalm 19. In this psalm two themes, the communication of God through creation (vv. 1-6) and the law (vv. 7-14), are joined together in one song. Verses 1-4 are particularly important for this examination. The psalmist declares,

> The heavens are telling the glory of God;
>   and the firmament proclaims his handiwork.
> Day to day pours forth speech,
>   and night to night declares knowledge.

There is no speech, nor are there words;
   their voice is not heard;
yet their voice goes out through all the earth,
   and their words to the ends of the world. (NRSV)

Obvious similarities in tone, structure, and theme exist between Psalms 8 and 19. Both are hymnic songs of praise extolling God and the grandeur of creation. Weiser suggests that both poets "contemplate with awe the majesty of God revealed in creation, and the composition of their songs is the fruit of the rapture which was aroused in them by their moving experience of God in nature."[17]

 In vv. 1-2 of Psalm 19 one sees again the reference to God's glory proclaimed by the heavens. The creator is known by the divine handiwork of creation. The implication here, according to Weiser, is that "the whole of Nature is in the service of a Supreme Being; its duty is to sing the praise of God and to be the vehicle of his revelation."[18] In vv. 3-4 the key image is creation as the medium of divine communication and knowledge. God's creation is not mute; it functions as a vehicle of divine language; God's speech, voice, and word are disclosed in the design and beauty of the natural world. Furthermore, creation imparts knowledge,[19] a reminder of the function of Wisdom, who orders creation and instructs in the ways of righteous living those who seek Her. Commenting on these verses Weiser suggests that

> the grandeur of Nature reveals to [the text's author] . . . the majesty of its Creator, but he realizes that the created world is at the same time a vehicle of the revelation of the divine wisdom and order ("his handiwork"), which it passes on from day to day in an unbroken tradition like a secret knowledge (v. 2). Nature itself is the record of creation, an essential part of the self-revelation of God to the whole world, and in that record God has entered by means of powerful signs the story of the genesis of the world and of its laws.[20]

Theological Reflection: Creation-in-Crisis as Revelatory Event

The preceding examination substantiates the experience of God's self-disclosure in creation as an important theme in biblical creation theology. The emergence of the creation paradigm for biblical interpretation and the subsequent claim that creation is the principal horizon of biblical theology gives contemporary theologians a unique opportunity to provide a theological interpretation of the meaning and content of the ecological crisis. If one unites the horizon of biblical creation faith with the horizon of our contemporary ecological crisis, one would appear to have what Hans-Georg Gadamer calls a "fusion of horizons."[21] Theologically, this fusion of horizons requires us to interpret ecological degradation as creation-in-crisis. This final section discusses the implications of the biblical experience of God's revelation in creation as the primary hermeneutical lens through which the ecological crisis must be theologically interpreted as a unique disclosure of God. It aims at making a modest and preliminary advance toward a creation-ecological model of revelation.

The Status of Creation in the Theology of Revelation

How one deals with creation in biblical interpretation and theological reflection is dictated, in large measure, by one's confessional location and methodology. Sirach is canonical in the Catholic tradition and thus, for Catholics, it can be used with "authority" in biblical and theological interpretation. Creation has always held a place—albeit ambiguous and secondary—in a Catholic theology of revelation. For example, Thomas Aquinas is clear in the *Summa Theologica* that through the use of human reason something of the nature of God can be derived from creation.[22]

A similar line of thought is contained in the Catholic Church's First Vatican Council, which admits to the possibility that God can be known—"through the light of human reason."[23] The Council speaks about the "natural manifestation" of God in creation and that knowledge of God through the medium of creation constitutes a type of natural revelation that is accessible through rational reflection. The Council, however, clearly established a distinction between the primacy of "supernatural revelation" and the secondary status of "natural revelation."

Contemporary theological discourse on revelation continues to use the distinction between "natural," "general," and "universal" self-revelation of God in creation and asserts that the "revealed," "special," "supernatural," and "historical" self-disclosure of God lies in the history of Israel and the person of Jesus Christ. It is the position of this article that, from the perspective of creation as the horizon of biblical theology, these distinctions are spurious. In other words, these distinctions and categories are not used in the biblical tradition and cannot be supported on the basis of biblical interpretation. In *Biblical Faith and Natural Theology*, James Barr claims it is exceedingly difficult to distinguish between revealed and natural theology in the biblical text and concludes "that 'revelational' theology and 'natural' theology were irretrievably mixed up with one another."[24] From a biblical perspective Barr raises a good question: "If one believes that God has revealed himself in his creation and continues to do so, why is that 'natural' theology and not 'revealed'?"[25] The biblical witness surely recognizes that God is disclosed in creation and through God's salvific acts in history. There is, nevertheless, one God, and God discloses God's self in manifold ways. Creation is the original medium and backdrop. All that can be construed as revelatory of God occurs in and through creation, including the history of God's salvific acts and such pivotal events as the Incarnation.[26]

Revelation and the Ecological Crisis

If one uses humanity's current situation as the point of departure in this hermeneutical-theological analysis, it is undeniable that, from a scientific perspective, the earth and its natural systems are in serious jeopardy. A full analysis of the litany of environmental problems and their severity is beyond the scope of this present reflection. This article assumes that the ecological crisis is self-evident to anyone who is willing to engage the overwhelming scientific evidence. The nature of this crisis (which from a scientific view is a crisis of nature) has become an opportunity for those whose lives are shaped by biblical faith to rediscover nature as creation.[27] Consequently, the ecological crisis is best understood theologically as creation-in-crisis and ought to be viewed through the biblical lens of creation. Creation continues to unfold and therefore God's self-disclosure in creation continues as well. This divine self-disclosure is available to humanity today as it was to the ancient sages and poets of Israel's wisdom-creation hymns. We too have the capacity to be awe-inspired and marvel at the beauty and sublimity of creation. However, the very fact that creation is in crisis advances the nature of the current situation to an unprecedented level. It requires one to ponder the possibility that the ecological crisis of creation is a unique revelatory event in time and history.

Consider for a moment the scope and range of the crisis. It is global and universal. There is not a species, ecosystem, biome, or human society on the planet that is unaffected. In other words, the entire ecosphere of the earth is threatened. Moreover, it is a crisis of history. In the history of geologic time, humanity is witnessing a collapse of biodiversity the likes of which the planet has not experienced in the last 65 million years. By some estimates this anthropogenic process of extinction results in the loss of 27,000 species a year. Harvard biologist E. O. Wilson argues that "we are in the midst of one of the great extinction spasms of geological history."[28]

The ecological crisis is also a crisis of human history and society. For the first time in history the human species has become shockingly aware of the fact that our whole manner of being and doing on the earth is unsustainable. The crisis has impacted nearly every human discipline of knowledge of the modern era. In particular, humanity is being forced—for the good of our own survival—to re-evaluate the social, political, and economic institutions that have in large measure caused this crisis. The human species is at a crossroads in time and history. The language of sustainability has erupted into human consciousness and offers a hopeful vision and model of human existence as we face an uncertain future. This development is nothing short of revolutionary and its implications are revelatory.[29]

Humanity is confronted with the "spasm" of creation and history. In the language of contemporary theology one may interpret this eruption or interruption as a unique revelatory moment. Theologian John Haught claims that "from one point of view revelation is the 'interruptive' utterance of a word of promise into what otherwise may be seen as a cosmic void."[30] As humanity stands before an uncertain future we are confronted with the disturbing interruption of the human project and search for a word of promise and hope. According to Haught,

> the uncertainty of the future into which history is taking us would be unbearable unless we are guided by some vision of fulfillment. The quest for revelation may therefore be understood, in the present context at least, as the seeking of a resolution to the uncertainty that confronts us as we peer into the unknown outcome of historical events.[31]

Characteristics of a Creation-Ecological Model of Revelation

Returning to the biblical understanding of creation as the self-disclosure of God can assist in articulating some preliminary reflections on a creation model of revelation. Avery Dulles's classic discussion and typology of revelation, *Models of Revelation*, is insightful as a frame of reference.[32] Dulles offers five models for analysis: revelation as doctrine, history, inner experience, dialectical presence, and new awareness. While it is important to note that creation is virtually absent from his examination, Dulles's fifth model—revelation as new awareness—is closest to the trajectory of this reflection. According to Dulles, this model of revelation is best represented by Karl Rahner—with possible influence from Pierre Teilhard de Chardin. In his interpretation of Rahner's view, Dulles suggests that revelation in this model should be understood "as the process by which God, working within history and human tradition, enables his spiritual creatures to achieve a higher level of consciousness."[33] A creation paradigm would reinterpret this statement and define revelation as God working in creation and human history, resulting in a new mode of human awareness that sees, in a fresh light, the interrelatedness of God, creation, and the human project.

Creation-in-Crisis as New Awareness

The interruption of the present crisis is producing a transformation of consciousness. A creation-ecological model of revelation interprets this new emergence of human awareness as an ecological shift in human self-understanding. Ecological consciousness is characterized by a critical awareness that the earth's ecosphere is an intricate network of biotic and abiotic relationships and a new perception of humanity's place within that complex web of life. On the individual level it is cultivating what Daniel Chiras calls the "ecological self," the personal capacity to "blend into the landscape" and "develop a sense of union and empathy with other beings."[34] On the macro level of human institutions it means imagining a new paradigm of human socio-economic existence that is shaped by a vision of sustainability and ethical responsibility to future generations. On the theological level, it means cultivating a sacramental consciousness which is the ability to see and experience the earth as a disclosure of God's sacred presence. Combined, an ecological-sacramental consciousness recognizes creation and its ecological design as a revelatory medium, as an invitation to engage in a new conversation with God.

Creation-in-Crisis as the Language of Revelation

The examination of wisdom-creation theology indicates that the sages and poets of ancient Israel encountered creation as the language of God. God's creation is not silent, but functions as a vehicle for God's self-communication. Woman Wisdom calls to humanity; God's speech, voice, and word are revealed in the awe-inspiring quality of creation. Humanity continues to witness the beauty and magnificence of creation, but today creation is in crisis and the agony and groaning of creation is a revelatory word. Recent theological perspectives, notably liberationist approaches, argue that the voice of the poor and oppressed is one avenue for hearing God's disclosure in the intolerable experience of unjust suffering. Haught claims that "social outcasts, oppressed and rejected people have been the constant mediators of revelation."[35] The creation model of revelation expands this notion to include the suffering of all creation and seeks to expose the intrinsic institutional links between the oppression of people and the oppression of all creation. The work of social and ecological justice becomes then a harbinger, a revelatory promise, and an anticipatory ethic in the hope of creation's renewal and restoration.

Creation-in-Crisis as Divine Instruction

Another characteristic of creation theology that seems applicable to a creation-ecological model of revelation is the idea that Woman Wisdom imparts knowledge and instructs the seeker of Wisdom in the paths of justice and righteousness. This idea is based on the notion that Wisdom renders creation intelligible—to some degree—within human limits. Through this study and rational reflection, Woman Wisdom will enable those who seek Her to better understand the resplendent design of creation and even come to "know" God. The creation model insists that human reason play a role in the appropriation of revelation. This does not mean revelation is reduced to a matter of data or information about the natural world, but that there is a cognitive dimension to discerning and understanding the signs of the times.

A theology of revelation must take into consideration the new knowledge achieved by science, especially ecology and its related fields. Is it possible that the "wisdom" of ecology and the environmental sciences is revealing a great deal about the potential disorder, even chaos, that living out of harmony with creation can engender? Haught suggests that "science can provide helpful assistance in our attempts to understand the circumstances within which the mystery of God is disclosed."[36] One must remember, however, that knowledge is not simply a matter of rationally acquiring the facts about nature, but also of participating in a relationship with God-in-creation.

Creation-in-Crisis, Divine Immanence and the Relationality of God

The ecological crisis has already impacted Christian theology. Attempts to produce ecological theologies that reimagine the relationship between God and creation have produced fresh insights. Central issues in these theological projects have been the immanence and the relationality of God, which are key ideas in Israel's creation theology. On the whole, Western theology and classical theism have not done well with either of these qualities of God, but they are essential for a creation-ecological model of revelation.

One of the hallmarks of wisdom-creation theology is the idea that God, through Woman Wisdom, is immanently present in creation. Creation, on the other hand, is a community of being or an ontology of communion in which all creatures stand in profound relationship to each other and God. James Crenshaw claims that the wisdom sages introduced the notion of Woman Wisdom to mediate the tension between God's transcendence and God's immanence in creation.[37] Perdue maintains that, in the Wisdom tradition, "God's immanence and compassionate humaneness are portrayed in expressions of divine care for the good creation and its mortal creatures. The God of the sages acts in justice and love to create, sustain, and bless all life."[38] The presence of God, the sacramentality of the universe, and the creation model of revelation are dependent on an adequate understanding of God's immanence and relationality. From this perspective, the self-communication of God does not occur from "outside" but from within the profound depths of creation. According to Teilhard de Chardin, "God never reveals himself from outside, by intrusion, but from within, by stimulation and enrichment of the human psychic current, the sound of his voice being made recognizable by the fullness and coherence it contributes to our individual and collective being."[39]

Conclusion: Disclosure and Response

The disclosure of God in biblical creation theology is not a matter of revealed truths shaped in a manner of propositions but an invitation to participate in relationship. God's revelation is the self-communication of God in, through, and to creation, a communion of being bound together by common ground. These organic bonds of love are disclosed through the relational order of creation, which is, above all else, governed by ethical considerations. In the biblical tradition, particularly in the Old Testament, the response to God's self-disclosure is knowledge. Knowledge of God arises from the experience of and relation to the divine milieu of creation. It requires one "to do God's will." The relational order of creation, sustained by the abiding presence of Wisdom, is a moral order that requires the human response of justice and righteousness. This response to the disclosure of God seeks to maintain the integrity of creation and becomes itself a hopeful witness to the promise of God's revelation.

Notes

[1]For an excellent summary of the paradigm shift in Old Testament interpretation and theology, see Walter Brueggemann's article, "The Loss and Recovery of Creation in Old Testament Theology," *Theology Today* 53:2 (July 1996): 177-90.

[2]The language of "primary horizon" used here and in Brueggemann's article noted above means that creation has become the foundational starting point in contemporary biblical interpretation.

[3]Hermeneusis is used here in distinction to the noun hermeneutics and the adjective hermeneutic(al) and refers to the active process of interpreting contemporary ecological conditions as creation-in-crisis.

[4]Brueggemann, "The Loss and Recovery of Creation in Old Testament Theology," 188.

[5]Gerhard von Rad, *Wisdom in Israel* (Nashville: Abingdon Press, 1972).

[6]Ibid., 163.

[7]Ibid., 175.

[8]Ibid.

[9]Leo Perdue, *Wisdom and Creation: The Theology of Wisdom Literature* (Nash-

ville: Abingdon Press, 1994); see especially Perdue's summary and conclusions, 325-42.

[10]Ibid., 279.

[11]Ibid.

[12]Ibid.

[13]Ibid., 280.

[14]Artur Weiser, *The Psalms: A Commentary* (Philadelphia: The Westminster Press, 1962), 140.

[15]Ibid., 140.

[16]Ibid., 142.

[17]Ibid., 197.

[18]Ibid., 198.

[19]It is important to bear in mind that knowledge in the Old Testament context is not propositional or speculative but primarily experiential. Knowledge is not contained in objective theoretical statements about the natural world but through the "knowing" that arises in the experience of relatedness.

[20]Weiser, *Psalms*, 198.

[21]Hans-Georg Gadamer, *Truth and Method* (New York: Seabury Press, 1975), 273.

[22]St. Thomas Aquinas, *Summa Theologiae*, vol. 1, The Existence of God, Part One: Questions 1-13, ed. Thomas Gilby, O.P. (Garden City, N.J: Image Books, 1969), 166-94.

[23]See Latourelle's discussion of creation and revelation in Rene Latourelle, S.J., *Theology of Revelation* (New York: Alba House, 1987), 332-40.

[24]James Barr, *Biblical Faith and Natural Theology: The Gifford Lectures for 1991 Delivered in the University of Edinburgh* (Oxford: Clarendon Press, 1993), 151.

[25]Ibid., 115.

[26]The reader is cautioned not to misinterpret this assertion. It is simply recognizing that creation is prior to the Incarnation and that the Incarnation could not have occurred without creation, that it occurred within creation, and that it points to the eschatological redemption of creation. From the view of Christian faith, the faith in and the hope for the future salvation of creation is not possible without the Incarnation.

[27]There is an important distinction to note between the concept of nature and creation. There is no concept of nature in the Old Testament. Nature, derived from the Greek worldview, is by scientific definition a self-sustaining system replete with its own internal laws. Creation, a biblical-theological concept, recognizes that creation is not self-sustaining but is continually dependent on the presence of God. In the Wisdom tradition it is the function of Woman Wisdom who sustains and maintains creation.

[28]E. O. Wilson, *The Diversity of Life* (New York: W. W. Norton, 1992), 280.

[29]For a more comprehensive understanding of what is meant by sustainability, see my "Sustainability: An Eco-Theological Analysis," in *All Creation Is Groan-*

ing: An Interdisciplinary Vision for Life in a Sacred Universe, ed. Carol J. Dempsey and Russell A. Butkus (Collegeville: Liturgical Press, 1999), 144-67.

[30]John Haught, "Revelation," *The New Dictionary of Theology*, ed. Joseph Komonchak et al. (Wilmington, Del.: Michael Glazier, 1987), 888.

[31]Ibid., 889.

[32]Avery Dulles, *Models of Revelation* (Garden City, N.Y.: Doubleday, 1983; reprint, Maryknoll, N.Y.: Orbis Books, 1992).

[33]Ibid., 100.

[34]Daniel Chiras, *Lessons from Nature: Learning to Live Sustainably on the Earth* (Washington, D.C.: Island Press, 1992), 47.

[35]Haught, "Revelation," 892.

[36]Ibid., 898.

[37]James Crenshaw, "In Search of Divine Presence," *Review and Expositor* 74 (1977): 365.

[38]Perdue, *Wisdom and Creation*, 327.

[39]Pierre Teilhard de Chardin, *Christianity and Evolution* (New York: Harcourt, Brace & Jovanovich, 1971), 143.

From Malachi to Matthew:
A Gift of the Tradition

Patricia McDonald

An excellent and thought-provoking paper at the annual meeting of the Society of Biblical Literature last November drew my attention to the last few verses of the book of Malachi.[1] The presenter, Anathea Portier-Young, demonstrated how this text put before readers what was necessary for Israel's continued flourishing in the land: attentiveness to the Mosaic tradition and, therefore, attentiveness to one's parents and children. Malachi concludes with the Lord's promise to send the prophet Elijah to empower the people so that they could, finally, get it right and so that the earth would be delivered from the curse that would otherwise come upon it. As a fitting transition to the New Testament, it raised for me the following question: what, if anything, is supposed to happen when a Christian reader of the Bible turns the page from the end of the Old Testament[2] to the beginning of the New?

As is often the case, the question was less simple than I had at first thought. So the first two parts of what follows relate to doubtful assumptions inherent in the question itself. The first part treats the order of books at the end of the Old Testament canon and thus examines the material relationship that Malachi and Matthew have in the tradition. The second part considers whether page turning is a necessary part of the move from the Old Testament to the New. (It is not.) In the third section, "From Malachi to Matthew," we are finally able to make some exegetical moves and draw conclusions about the texts and also about the process that brought us to those texts.

The Canonical Issue

Almost as soon as I had asked about the rhetorical effect of moving from Malachi to Matthew, a logically prior question demanded attention. Granted, the various English Bibles that I use have Matthew following Malachi, at least if one discounts the Apocrypha that the New Revised Standard Version sandwiches between the Old and New Testaments. My Hebrew Bible, however, concludes with 2 Chronicles, even though the tenth/eleventh-century manuscript on which it was based, Codex Leningradensis, ended with Ezra and Nehemiah. Different again, Rahlfs's two-volume edition of the Greek Old Testament has as its final chapter the stories of Bel and the dragon from the book of Daniel. This deuterocanonical material reminded me of the Council of Trent, which, in its Fourth Session, promulgated a list of the canonical books of the Old and the New Testaments. In that list, the final Old Testament book is 2 Maccabees. So far, then, and with minimal exertion, I had found four different Old Testament endings in texts older than the NRSV (or any other English Bible in common use), none of them the Book of Malachi.[3]

A little more research yielded six more ways in which the Tanak or the Old Testament was concluded during the early centuries. As the chart below shows,[4] they are: Job, Esther, Ben Sira, Ezekiel, the Song of Songs, and, finally, Malachi as the last item in the Book of the Twelve Minor Prophets.

1. Second Chronicles	Babylonian Talmud, *Baba Bathra* 14b (c. 200 C.E.); Innocent I's list from his letter to Bishop Exsuperius of Toulouse (c. 405); modern Hebrew Bibles
2. Daniel	Athanasius's Festal Letter of 367; Codex Vaticanus; Cyril of Jerusalem (315-86); Rahlfs's edition of the Greek OT
3. Job	Codex Sinaiticus
4. Esdras (Ezra-Nehemiah)	Melito of Sardis (c. 170, in Eusebius, *Ecclesiastical History*); Cassiodorus

	(485-580), *Institutiones* I.11.3; the Aleppo and Leningrad Codices
5. Esther	Origen; Hilary (some add Tobit and Judith, he says); Epiphanius; Jerome in Prologue to Vulgate version of Samuel and Kings; Codex 54 (copied c. 1056); Hugh of St. Victor (d. 1141)
6. Ben Sira	Codex Alexandrinus text, although the list of contents concludes with the Psalms of Solomon, of which the text is not given
7. Ezekiel	Augustine, *On Christian Teaching* II.13
8. Second Maccabees	Councils of Rome (382) and Hippo (393); the Septuagint, according to Cassiodorus; Trent and subsequent RC versions (e.g., Vg edition of 1922; Douai-Rheims)
9. Psalms	Pseudo-Chrysostom
10. Song of Songs	Rufinus
11. Malachi	Augustine, according to Cassiodorus

Obviously, my casual assumption that the transition from the Old Testament to the New traditionally took the reader from Malachi to Matthew was very wide of the mark. The data give no support at all to the hypothesis that the present arrangement of books was intentionally set up by some early compiler whose work was then widely accepted and promulgated.

Variation in the place of the Book of the Twelve Minor Prophets within the prophetic canon is one factor that prevented Malachi from being at the end of most ancient manuscripts or listings. The Twelve often appear first among the writing prophets and, in such manuscripts, Malachi could never conclude a canon. Most of the available fourth- and fifth-century Christian sources are of this type. They include Athanasius, in his Festal Letter of 367, Cyril of Jerusalem, Jerome in his 394 Letter to Paulinus (*Epistle 53*), Codex Vaticanus, Hilary of Poitiers, Codex Alexandrinus, and Augustine (*On Christian Teaching*). That is impressive testimony to a tradition that was discarded or fell by the wayside!

Our modern arrangement, with the Twelve as the conclusion to the prophets, is found in the Jewish tradition, namely, the Babylonian Talmud (*Baba Bathra* 14b), the two ancient Tiberian codices associated with Aleppo and Leningrad, and modern editions of the Hebrew Bible. All of these, however, locate the Hagiographa (the Writings) after the Prophets, which means that Tanak does not conclude with Malachi. The same is true of Codex Sinaiticus, where the Twelve also seem to follow the other Prophets and are (it seems) followed by the Wisdom Literature.[5] A third positioning of the Twelve is found in the writing of the second-century Melito of Sardis: he has them in the middle of the Latter Prophets, after Isaiah and Jeremiah but before Daniel and Ezekiel.[6] Origen's list of the prophets omits the entire Book of the Twelve, presumably in error.

So how did we get from this non-uniform situation to the point at which modern Bibles in English, whatever their denominational affiliation, conclude the Old Testament with Malachi, when practically all the ancient witnesses, Jewish or Christian, do not? In fact, the pattern is essentially set by the sixteenth century, by which time Christian printed Bibles all had the Twelve Minor Prophets as the last item in the collection of prophetic books and also concluded their essential Old Testament with the prophetic books (usually followed by one or more books of less certain canonicity). Let us look in more detail at these two elements as they appear in the earlier part of the tradition: the position of the Twelve and the position of the prophetic corpus, and then consider briefly the situation in the sixteenth century, and the transition from there to the present within English-speaking Roman Catholicism.

The Position of the Twelve

Having the Twelve as the last of the named prophets is characteristic of the Jewish tradition. It also had the sanction of Jerome, inasmuch as he reported it as the Jewish order in his "helmed prologue" to the Books of Samuel and Kings that he translated into Latin from the Hebrew between 390 and 405. Significantly, this is the order that the influential Cassiodorus gives for Jerome in the sixth century,[7] even though Jerome had another listing in which the Twelve preceded Isaiah and the others.[8] Furthermore, Cassiodorus also reports Augustine as putting the Minor Prophets after the conventionally listed "Isaiah, Jeremiah, Ezekiel and Daniel," even though this is not the case in Augustine's own work, *On Christian Teaching*, where Daniel and Ezekiel are also transposed. Similarly, the Old Testament canon that Cassiodorus gives "according to the old translation and according to the Septuagint"[9] has the Minor Prophets following the four major ones. So, whatever variation there was even as late as the times of Jerome and Augustine, by the time of Cassiodorus the listing of the prophets in the Latin Bible had become stabilized. Cassiodorus suggests as much in his *Institutiones*, which is essentially his library catalogue. In volume one, he says that the Bible is normally in nine volumes, of which the third is "the four Major and twelve Minor Prophets."[10] Cassiodorus is, therefore, a witness for what had become the accepted Christian practice of positioning the Twelve as the conclusion of the prophetic books of the Old Testament.[11]

The Position of the Prophetic Corpus

On the other hand, the lists that Cassiodorus gives in the sixth century also testify that, at least in the traditions with which he was familiar, Matthew does not follow directly on the prophetic books. This is because Jerome, "the old translation and the Septuagint," and Cassiodorus's own nine-volume Bible have other Old Testament works following the prophets. In his account of Augustine's ordering of the books, the New Testament does follow Malachi but opens with the Epistles, not Matthew. There are earlier witnesses to an arrangement in which the gospels come immediately after the prophetic corpus, but in them[12] the Twelve come first in the list of prophets, not at the end.

The Sixteenth-Century Situation

In Cassiodorus, then, the prophetic corpus concludes with the Twelve (and, hence, with Malachi) but does not form the final part of

the Old Testament. Even before the earliest printed Bibles were produced, however, the prophets had become the last significant item of
the Old Testament canon. The Council of Florence, for example, in its
1442 Bull of Union with the Copts, lists the biblical books in what
became the standard order: the Old Testament finishes with the Minor
Prophets, followed by 1-2 Maccabees.[13] In the following century, both
Martin Luther (1535) and those responsible for the Sixto-Clementine
Vulgate of 1592[14] produced texts in which the Old Testament ended
with Malachi (plus 1-2 Maccabees in the Roman version). That the
Reformers and their opponents agreed on this matter is strong evidence that the prevailing manuscript tradition had that form, whatever
its predecessors.[15]

The Final Stage: From 1590 to the Present

The final stage of development of the canon in Bibles sponsored
by Anglophone Catholics is very recent and easy to trace. From Trent
until the new versions of the 1960s, English-speaking Catholics used
the Douai-Rheims-Challoner version of the Bible. Like its *Vorlage*,
the Clementine Vulgate,[16] and the list of canonical books from the
Council of Trent, the Douai Old Testament concluded with 1 and 2
Maccabees, preceded by Malachi. Ronald Knox's translation into
English from the Vulgate (1944-50) kept the same order. The situation changed with the publication of *La Bible de Jérusalem* in 1956,
the Jerusalem Bible ten years later, and the New American Bible in
1970.[17] In all three of these, 1 and 2 Maccabees were moved to a position between Esther and Job, namely, at the end of the "historical"
section. So far as I am aware, there is no ancient testimony to this
sequence, although Augustine had something like it.[18]

In making such a change, was the church being unfaithful to its
tradition? I do not think so, and for two reasons. First, there is no
evidence that Trent's concern in April of 1546 was with the order of
books. The main purpose of the conciliar decree was to rectify the
mayhem caused by individual interpretation of Scripture and the un-
controlled state of the biblical text. In fact, the delegates at Trent adopted
the list that had been made earlier at the Council of Florence and, by
majority vote, decided not to discuss its details.[19] Second, relocating
1-2 Maccabees in new translations of Scripture is well within the terms
of *Divino Afflante Spiritu*, Pius XII's 1943 encyclical on biblical stud-

ies that set out in detail the need for critical biblical scholarship. One theological consequence of the move was to embed more deeply in the Old Testament an important example of pre-Christian teaching on the afterlife: 2 Maccabees 12. Another was to leave Malachi as the concluding book of the Old Testament canon, as was already the case in other Christian Bibles.

Turning the Page?

So are we at last in a position to consider the transition from Malachi to Matthew? Almost. There is, however, one other feature to note. For, just as the juxtaposition of those two books represents a relatively narrow part of the tradition, so does the solitary reading of the Bible. Admittedly, some of the literate monks, nuns, and clerics would have read the Bible as individuals, on occasion, but this was not the normal way for people to encounter the sacred text, especially in the Catholic form of the tradition. Rather, they knew the Bible from their experience of the liturgy. In this, they resemble most modern Christians, who are also more likely to listen to biblical readings in church than they are to read the Bible on their own. Listening, being both aural and communal, is a different experience from turning the pages.

In the liturgical reading of Scripture, the controlling factor is the Lectionary, which determines the parts of Scripture that are used and how they are combined. In the current form of Latin-rite Catholicism, on Sundays and feast days more or less sequential readings from the gospels and the other New Testament writings are accompanied by varied Old Testament readings, including psalms. For weekdays is specified the continuous reading of a text from, first, either the Old or the New Testament and then a gospel, the two being separated by a psalm. In this context, the congregation experiences the transition from the Old Testament to the New not as turning a page but (at least on weekdays) as a move from sitting to standing, at the conclusion of the psalm. I would wager that no liturgical assembly ever listened to the end of Malachi followed immediately by Matthew's genealogy. This is a second reason why my initial question is not one that has the sanction of long usage in the church: even when Malachi was followed by Matthew in printed Bibles, most people did not experience the juxtaposition, because it did not occur in the Lectionary.

From Malachi to Matthew

Malachi does, of course, have strong connections with the gospel tradition, but they are with Luke,[20] not Matthew;[21] and so far as I am aware, no edition of the New Testament except Marcion's began with Luke. Yet even though there are no thematic links between Malachi and Matthew, I still think that turning the page from one to the other does throw some light on a particular set of emphases in Matthew.

The Jerusalem Connection

First, each text has an implied or explicit link with Jerusalem and a claim that Israel's relationship with the Lord is not what it should be. Malachi accuses Israel of being unaware of the Lord's action on its behalf (1:2-5). In a world where the Lord's name is "reverenced among the nations" (1:14), Israel's failure to give the "honor due to" the Lord as father and master (v. 6) is given ritual expression in the sacrificial offerings of "what has been taken by violence or is lame or sick" (v. 13). The primary responsibility for this state of affairs belongs to the priests, as Malachi's second chapter makes clear. Although the prophet does not name Jerusalem in this connection until 2:11 (and see also 3:4), readers could not fail to be aware that the Temple in Jerusalem is the site of this highly inappropriate activity at the heart of Israel's communal life. That these defective sacrifices do indeed reflect people's general attitudes becomes clear in chapter 3, where the prophet claims that Israel has turned aside from the Lord's statutes (3:7) specifying short-changing the Lord on tithes (3:8-10) and, generally, regarding service of God as a waste of time (3:14).

Matthew does not name Jerusalem in his opening chapter either, but his use of the genealogy to present Jesus as the Messiah/Christ relies heavily on references to King David. In addition to David's inclusion as son of Jesse and father of Solomon (1:6), he is named (along with Abraham, whom he precedes) in the opening of the genealogy in 1:1 and again, in its summarizing conclusion: "So all the generations from Abraham to David are fourteen generations; and from David to the deportation to Babylon, fourteen generations; and from the deportation to Babylon to the Messiah, fourteen generations" (1:17).

Here, it becomes evident that David is the major organizing principle of Matthew's list. Not only is he on a par with Abraham and the Babylonian exile, those two major and formative elements of Israel's experience, but his name, DWD, has the numerical value of "fourteen" (4+6+4) that structures the entire genealogy. Although Matthew 1 does not specify Jerusalem as the city that the ubiquitous David adopted as his capital, the second chapter opens with the magi finding their way to that city (2:1), where the news of their quest frightens Herod "and all Jerusalem with him" (2:3). Here again is depicted inappropriate behavior of Israelites under the leadership of a Jerusalem-based figure, in this case Herod the Great.

It is important to notice that one of Matthew's chief concerns in these first two chapters is to establish the identity of Jesus as the Messiah, the Lord's anointed one: Christos is used in 1:1, 16, and 17; in 1:18 Jesus' birth is specified as that of *Iēsous Christos*; in 2:2 the magi term him "the newborn king of the Jews" (in mute contrast to "Herod the king" in 2:1), and in response to their request for information, Herod sends for "all the chief priests and scribes of the people" to find where "the Christ" was to be born (2:4). Yet, as we shall see from what Matthew says about Jesus' origins, Jesus is no ordinary successor to David.

On Paternity, Its Correlations and Consequences[22]

The second element of continuity that may occur to the reader who moves from Malachi to Matthew concerns the relation between generations. In its present form, the prophetic book ends with the Lord's promise to send Elijah to "turn the hearts of fathers to their sons and the hearts of sons to their fathers, lest I come and strike the land with a curse [or with doom]."[23] The final word is thus *herem*, ban. It denotes the removal of something from profane use, often with the idea of its destruction, and the way that it may be avoided is by sons being actively concerned about their fathers and vice versa. God will send help so that people will find themselves able to do this: that is to be Elijah's function.

In a very different mode, the opening of Matthew comes at this same idea of the connectedness between generations. For the evangelist first announces and then more or less delivers "[a]n account of the genealogy of Jesus the Messiah, the son of David, the son of Abraham" (1:1, to v. 17). Here is a bare-bones account of what has happened since God's choice of Abraham: men have begotten sons, and the end point is "Joseph the husband of Mary, from whom Jesus was born, who is called the Christ" (Matt 1:16; the "whom" here is feminine).

So what the reader finds when turning the page from Malachi to Matthew is certainly not the divine curse that was the last word of Malachi. Nor does Matthew mention the expected means by which that curse was to be avoided: the account of a reconciliation effected by a human being, in the person of the Prophet Elijah. The evangelist's version of that will come two chapters later when John the Baptist appears in the desert wearing Elijah's leather belt (cf. 2 Kings 1:8) and insisting on evidence of repentance (Matt 3:1-12; see also 11:7-19). In Matthew 1 there is, rather, a prosaic listing of fathers and sons that bears implicit witness to God's fidelity through the ages.

The evangelist's introduction and conclusion to the genealogy (vv. 1 and 17) draw particular attention to three key points in the sequence. They are Abraham, who first received God's promise of land and offspring; David, God's anointed one, whose reign represented the high point of Israel's success as a nation; and [Jesus] the Messiah (the anointed one), who represents the Lord's latest activity on Israel's behalf and whose story will be told in what follows. Note that Jesus is linked to Israel, not in the way that all generations from Abraham had been, but through his being "named" by Joseph (1:21, 25) and through his mother, who is "betrothed to Joseph" (1:18). Jesus is, therefore, an integral part of Israel—and yet not in quite the same way as his predecessors from Abraham to Joseph.

Another aspect of Jesus' identity is that he, whom the genealogy presents as the culmination of Israel from Abraham onward, is also God's son. Matthew does not present this as metaphorical, since Joseph is not Jesus' biological father. In this Gospel, Jesus is "really" God's son, even though Matthew does not say so as bluntly as did Gabriel in Luke 1:35. Rather, Matthew first presents Jesus as belonging to Israel, through Joseph (and Mary). Next, he twice attributes Jesus' conception to the Holy Spirit (1:18, 20). Finally, God acknowledges Jesus as "my son" in the way that Israel also was in Hosea 11:1: by being called out of Egypt by God. This Matthew expresses by quoting Hosea in 2:15. It allows him to have God say about Jesus, "Out of Egypt I called my son." So Jesus is God's son uniquely through his conception by the Spirit and also through his essential connectedness with God's son, Israel, both genealogically (although indirectly) and by his reliving a key element of Israel's history when the Lord brings him out of Egypt.

Matthew's text both contrasts with and develops what is found in Malachi. In Malachi 1:6, God asked rhetorically, "If I am a father, where is the honor due me?" Here, the expression is figurative. Matthew, though, takes up the theme of fatherhood in a way that is literal, at least to begin with, and much more important. First, there is a recapitulation of Israel's flourishing from Abraham to the Messiah. Even though "father" is nowhere used here (nor elsewhere in the first four chapters of the gospel), the successive "begettings" make it clear that the mechanism is understood to be human fatherhood (with the occasional mother deemed worthy of mention). The Christ thus belongs within that history. Second, however, God's begetting of Jesus is at least hinted at, since he is conceived by the Holy Spirit (1:18, 20) and called forth from Egypt by God.

The divine fatherhood and its consequences are one of the very strong emphases of the Gospel according to Matthew. The primary datum is God as Jesus' father, established in the infancy story, along with two other aspects of the child's identity: those of savior (1:21, although that is not, in fact, what "Jesus" means) and "Emmanuel, which means 'God is with us'" (vv. 22-23). Thus, in contiguous verses Matthew notes first that Jesus "will save his people from their sins" (1:21) and then that he fulfills the prophecy about the child to be called "Emmanuel" (1:22-23). Even though the full implications of these statements come only later in the narrative, Matthew's community would have been aware that in Israel's tradition, the Lord is the one who saves and is characteristically present with Israel. So, for example, after the account of the crossing of the Red Sea, the editor of Exodus notes, "Thus the LORD saved Israel that day from the Egyptians" (Exod. 14:30), and later Moses makes clear that Israel's identity as a people is bound up with the Lord's presence with them (see, for example, 33:15-16). Matthew will develop both those themes later on, but before doing so, he expands on the theme of God's fatherhood of Jesus and its consequences.

This begins in chapter 5, where it transpires that God is not only Jesus' Father, but also the "heavenly Father" of believers. Seventeen times in the Sermon on the Mount (Matthew 5-7), *pater* is used to designate God as Jesus' Father or as the Father of his followers. These chapters can be read as basic teaching about what it means to have God as one's Father.

The word *pater* is not used in chapters 8-9, but between chapters 10 and 26 it occurs a further twenty-seven times to designate God. (Only four of these seventeen chapters are without it.[24]) Particularly notable is the saying, found in Matthew alone, in which Jesus tells his followers, "And call no one your father on earth, for you have one Father—the one in heaven" (23:9). This is immediately linked with Jesus as the Messiah, for the following verse is: "Nor are you to be called teachers, for you have one teacher, the Messiah" (23:10). Here, as in the infancy narrative, God's fatherhood is connected with Jesus as the Messiah.

What is happening in Matthew, then, can be seen as a radical but beneficent adjustment of the plan laid out in Malachi. It is not that Elijah (the Baptist) causes conversions of people so that they behave as they should toward their nearest relations—although he does try, in a rather counterintuitive manner (3:7-12). Rather, God's paternity of Jesus (and of Israel) is extended to Jesus' followers in a way that is intimately connected with Jesus' own sonship, which, in turn, is recognizable quintessentially in his death (see 26:54).

Matthew is thus much more explicit than Malachi 1:6 in specifying what being God's children should mean for Jesus' followers. Indeed, according to the Sermon on the Mount, being children of God characterizes Matthew's community and shapes their life in a way that is analogous to God's presence with Israel in the Old Testament, including the Torah to which Malachi referred in 4:4 (3:22 in the Hebrew). In the final verse of the gospel, the two motifs of divine Fatherhood and Presence come together: the church is to baptize in the name of the Father, the Son, and the Holy Spirit, and Jesus (who was Emmanuel in 1:23 and the Messiah throughout) is to be with his disciples, not only when they gather in his name (18:20) but even "to the end of the age" (28:20). It is, of course, a saving presence.[25]

Conclusion

Looking for the connections and contrasts between Malachi and Matthew can draw the reader's attention to particular aspects of Matthew's theology. It is certainly not the case that without the juxtaposition, people would miss the evangelist's presentation of God as

Father and Jesus as the Messiah who is forever present with the community. Yet considering the two books together does make these themes stand out.

Interestingly, nothing in the history of the biblical canon makes it inevitable that people of our day would be able to develop their thought about the significance of Jesus by reading Matthew in light of Malachi. For most of the Christian era the two books had no particular connection with each other, either ideological or in the arrangement of the canon. The majority of Old Testament lists did not end with Malachi, and, prior to the age of printed Bibles, the manuscripts usually consisted only of one or two books.[26] Even when manuscripts came to take the form of codices rather than scrolls, there were physical limits to how much of the Bible could be bound in one volume while still being usable and able to stay in one piece over long periods of time.[27] Yet, despite the apparent improbability of its happening, the Twelve came to conclude the prophetic corpus and the Writing Prophets were eventually placed at the end of the Old Testament, so that Malachi abutted on Matthew. For Catholics, the final stage of this did not happen until the middle part of the twentieth century. So the juxtaposition of the two books is not something that was worked out logically or even something that is deducible from the physical evidence available. Nor did it arise in the liturgy. It is simply a gift of the tradition.

It is not, however, just any kind of gift, but one that is inherent in the material conditions by which the biblical tradition was passed down through the centuries. As oral material was recorded in writing, first in scrolls, later in codices, and finally in the various generations of printed Bibles, new intertextual relationships appeared. This resulted in fresh understandings of the text. For example, until Paul's letters were bound together, people could not read them in light of each other; once they began to do this, new aspects of Paul's teaching became obvious. The Malachi-Matthew juxtaposition is another instance of the same phenomenon.

There is a profound fittingness to this. For the Christian tradition itself stems from belief in the incarnation of God in Jesus of Nazareth. As an aspect of particularity in time and place, materiality is thus of the essence of God's self-communication and of Christians' response to that revelation. In other words, the world is sacramental. Although the revelation itself (in the life of Jesus) and the church's witness to it in the biblical books are both "given," people's understanding of them continues to develop. The material conditions of the Bible's transmission are one source of that development. Those inclined to think of the Bible as having dropped from heaven in its completeness will find this problematic. It is otherwise for people who experience the world, in all its messiness, as mediating God's presence. They are more likely to find here yet another cause for wonder and delight.

Notes

[1] Anathea Portier-Young, "Moses and Elijah in Malachi 3:22-24," Annual meeting of the Society of Biblical Literature, Nashville, November 20, 2000. (Note that in the New Revised Standard Version and its antecedents, Malachi 3:19-24 is given as 4:1-6.)

[2] Contrary to some recent usage and in line with the convincing arguments advanced by A.-J. Levine elsewhere in this volume, I shall use the traditional term, Old Testament, to denote the thirty-nine or forty-six books of Jewish origin that Christians adopted as the first part of their Bible. The Jewish canonical scriptures (consisting of the Law [*Torah*], the Prophets [*Nevi'îm*] and the Writings [*Kᵉtûbîm*]) I shall usually refer to as Tanach and occasionally as the Hebrew Bible.

[3] For the Hebrew, see A. Alt et al., eds., *Biblia Hebraica Stuttgartensia* (Stuttgart: Deutsche Bibelstiftung, 1967/77), XI. A two-volume edition of the Greek Old Testament is Alfred Rahlfs, ed., *Septuaginta* (Stuttgart: Deutsche Bibelgesellschaft, 1935, 1982). For the decree of the Council of Trent, see, for example, Norman Tanner, S.J., ed., *Decrees of the Ecumenical Councils*, vol. 2 (London: Sheed & Ward; Washington, D.C.: Georgetown University Press, 1990), 663-64.

[4] Most of the information on the chart comes from Alfred C. Sundberg, Jr., *The Old Testament of the Early Church*, Harvard Theological Studies, vol. XX (Cambridge: Harvard University Press and London: Oxford University Press, 1964), 58-59. Sundberg includes references. See also F. F. Bruce, *The Canon of Scripture* (Downers Grove, Ill.: InterVarsity Press, 1988), 97 and 68-114.

[5] The first editors of the whole Mount Sinai codex, Helen and Kirsopp Lake, give as the original Old Testament order of the manuscript: Genesis, Numbers, 1 Chronicles to Tobit, Tobit to Judith, to Jeremiah and Lamentations, and Joel to Job. See *Codex Sinaiticus Petropolitanus et Friderico-Augustanus Lipsiensis* (Oxford: Clarendon Press, 1922), ix. Ezekiel and Daniel are missing, as are three of the Twelve (Hosea, Amos, and Micah), but Kirsopp Lake deduces from the two sets of numbering on the sheets that, apart from possibly one gathering at the end of the Old Testament (probably of eight leaves), no part of the original manuscript is missing.

[6] This is preserved by Eusebius, *Ecclesiastical History* 4.26.12-14.

[7] Cassiodorus, *De institutione divinarum litterarium* XII, PL 70, 1125.

[8] See Jerome's list in *Epistle 53*, his Letter to Paulinus of Nola, dated 394.

[9] *De institutione divinarum litterarium* XIV, heading.

[10]See Margaret T. Gibson, *The Bible in the Latin West*, The Medieval Book, vol. 1 (Notre Dame and London: University of Notre Dame Press, 1993), 3.

[11]Jewish influence on the Christian canon may be operative in this case as in others. See Albert C. Sundberg, Jr., "The 'Old Testament': A Christian Canon," *Catholic Biblical Quarterly* 30 (1968): 143-55, 149.

[12]For example, Athanasius's Festal Letter of 367 and Augustine in *On Christian Teaching*.

[13]See Tanner, *Decrees of the Ecumenical Councils*, vol. 2, 572. The Decree was issued from the Council's Fourth Session, 4 February 1442.

[14]They included Robert Bellarmine and William Allen. See S. L. Greenslade, ed., *The Cambridge History of the Bible: The West from the Reformation to the Present Day* (Cambridge: Cambridge University Press, 1963), 68-69, 207-11.

[15]On the intricacies and uncertainties of the medieval Vulgate manuscript tradition, see, for example, G. W. H. Lampe, ed., *The Cambridge History of the Bible, Volume 2: The West from the Fathers to the Reformation* (Cambridge: Cambridge University Press, 1969), chapter V, "The Medieval History of the Latin Vulgate," 102-4.

[16]The original Rheims version of the Vulgate had been made from the pre-Sixtine text in 1578-82 (Greenslade, *The Cambridge History of the Bible*, 211) but was later "'conformed to the most perfect Latin edition,' the Sixto-Clementine of 1592" (163).

[17]The New American Bible volume containing the books from Isaiah to Malachi first appeared in 1961, although the full Bible was not published until 1970.

[18]In *On Christian Teaching*, Augustine's presentation of the canon includes the following sequence: Tobit, Esther, Judith, 1-2 Maccabees, 1-2 Esdras. (See Sundberg, *The Old Testament of the Early Church*, 59.) Cassiodorus's list for Augustine reverses the last two elements of this.

[19]See Peter G. Duncker, "The Canon of the Old Testament at the Council of Trent," *Catholic Biblical Quarterly* 15 (1953): 277-99. Then, according to Greenslade (*The Cambridge History of the Bible*, 201), the Council Fathers proceeded to lose the document from Florence, the Bull of Union with the Jacobites. The list from the same Council's Bull of Union with the Syrians is extant, however; see n. 13, above.

[20]Connections between Luke and Malachi include the use of Malachi 3:23-24 (4:5-6) in Luke 1:17; the image of the "dawn of righteousness" in Malachi 3:20 (4:2) taken up in the Benedictus (Luke 1:78-79); and, perhaps, an allusion to Malachi 3:1b in the twofold coming of Jesus ("the Lord," Luke 2:11) to the Temple, as a baby (2:22-38) and at twelve years (vv. 41-49). The first part of Malachi 3:1 is quoted in Luke 7:27 and its parallels, Mark 1:2 and Matthew 11:10. There may be an allusion to Malachi 1:11 in Luke 13:29.

[21]In addition to the quotation of Malachi 1:11 in Matthew 11:10, Matthew 11:14-15 alludes to Malachi 3:1, 23.

[22]In Malachi and in Matthew's Gospel as a whole, the theme of paternity need not be gender-exclusive, but fatherhood is clearly the issue in Matthew 1-2.

[23]The NRSV and its predecessors, along with the Jerusalem Bible, have "a curse," while the New American Bible has "doom." The reference is to Malachi 3:24 (4:6 in NRSV and its predecessors).

[24]They are chapters 14, 17, 19, and 21.

[25]The story of the storm in 8:23-27 can be read as paradigmatic of the experience of Matthew's community. Jesus is, indeed, with them and available to save those who call on him, even though he may seem to be "asleep."

[26]An exception is that the Twelve Minor Prophets were usually transmitted together, in Jewish and Christian tradition.

[27]See, for example, Lampe, *The Cambridge History of the Bible*, 108-9.

Paul the Enforcer: Using Rhetoric to Deconstruct an Image and to Reconstruct Theology

Maria Pascuzzi

Both figuratively and, in some cases, literally, Paul's legacy has become what has recently been termed "an ideological weapon of death,"[1] aiding and abetting systems of domination and oppression. As is well known, Paul's thoughts have, in many instances, formed the scriptural battleground upon which women's issues, views, and aspirations have been contested.[2] Some have viewed Paul as the person responsible for creating a rigid, dogmatic Christianity quite divorced from Jesus.[3] Others point to Paul as the root cause of modern anti-Semitism, which, they claim, had its origin in Paul's sharp polemic against Jews as reflected in 1 Thessalonians 2:14-16, a text often cited to illustrate Paul's animosity toward the Jews. References to 1 Corinthians 6:9 in the context of discussions on natural law and "intrinsically evil" acts[4] are implicit reminders to gay and lesbian persons that they too may be among those whom Paul states "will not inherit the kingdom."

Having been the authoritative voice cited in the service of so much abuse, oppression, and discrimination, it is no wonder that Paul is perceived by many as imperious or that he is the object of widespread hostility.[5] Thus, while it is hardly a surprise to read that Paul has won the distinction of being "the most attacked person in the New Testament"[6] or that "few figures in Western History have been the subject of greater controversy than Saint Paul"[7] or that "few have caused more dissension and hatred,"[8] it is certainly ironic that the one who purposed to be "all things to all people" (1 Cor 9:22), for the sake of the gospel, has evolved into something of a stumbling block to so many.

The fact of this widespread hostility to Paul can hardly be denied. Whether or not, however, Paul is responsible for everything negative imputed to him is quite another question, one that is now being addressed in various studies.[9] The purpose of this brief study will be to 1) consider some factors that may contribute to negative perceptions of Paul as imperious and that continue to exacerbate the antipathy toward him; 2) take one text where, more often than not, Paul is shown to be at his imperious worst and then consider that same text through the lens of rhetoric to see whether a more positive assessment of Paul is warranted; and, finally, 3) in view of the rhetoric, to recover valuable theological insights that may have relevance but risk being overlooked when the man responsible for them is perceived as an inflexible autocrat.

Some Factors Contributing
to the Current Disaffection with Paul

Why Paul is so insufferable to so many today may have less to do with Paul than with interpretations of him and his thought that have come forth from European scholars who have dominated Pauline studies during the past two hundred years. This is the recent suggestion of Robert Jewett, who claims that European scholars, predominately white and male, have, in essence, refashioned Paul and recast his thought in view of their own eurocentric intellectual and cultural traditions.[10] Jewett signals a number of features characteristic of this tradition that have conditioned the study of Paul and contributed to misrepresentations of him and misunderstandings of his thought.[11]

Two of these features that seem to have had a great impact on presentations of Paul and interpretations of his letters are a preoccupation with the notion of an "imperial self" at the top of the ladder and a tendency to advance ideas in a polemical way. As will be seen below, one can still read articles and commentaries in which the authors underscore or make absolute Paul's unique authority and then consider his "opponents" contentious, headstrong, or the like. Even more notable is the tendency to showcase Paul as the irascible protagonist. In a recent commentary on 1 Corinthians, Paul is featured as battling his way against a fractious community, re-asserting his authority and re-establishing unity, order, right thinking, and right praxis. The author writes:

> Paul is taking them on at every turn. There is little to suggest that he is informing or merely correcting; instead he is attacking and challenging with all the weapons in his literary arsenal.[12]

> Paul is on the attack, contending with them, arguing with them, trying to convince them that he is right and they are wrong. . . . Thus the letter is basically the Apostle Paul vis-à-vis the whole congregation.[13]

Though produced in the 1980s, this commentary comes quite close to replicating the portrait of Paul advanced by a European scholar almost a century before in which Paul is featured as an indefatigable spokesman of the gospel who, assailed by enemies at every point in his work, remained fearless and willing to push on to certain victory.[14] This Paul is the lone intellectual warrior, battling, winning, never short on energy or force to compel belief in the gospel. This is the Paul holding the sword, the towering and imposing figure sculpted in stone that has stood for just over a century at the Basilica of Saint Paul Outside the Wall in Rome, adding graphic expression to the eurocentric view of an irascible, imperious Paul who still lives on in the pages of contemporary commentaries and articles.

When Paul, who chastises, corrects, shames, uses irony, expresses anger, dismay, and sarcasm, is viewed through eurocentric categories, he will be the imperial great man who thinks he has the right to impose his will and enforce his gospel. It is understandable that we would wish to distance ourselves from such a person. However, it is also possible to consider Paul, who chastises, corrects, expresses anger and shock, and so on, within the intellectual and cultural tradition of his own Greco-Roman world and discover that these same literary devices and expressions point to a different type of individual altogether: one who knows how to employ rhetorical strategy, whose texts illustrate that he would rather eschew force for persuasion; in sum, someone who is quite capable of crafting rhetorically sophisticated arguments aimed at moving the communities he founded to adhere more fully to the gospel message rather than simply commanding that they do so.[15]

Fortunately, since the pioneering work of Wilhelm Wuellner,[16] Paul's letters have been increasingly studied under the aspect of rhetoric,[17] that is, as arguments aimed at persuasion and not simply or exclusively as *Briefgattung*.[18] This new phase in contemporary biblical scholarship[19] has alerted readers to the rhetorical techniques employed by Paul to persuade his readers. In particular, the rhetorical approach to Paul's letters constitutes a serious attempt to understand Paul within the context of the intellectual and cultural tradition of his own Greco-Roman[20] world, and insights resulting from the application of rhetorical criticism have already significantly advanced our understanding of the dynamics of Paul's letters. This method, as I hope to show vis-à-vis the text of 1 Corinthians 5, can be fruitfully employed in the effort both to rescue Paul from negative umbrage and gain further insight into and a greater appreciation for his message.

1 Corinthians 5: Enforcing Paul or Persuading Paul?

1 Corinthians 5 is just one of the many texts that could be cited to illustrate how negative portrayals of Paul, many times unfounded, can impede both the appreciation of his method and the appropriation of his message. The text concerns a situation of immorality in the Christian community at Corinth. Paul had spent eighteen months evangelizing there and apparently after his departure problems developed in the community that challenged both its unity and status as a holy community. One of these problems, treated in 1 Corinthians 5, was that a community member was involved in an on-going sexual relationship with his step-mother,[21] a relationship considered incestuous and proscribed by both pagan and religious law.[22] For some reason, there were members of the community who were boasting about this relationship, perhaps seeing it as a reflection of the freedom and liberation that Paul probably preached as the hallmark of Christian existence.[23]

Some scholars who view the entire situation of 1 Corinthians as reflecting a polemical relationship between Paul and the Corinthians are inclined to understand the incestuous relationship and boasting as conscious acts of disobedience intended to challenge Paul's authority in a public way.[24] As a result, the Corinthians are usually depicted as insolent and disobedient while Paul, on the other hand, is depicted as the champion of truth and morality who must squelch the boasting, discipline the sinner, and re-establish his authority.

It is not at all certain, however, that 1 Corinthians reflects Paul's struggle to re-establish his authority in a situation where it is presumed to have seriously eroded.[25] If this is so, it may be unwarranted to construe 1 Corinthians 5 as one episode in this larger battle and, even further, to construe Paul's purposes in this chapter as nothing more than a magisterial and unilateral exercise of authority. When the politics of authority and obedience are brought into the foreground, it is Paul the autocrat who is spotlighted. In fact, it has been alleged that 1 Corinthians 5 represents a case of ecclesiastical discipline carried out in a completely undemocratic, highly authoritarian manner by the Apostle Paul, which should be sufficient proof to set aside any false contemplation of the beginnings of early Christianity as embodying collegiality.[26] It has also been suggested that in 1 Corinthians 5, Paul attacks his enemies to enhance his own prestige and arrogates to himself the identity of the ascended Christ in order to enforce his judgment.[27] Thus Paul is the enforcer of discipline; the community's task is simply to obey. When Paul is represented in this manner and his intention is said to be little more than the imposition of his will on a community of believers, it is quite easy to see how and why the negative assumptions at the basis of the contemporary alienation from Paul are simply reinforced.

Unfortunately, those who hold such views fail to recognize the carefully structured rhetorical argument that Paul sets forth in this chapter; through it he aims to persuade the community that this case of immorality is ultimately detrimental to its own well-being, and therefore, that some sanctioning action must be taken against the man. Although it is true that Paul outlines the sanctioning procedure (5:3-5), it is not true that Paul expects the community to do what it is told as an act of unreflective obedience. If it were, there would be no need for Paul to advance any reasons at all. Yet he does, and once the text strategy is disclosed, it will become evident that Paul has carefully crafted a persuasive argument intended to move the community to act on its own behalf.

Paul's Argumentative Strategy

Paul's argument unfolds in three phases. First, following good rhetorical convention, Paul begins his argument in v. 2 by shaming the community,[28] reminding them that even pagans would not tolerate such

an arrangement.[29] According to the handbooks of rhetoric, a good persuasive argument that was intended to move an audience to change its
behavior usually began with an appeal to emotions[30] since, as Aristotle
noted, "the emotions were all those affections which cause men to
change their opinion in regard to their judgements."[31] Moreover, among
the emotions to be tapped, "shame" was one of the most powerful if
one were attempting to induce an audience to modify its views and
change its behavior, since, as Cicero observed, the desire not to be
disgraced was the strongest incentive to change one's thoughts or behavior.[32]

When Paul's rhetorical technique is not recognized, it is easy to
misconstrue his intentions[33] and to read this reference to the pagans as
an indication of Paul's preoccupation with scandal, which is then assumed to be the reason for the very severe sanction announced at 5:3-
5.[34] Knowledge of rhetorical theory, however, allows us to take this
shaming section for what it really is, namely, a rhetorical device skill-
fully employed by Paul to induce change that is evidence of some
rhetorical sophistication.

Moreover, by referring to the pagans, Paul insinuates that there
exists a societal consensus that such relationships are wrong. If pagans consider it wrong, then everyone must consider it wrong. This
universal moral standard is set out as the standard against which
Corinthian judgment and behavior are initially critiqued. In other words,
it is not Paul's moral reasoning that is first cited as a critical standard.
From the vantage point of rhetorical strategy, one can see that Paul
actually avoids reproaching the community as an individual figure of
unique authority.[35] Instead, he cleverly exploits the convergence of
the world's values with Christian values as a point of departure for his
argument.[36]

In addition, attention to the rhetorical strategy of shaming also allows us to recognize that, in all probability, Paul actually had a positive relationship with the community, since, as Aristotle observed, the
evocation of shame depends on the fact that the one attempting to
evoke shame be esteemed and admired by the group or individual
addressed; otherwise, no matter how grave the matter, shame will not
be experienced.[37] This appeal to the Corinthian emotions is the first
step in Paul's persuasive strategy.

The third part of the argument, located in vv. 9-13,[38] is an appeal to
the Corinthians to consider the community member for what he really

is, an immoral person. Here again, in good rhetorical fashion, Paul uses the technique of comparison or classification.[39] By classifying the one calling himself a brother with other sinners, Paul is able to expose the community member as a sinner of rank. By bringing the community to view the brother no longer as one in whom to boast, but rather as one comparable to other immoral persons from whom the community would naturally desire to be separate, Paul effectively drives a wedge between the community and the sinful brother. Having evoked powerful sentiments of abhorrence and alienation, Paul has again given the community reason to feel exigent about removing the sinful brother from its midst in order to protect itself from his corrupting influence. Without resorting to force, Paul uses a powerful rhetorical tactic to engage the emotions of the community. In this way, the community's own sense of repugnance becomes the motivating force that will ultimately compel it to change its judgment and deal with the erring brother.

In the middle section of the argument, vv. 6-8, again in good rhetorical fashion, Paul appeals to the common sense of the community, citing a maxim with which they could all agree: "a little leaven leavens the whole lump of dough." Then through analogy, Paul compares the community to a whole lump of dough or loaf (*phyrama*), which is meant to be unleavened (*azyme*), a term which in this context means "sin-free." This is so because Christ, the Paschal Lamb, has been sacrificed, creating the condition of sinlessness that obtains in the community as a whole. Here Paul does not appeal to the emotions of the community; he reasons with them in view of the status that is theirs through the atoning death of Christ. The necessity to preserve the sinless status of the community is the central argument advanced by Paul to persuade the community to deal with the offender.

Thus, a close look at the text and a careful consideration of Paul's use of rhetoric reveals that there is no enforcer demanding that the community obey orders and carry out a sanction. The Paul who writes in response to this situation has set out a carefully constructed persuasive argument, beginning with an appeal to the emotions (argument based on *pathos*), continuing with an appeal to the Corinthians' reason (*logos*), and ending with another appeal to their emotions (*pathos*). Paul has already sized up the situation and has a plan for how to deal with it. This is clear especially in view of 5:3-5.

Nonetheless, Paul goes forward to craft an argument in order to provide the community with three separate arguments or motives for why they should adopt a different perspective on the brother's behavior, desist from boasting about it, and actually do something to sanction the man. Paul clearly expresses dismay that the community has not taken appropriate action. He shames the community. He dramatizes the menace the brother poses to the holiness of the community—even a little yeast can corrupt the whole—and he creates an urgent, black and white situation: preserve the holiness, the sinless state, of the community by ejecting the sinful presence, or suffer corruption as a whole. But the choice to act resides finally with the community and, through persuasive argument, Paul hopes to move the community to choose its own corporate well-being.

The rhetoric of the text underscores that the practical aim of this passage is to persuade the community to modify its judgment and behavior. This does not mean that in responding to this situation, as he did, that Paul could not have had ulterior motives that related specifically to a personal desire to reassert his authority, as some claim. Readers and hearers have no way of knowing this. What I am suggesting, though, is that the text rhetoric does not lend support to claims that Paul was flexing his muscle here to enforce his will or that he was reasserting his authority in a situation alleged to pose an intentional challenge to that authority by the Corinthians. On the contrary, the rhetoric of the text would seem to suggest that there is no justification for reading this text through the lens of polemic that unnecessarily and even, it seems, erroneously shifts attention to the "politics-of-authority" rather than to the issue at stake and Paul's response to it. Once this lens is peeled away, we can begin to appreciate the rhetorical strategy at work and finally begin to ask about the theology that informs this argument and what contemporary relevance it may have.

Recovering Theology: The Primacy of the Community

In 1 Corinthians 5, Paul's central argument for the sanctioning of the sinful brother turns on his insistence that the community forms one sinless whole. Paul's insistence on this fact derives from his understanding not only of the atoning quality of Christ's death and its sanctifying effect on the community of believers (1 Cor 5:7) but the further awareness that in Christ, through baptism,[40] Christians are not simply cleansed individuals but are constituted members of one cleansed whole, the Body of Christ, as we read elsewhere throughout his writings (for example, Romans 6:1-11; Galatians 3:27-28; 1 Corinthians 12:13; 1 Corinthians 6:11 and further 1 Colossians 2:11-12 and Ephesians 4:5).

Paul's deep convictions about the sinless status of the *ekklesia* as a whole clearly inform his response to the incest situation. He communicates the substance of his understanding of the *ekklesia* as one and sinless[41] in the metaphoric language, the simple picture-words, of leaven and lump of dough. Within the context of this particular argument where Paul is arguing for the preservation of the sinless status of the whole community, the maxim, "a little leaven leavens the whole lump," apparently functions as an ecclesial metaphor. Through it, Paul is able to communicate the idea that the Christian community constitutes one moral environment. This sinless status is a result of Christ's atoning death (1 Cor 5:7) but it obtains *within* the community as a whole, the Body of Christ, into which each believer is baptized and constituted part of the sinless community.

This moral environment has its own ecology about which each individual member must be concerned. In fact, as Paul argues, the sin of one member of the community can upset and compromise the moral ecology of the whole community. Why is this so? Because a Christian can only act as a member of a community,[42] and participation in this community is, on analogy with leaven, dynamic; it is power either to contribute to the continued sanctification of the whole or to introduce pollution into the community by exposing it to the reign of sin. For Paul, no one redeemed and baptized into Christ can divest himself or herself of this power to affect the whole. Once part of the body, the Christian cannot withdraw into neutrality. For Christians, then, this very fact means that they are not "bounded" persons—separate entities—able to act autonomously; rather, they are "bonded" and connected persons who must be responsible for the life of the whole community. To borrow an image suggested by the metaphor, the Christian community rises or falls as a whole.

In 1 Corinthians 5, Paul does not engage in theoretical discourse about the exercise of individual freedom or rights or the motives of the individual or the community. Rather, Paul's focus is teleological; his concern centers on the negative consequences for the community resulting from an individual choice, in this case the choice to live as a member of the community while simultaneously living a life of *"porneia."* Even when these negative consequences are not perceived by the community, as appears to be the case in 1 Corinthians 5, Paul insists that the community risks suffering the consequences nonetheless, and so Paul exhorts the community to be vigilant about its common sanctified life. When Christians consider the implications of Paul's religious message, they realize that they are faced with a message that has contemporary relevance but which is at the same time difficult and challenging.

In what is widely acclaimed as a benchmark study of American culture, sociologist Robert Bellah notes that radical individualism is perceived as one of the major factors contributing to the unraveling of the moral and ethical life of the nation and to the destruction of freedom itself. In the language of radical individualism, the individual is understood to be antecedent to society and the self is perceived as the only or main form of reality.[43] The self becomes the criterion for the validation of choices.[44] Within this conceptual world, the exercise of freedom can turn out to be little more than an exercise in self-realization that becomes the ultimate goal, unfortunately replacing any concern for the common good. What Bellah calls for to counter the destructive ethos of radical individualism is a re-hearing and re-adoption of the biblical ethos that places primacy on the community and stresses the interrelatedness of all persons. In this regard, Paul is not a lone biblical voice, but perhaps one of the most forceful in his insistence on the primacy of the life of the community.

Not all Christian living, either in the Corinthian community or in Christian communities today, is subverted by radical individualism. However, those who are caught up in the ethos of radical individualism and value it more than the life of community and its well-being will undoubtedly find it difficult to appropriate what Paul had to say in 1 Corinthians 5 in a meaningful way. In fact, Paul's religious message, that the community takes precedence over the individual, may even be disturbing. As Leander Keck has observed, perhaps therein lies the test of the relevance of Paul's message: that it has the potential to be as much a disturbance to one's own ethos and ethics as was originally intended.[45] If this is so, then one might have reason to feel antagonism toward Paul, and such antagonism will be because one has at least read and understood Paul and been uncomfortable with his message and not because culturally conditioned presentations of Paul make him unappealing or irksome.

Notes

[1]See Neil Elliott, *Liberating Paul: The Justice of God and the Politics of the Apostle* (Maryknoll: Orbis Books, 1998), 9.

[2]For example, the oft-cited injunctions that women be silent in the assembly (1 Cor. 14: 36-38) and that wives be subject to their husbands (1 Col 3:18; Eph 5:21-23).

[3]See Friedrich Nietzsche, *The Will to Power,* Book 2, trans. W. Kaufmann and R. J. Hollingdale (New York: Vintage Books, 1968), 1, 167.

[4]See John Paul II, *Veritatis Splendor* (Rome: Editrice Libreria Vaticana, 1993), esp. secs. 49, 80 and 81.

[5]Commenting on this widespread hostility, J. Christiaan Beker remarks that "even intelligent church members dislike Paul because of his presumable arrogance, his doctrinal stance or his perversion of the gospel" (see *Heirs of Paul: Paul's Legacy in the New Testament and in the Church Today* [Minneapolis: Fortress Press, 1991], 100-01).

[6]Susanne Heine, *Women and Early Christianity: A Reappraisal*, trans. John Bowden (Minneapolis: Fortress Press, 1987), 82.

[7]See John G. Gager, *Reinventing Paul* (New York: Oxford University Press, 2000), 3.

[8]Ibid., 3.

[9]Neil Elliott's *Liberating Paul* and John G. Gager's *Reinventing Paul,* cited above in nn. 1 and 7 respectively, are two recent attempts to re-examine Paul and distinguish between what Paul said and the subsequent (mis)interpretation and (mis)use of what he said. Both titles hint at needed efforts to rehabilitate Paul and reconsider his message.

[10]Robert Jewett, *Paul the Apostle to America: Cultural Trends and Pauline Scholarship* (Louisville: Westminster/John Knox Press, 1994), 1-12.

[11]Some characteristics noted by Jewett are the penchant to systemize thought; the tendency to advance ideas in a polemical way; entrenchment in a system of social hierarchy; the preoccupation with the aristocratic notion of the "great man" or "imperial-self" at the top of the ladder. For the discussion of these characteristics, their impact on Pauline scholarship, and the legacy of eurocentric scholarship on how Paul is currently (mis)perceived and (mis)understood, see *Paul the Apostle to America*, 4-11.

[12]Gordon D. Fee, *The First Epistle to the Corinthians,* NICNT (Grand Rapids: Eerdmans Publishing Co., 1988), 6.

[13]Ibid., 10.

[14]Auguste Sabatier, *L'apôtre Paul. Esquisse d'une histoire de sa pensée*, 3rd ed. (Paris: Librairie Fischbacher, 1896), 136 and passim.

[15]In view of a number of recent studies, it is becoming increasingly difficult to argue against Paul's conscious use of rhetoric and the likelihood that he was formally trained in rhetoric; see, for example, Kieran J. O'Mahony, *Pauline Persua-*

sion: A Sounding in 2 Corinthians 8-9, JSNTSS, 199 (Sheffield: Sheffield Academic Press, 2000).

[16]Wilhelm Wuellner, "Paul's Rhetoric of Argumentation in Romans: An Alternative to the Donfried-Karris Debate over Romans," *CBQ* 38 (1976): 330-51.

[17]Among the numerous studies of Paul's letters under the aspect of rhetoric, see, for example, Hans Dieter Betz, *A Commentary on Paul's Letter to the Churches in Galatia* (Philadelphia: Fortress Press, 1979); Stanley Kent Stowers, *Diatribe and Paul's Letter to the Romans,* SBLDS, 57 (Chico: Scholars Press, 1981); Margaret Mary Mitchell, *Paul and the Rhetoric of Reconciliation: An Exegetical Investigation of the Language and Composition of 1 Corinthians* (Tubingen: J. C. B. Mohr, 1991).

[18]On the relationship between epistolography and rhetoric, see Abraham Malherbe, ed., *Ancient Epistolary Theorists* (Atlanta: Scholars Press, 1988), 2-6; also, David E. Aune, *The New Testament in Its Literary Environment* (Philadelphia: Fortress Press, 1987), esp. 157-58.

[19]On the revival of interest in rhetoric, its application to the New Testament, the variety of approaches embraced by the term rhetorical criticism, and an extended bibliography, see Duane F. Watson and Alan J. Hauser, *Rhetorical Criticism and the Bible: A Comprehensive Bibliography with Notes on History and Method* (Leiden: E. J. Brill, 1994).

[20]Whether only classical or modern rhetorical categories, or both, should be employed is debated; see C. Joachim Classen, "St. Paul's Epistles and Ancient Greek and Roman Rhetoric," in *Rhetoric and the New Testament: Essays from the 1992 Heidelberg Conference*, ed. Stanley E. Porter and T. H. Olbrichts, JSNTSS, 90 (Sheffield: Sheffield Academic Press, 1993) 265-91.

[21]Literally "with his father's wife" *(gynaika tou patros)*. This expression is used to refer to someone other than one's own mother, as implied by the double injunction at Leviticus 18:7 and 8, and is usually taken as a reference to one's stepmother. *Echein* (translated "is having") with *gyne*/woman or *aner*/man normally connotes sexual intercourse. Whether the two were married is not certain.

[22]See Gaius, *The Institutes of Gaius*, I, trans. William M. Gordon and Olivia F. Robinson (Ithaca, N.Y.: Cornell University Press, 1988), 63. At Leviticus 18:8 we read the biblical injunction against this type of relationship which was also frequently discussed in Jewish literature. See also Jub. 33:1-17; Philo, *Spec. Leg.*, III.22-25.

[23]Paul states no motives for the incestuous relationship or the community's boasting in it. It is usually assumed that the problems addressed in 1 Corinthians 5, indeed almost all the problems reflected in 1 Corinthians, stem from over-realized eschatology. See Anthony C. Thiselton, "Realized Eschatology in Corinth," *NTS* 24 (1977): 510-26.

[24]See infra n. 38.

[25]See my *Ethics, Ecclesiology and Church Discipline: A Rhetorical Analysis of 1 Corinthians 5* (Rome: Gregorian University Press, 1997), 25-46.

[26]See Ivan Havener, "A Curse for Salvation—1 Cor 5:1-5," in *Sin, Salvation*

and the Spirit: Commemorating the Fiftieth Year of the Liturgical Press, ed. Eugene F. Durken (Collegeville: Liturgical Press, 1979), 334-44.

[27]Graham Shaw, *The Cost of Authority: Manipulation and Freedom in the New Testament* (Philadelphia: Fortress Press, 1983), 70.

[28]Ancient rhetoricians agreed that emotional appeals were most effective at the start of the argumentation (see Cicero, *De Oratore*, II.77.310-11; Quintilian, *Institutio Oratoria*, VII, preface, 6; and further IV. 2.116.

[29]That incest was not found among the pagans is no doubt an exaggeration, setting up an implicit comparison between the pagans and the community. Such exaggerated comparisons allow the speaker to prove a point without extended argumentation. This technique is discussed in Aristotle, *Ars Rhetorica.*, II.24.4 and further, Quintilian, *Institutio Oratoria*, VIII.4.2.

[30]Proofs were of three kinds: those based on *pathos*, on *ethos* and on *logos*; see Aristotle, *Ars Thetorica*, I.2.3-7. Such proofs were called "entechnic" because the speaker himself invented them, cf. *Ars Rhetorica* I. 2. 2.

[31]Ibid., II.1.8; cf. also Cicero, *De Oratore*, II. 77.310-11 and Quintilian, *Institutio Oratoria*, Bk. 8.

[32]Cicero, *De Paritione Oratoria,* XXVI, 91.

[33]Failure to recognize Paul's rhetorical technique has also led to misinterpretations of Paul and misconstruals of his purpose in Galatians. See Lauri Thurén, "Was Paul Angry?: Derhetorizing Galatians," in *The Rhetorical Interpretation of Scripture*, ed. Stanley Porter and D. L. Stamps, JSNTSS, 180 (Sheffield: Sheffield Academic Press, 1999) 302-21.

[34]See, for example, Havener, "A Curse for Salvation," 341, and Charles Talbert, *Reading Corinthians: A Literary and Theological Commentary on 1 and 2 Corinthians* (New York: Crossroad Publications, 1987), 19.

[35]Paul allows himself to recede into the background elsewhere as, for example, at 2 Corinthians 8-9. For insightful comments on Paul's strategy here, see Kieran J. O'Mahony, *Pauline Persuasion*, 150-53.

[36]On the technique of calling upon universal values, see Quintilian, *Institutio Oratoria*, V.11.36.

[37]See Aristotle, *Ars Rhetorica*, II.6.1-13; a shorter discussion on shameful matters and persons in front of whom one feels shame is also found at Sirach 41:14-24.

[38]This third section of argument begins with mention of a "previous letter," which obviously included a warning about relations with immoral persons. It is generally agreed that the community had misunderstood Paul's previous instructions, although some would suggest that the misunderstanding was deliberate, intended to make Paul "appear ridiculous." See John Hurd, *The Origin of First Corinthians* (London: Routledge, 1965), 152, or to pose a blatant challenge to Paul's authority, see Fee, *The First Epistle to the Corinthians*, 221.

[39]See types of *amplificatio* in Quintilian, *Institutio Oratoria* VIII.4.1-2.

[40]The condition of sinlessness wrought through Christ's death and linked with the baptismal remission of sins (see, for example, Acts 2:38; 22:16; 1 Corinthians 6:11) is commonly recognized as a traditional eschatological theme.

[41]Unity and sinlessness were considered the distinguishing traits of the new *Helisgemeinschaft*, see, for example, Isaiah 11:11-14; Ezekiel 37:15-28; Joel 3:1-5; Isaiah 32:15; Zechariah 12:10.

[42]See Jerome Murphy-O'Connor, *Becoming Human Together: The Pastoral Anthropology of Paul* (Wilmington: Michael Glazier, 1982), esp. 175-81.

[43]Robert Bellah et al., *Habits of the Heart: Individualism and Commitment in American Life* (San Francisco: Harper, 1986), 47.

[44]Ibid., 79-80.

[45]Leander Keck, "Ethos and Ethics in the New Testament," in *Essays in Morality and Ethics*, ed. James Gaffney (New York: Paulist Press, 1980), 29-49.

SCRIPTURE IN TRADITION

Is the End of the Empire the End
of the World? Exegetical Traditions

Daniel Van Slyke

In the early fifth century, Latin-speaking Christians witnessed the traumatic events—including civil wars and barbarian invasions—that heralded the end of the empire in the West. Since the emperors had come to embrace Christianity in the previous century, political and social decline became a theological question. Why would Christ allow such trials to afflict the empire that professed faith in him? Christians turned to their sacred writings to discover how the seeming chaos of the fifth century fit into God's plan of salvation. Of the many possible interpretations of current events in the light of scripture, Bishop Quodvultdeus of Carthage (432/3-453) opted for one that is best described as apocalyptic. In his *Book of the Promises and Predictions of God*, he interpreted Rome's decline as the beginning of the tribulations that characterize the coming of Antichrist and the end of time. In so doing, Quodvultdeus appropriated two exegetical traditions with origins in the pre-Constantinian church. The first centers on 2 Thessalonians 2:7 and the second on the creation story in Genesis 1. In the two sections of this paper I examine, in turn, each of these two Western exegetical traditions and how Quodvultdeus makes use of them. What comes to light is both the originality of Quodvultdeus' apocalyptic thought for his time and his place within the broader context of several centuries of Christian reflection on these key biblical texts.

The Eschatological Significance of the Roman Empire

Tertullian believes that Rome is to continue as long as the world shall stand.[1] He has no doubt that the God of the Christians causes empires to rise and fall.[2] For this reason, if it is to be effective, prayer for the strength of the Roman Empire must be offered to the One who alone can grant such blessings. Christians do indeed offer such prayers.[3] The eschatological significance of the Roman Empire impels them to do so:

> There is another, even greater, obligation for us to pray for the emperors; yes, even for the continuance of the empire in general and for Roman interests (*statu imperii rebusque Romanis*). We realize that the tremendous force which is hanging over the whole world, and the very end of the world (*clausulam saeculi*) with its threat of dreadful afflictions, is arrested for a time by the continued existence of the Roman Empire. This event we have no desire to experience, and, in praying that it may be deferred, we favor the continuance of Rome (*Romanae diuturnitati fauemus*).[4]

The Roman Empire, Tertullian is convinced, is the last world empire. When Rome falls the tribulations of the end times will begin. Indeed, Antichrist can only arrive after the empire has been removed.

His scriptural source is 2 Thessalonians 2: "For the mystery of iniquity already worketh; only that he who now holdeth, do hold, until he be taken out of the way. And then that wicked one shall be revealed whom the Lord Jesus shall kill with the spirit of his mouth" (2 Thess. 2:7-8, Douay-Rheims translation).[5] Ancient Christians commonly interpret "he who now holdeth" as the Roman Empire, and the thing held back as Antichrist.[6] Ambrosiaster, for example, writes quite plainly that the Lord will not come until after the Roman Empire has been destroyed and Antichrist has appeared.[7] A Pseudo-Jerome interpolation of Pelagius' commentary on 2 Thessalonians 2 expresses the same idea and clarifies the passage with a reference to Daniel 7:24. The interpolation thereby indicates that ten kingdoms will be established, and when Rome is sufficiently divided Antichrist will arise.[8] This "one who holds" is also loosely associated with the various apocalyptic beasts of Revelation, and Quodvultdeus sees it in the beast ridden by the great whore.[9]

Earlier Lactantius summarized such traditions in the *Divine Institutes*:

> Even the general condition itself makes clear that the fall and ruin of things will be soon, except for the fact that with the city of

Rome being unharmed, it seems that nothing of that sort has to be feared. . . . That is the state which up to now holds up all things, and we must pray and adore the God of heaven, if His statutes and decrees can, however, be put off, lest that abominable tyrant come more quickly than we think, that one who works such great havoc and wipes out that light at whose destruction the world itself will collapse.[10]

Thus Lactantius, Tertullian, Ambrosiaster, and Pseudo-Jerome believe not only that Rome is the last empire, but also that Rome itself somehow holds back the end of time and the onslaught of Antichrist. Since Antichrist will wield worldwide political power, the worldwide power of Rome must be removed before Antichrist appears.

As Tertullian demonstrates, Christians interpreted the Pauline figure of "the man of sin, the son of perdition," in 2 Thessalonians as the "Antichrist" of Johannine literature.[11] Jerome witnesses to the longevity of this interpretation in the early fifth century. While Rome lies helpless before the barbarians shortly before its sack in 410, Jerome writes: "The one who holds him back is being removed, and yet we do not realize that Antichrist is fast approaching."[12] In this context one can properly understand the import of Jerome's lament that "the entire world perished in a single city."[13]

Augustine, too, follows this traditional interpretation of 2 Thessalonians. He believes the passage speaks of Antichrist, and he even concedes that one might interpret the thing restraining him as the Roman Empire.[14] Nonetheless Augustine exerts concerted effort to rid the Roman Empire of its eschatological significance. He also demonstrates more equilibrium than does Jerome after the fall of Rome: "Why panic, just because earthly kingdoms crumble? That's why a heavenly kingdom was promised to you, so that you wouldn't crumble away with the earthly ones. . . . Earthly kingdoms have their ups and downs."[15] "Heaven and earth will pass away: therefore why be astonished if at some time the City comes to an end?"[16]

Quodvultdeus does not share the serene view of the possible fall of Rome that tempers Augustine's reluctant acknowledgment of the eschatological significance of the empire. On two occasions Quodvultdeus cites 2 Thessalonians 2:7. He follows the standard interpretation of the "wicked one" as Antichrist.[17] He sees ten kings between the horns of the great beast in Daniel 7 and in the seven heads of the beast in Revelation 17, and these ten kings do indeed have apocalyptic significance, for Antichrist will find them upon his arrival.[18] The final king is Antichrist himself.[19] Quodvultdeus also believes that the one holding back Antichrist in 2 Thessalonians 2 is the Roman Empire. Hence he interprets these apocalyptic scriptural passages in reference to current political events.

Let us return to the whore and the beast in Revelation 17. Quodvultdeus quotes this vision at length. The whore is Babylon the great (Rev. 17:5). Quodvultdeus believes it is a temporal city enjoying world-wide domination, blasphemously claiming its rulers are gods and promoting idolatry.[20] The people of God who leave her (Rev. 18:4) are those who do not imitate her arrogance, but rather the humility of Christ.[21] He ends his discussion of the whore by applying to her the words of 2 Thessalonians 2:7-8: "so much that what now holds, may hold until it is taken out of the way; and then the wicked one will be revealed whom the Lord Jesus will kill with the spirit of his mouth."[22] Quodvultdeus repeats this sentiment elsewhere: "Indeed it is necessary to note that all these things are going to come about after the beast, that is after that kingdom is removed in which the woman sits 'drunk with the blood of the saints' (Rev. 17:6): While believing these things, we leave them to be seen by posterity."[23]

Quodvultdeus believes that the beast, that is the Roman Empire, has not yet been utterly destroyed and removed from the scene. Indeed, the Emperor Valentinian III still sat upon his throne while Quodvultdeus was writing, although his power was surely tottering.

Note the political import of Quodvultdeus' scriptural exegesis. Treating the texts of Revelation 17 and Daniel 7 as one continuous prophecy of the end times, he describes the character of the kings that will appear at the end times. Reflecting upon the three horns uprooted by the smallest horn (Dan. 7:7), Quodvultdeus writes:

> Therefore in my opinion, he is speaking either of the prior kings who savagely raged against the Christian religion, or the seven future ones who, after the first three have been destroyed, also will rage against the Church. Indeed he wishes us to understand all the Arian heretics when he says, "They will fight against the lamb and the lamb will conquer them"(Rev. 17:14). For they fight by exorcising and rebaptizing the members of the lamb that Christ has already consecrated with his own blood.[24]

By specifying that the kings represented in Revelation and Daniel are Arians who rebaptize Catholics, Quodvultdeus applies these apocalyptic prophecies to his own day.

Although he never mentions the Vandal king Geiseric by name, the bishop certainly has him in mind as one of these apocalyptic kings, for under Geiseric innumerable Catholics were rebaptized, sometimes forcibly, by Arian clergy.[25] Some of Quodvultdeus' African contemporaries saw the Vandal king as Antichrist himself,[26] but Quodvultdeus does not have such an exaggerated opinion of Geiseric. He believes that Antichrist is not a man but the devil himself, and so he does not demonize his tormentor. He sees Geiseric simply as one of the apocalyptic kings who precede Antichrist. The Arians are the agents of Antichrist who imitate his deeds and his pride and seduce many.[27] The fall of the Empire is a natural prerequisite to their rise to power. Indeed, Quodvultdeus does indicate that the Roman Empire is the last empire, in keeping with the vision of Daniel 2 and the interpretation he attributes to Orosius.[28] He expects that its fall will mean the rise of the Arian kings, who are soon to be followed by Antichrist and the end of time. Thus, Quodvultdeus re-appropriates the pre-Constantinian exegetical tradition on 2 Thessalonians that sees Rome as the last empire, modifying it in order to understand the political and religious developments of his own time.

The Ages of the World

Quodvultdeus interprets the six days in which God created the world as six ages (*aetates saeculi*) of the world's existence. Just as God created man on the sixth day, so the Word of God became man in the sixth age, at the close of which the world will come to an end.[29] These views of the fifth-century bishop of Carthage demonstrate the longevity of this exegetical tradition that erected a schema of history from the scaffolding of the first creation story in Genesis.

In his commentary on the book of Daniel, Hippolytus explains that just as the world was created in six days, so it is to last six thousand years, since a day of the Lord is like a thousand years (Ps. 89:4). The seventh day, on which God rested, indicates the repose of the saints. By Hippolytus' calculation Christ was born fifty-five hundred years after the creation of the world.[30] Thus, only five hundred years extend from the birth of Christ until the end of the world. Hippolytus affirms this by insisting that the fourth beast mentioned in Revelation, the Roman Empire, will dominate the world for only five hundred years. Then the end will come, when Antichrist persecutes the saints and Christ returns.[31] But these events cannot unfold so long as the fourth beast—that is, Rome—reigns.[32]

This tradition is common among African authors. According to Tertullian, the saints will soon be recompensed on earth for their earthly sacrifices; they will enjoy a millennium of earthly rule in Jerusalem.[33] At the end of that rule, during which period the resurrection of the saints will be completed, the world will be destroyed.[34] Cyprian acknowledges seven ages of a thousand years each, represented by the seven Maccabee brothers.[35] The seventh age will be a millennium of rest or of rule for the saints following six thousand years of labor.[36] Cyprian also believes that the world is failing, growing old and passing away.[37] The first six thousand years are almost over, and the time of Antichrist with which the sixth age ends is on the horizon.[38] Tyconius writes tersely: "The world's age is six days, i.e., six thousand years."[39] From the perspective of many ancient Christians, the six or seven ages of a thousand years each fits in well with the thousand years during which the saints are said to rule with Christ in Revelation 20:6.[40] The final thousand years corresponds with the seventh age. Such belief in a lengthy period of earthly rule for the saints is referred to as millenarianism, or, from the Greek, chiliasm.[41]

In a work that Quodvultdeus read, Lactantius clearly demonstrates belief in both the millennium reign of justice and the seven ages.[42]

> God completed the world and this admirable work of the nature of things in the space of six days, as the story is contained in the secrets of Sacred Scripture, and the seventh day, on which He rested from His labors, He sanctified. This, however, is the Sabbath Day, which in Hebrew took its name from the number, whence the sevenfold number is legitimate and full. . . . Therefore, since all the works of God were completed in six days, it is necessary that the world remain in this state for six ages, that is, for six thousand years. The great day of God is terminated by the circle of a thousand years, as the prophet indicates who says: "In thine eyes, O Lord, a thousand years are as one day." And as God labored six days in building such great works, so His religion and the truth must labor during these six thousand years, while malice

prevails and dominates. And again, since He rested on the seventh day from His completed labors and blessed that day, so it is necessary that, at the end of the six thousandth year, all evil be abolished from the earth, and that justice reign for a thousand years, and that there be tranquility and rest from the labors which the world is now enduring for so long.[43]

During the millennium when the Son of God will rule the earth with justice, the devil will be bound in chains.[44] "But the same one, when a thousand years of this reign, that is, seven thousand years in all, begin to be terminated, will be let loose at last; and, when let out from custody, he will proceed and stir up all the peoples."[45] Thus, according to Lactantius, the final apocalyptic battle in which the wicked are definitively defeated comes after the millennium of Christ's rule on earth.[46]

Quodvultdeus parts from this opinion. The very structure of his *Book of the Promises*, organized as it is according to salvation history, does not allow for any reign of the saints on earth. Lactantius' influence on Quodvultdeus is important, however, insofar as both attempt to calculate the end times. Lactantius assures his audience that,

when six thousand years have been completed . . . [end times] may be known from the signs which have been predicted by the prophets. For they foretold the signs by which the end of time was both to be expected by us and feared, even unto the single days. Since, however, this summary is being completed, those who wrote on the times, gathering material from the sacred books and from various historians, show how large the number of years is from the beginning of the world. Though they may vary and disagree somewhat in the sum-total, however, the entire expectation or length of time left seems to be no greater than two hundred years.[47]

Citing a general consensus among "those who wrote on the times," Lactantius concludes that the sixth age will end within two hundred years. Since he writes in the first or second decade of the fourth century,[48] his projected *terminus ad quem* for the end of the sixth age is somewhere between 500 and 520. The African bishop Hilarianus, who wrote his chronicle in the year 397,[49] predicted a similar date for the return of Christ, corresponding to the year 498.[50] Supulcius Severus provides another example.[51] Augustine is well aware of Christians who predict that the end will come around five hundred years after Christ, although he clearly does not share that opinion.[52] The late sixth century *Paschale Campanum* records that some extremists announced the coming of Antichrist in the years 493 and 496.[53] Thus, there is ample precedent for Quodvultdeus' position, for he too subtly indicates that the end of the age will come around the year 500.

This becomes most evident when Quodvultdeus develops his interpretation of Daniel 9:24 and Revelation 20:2:

> "from the coming forth of the words" [that is, the prayer of Daniel in Dan 9:24] when by Daniel 70 weeks were assessed to come until Christ the leader. For at that time Michael and his angels waged war against the devil, and the angel showed this to Daniel, saying that he had been sent in order to fight against the prince of the kingdom of Persia. And there is no one to help me, he said, except Michael your prince (Dn 10:21). In this war the devil was defeated, thrown down and bound. Just as it was shown to that same prophet [Daniel] in the beginning, so too it was shown to John in the end of time (cf. Rv 12:7-12): that those 490 years, plus those which extend from the coming of the savior until the loosening of the devil, conclude the thousand years during which the devil was bound "in order that he might no longer seduce the nations" (Rv 20:3) whom before he had beguiled into idolatries.[54]

Ostensibly following Jerome's commentary on Daniel,[55] Quodvultdeus holds that seventy weeks of years, or four hundred ninety years, extend from Daniel's prayer until Christ's second coming. He then relates Daniel 9:24 to the thousand years during which the devil is bound in Revelation 20:2. These thousand years, Quodvultdeus believes, began with Daniel's prayer, for it was then that Michael and his angels bound the devil. Thus, the first four hundred ninety years of the thousand had passed by upon Christ's first coming. From that point, Quodvultdeus strongly implies, five hundred ten years of the thousand remain before the devil is unchained and the *dimidium temporis* begins. Thus he believes that the devil is to be unchained around 510—that is, about sixty years after he is writing.[56]

Although the specific means of calculation may differ, Quodvultdeus' date for the end of the world is quite close to the dates

offered by Lactantius and the others mentioned above. All such predictions are based on the notion that the final age of the world will
last, quite literally, a thousand years. However, Quodvultdeus is unlike Lactantius and Tertullian insofar as he is not a millenarian. In this
he learns from the theological developments that took place in the two
or three generations preceding him. Influential Latin authors such as
Ambrose and Jerome had begun to deny a thousand-year earthly reign
of the saints in the previous century,[57] holding to the six ages or six
thousand years, but ceasing to interpret these periods literally.[58]

Augustine especially repudiates millenarianism and any attempt to
predict the end times.[59] This becomes clear in his development of the
six ages, with the seventh being eternity, the Day of the Lord. The
world, Augustine holds, passes through the same ages as a man: infancy, boyhood, adolescence, youth, middle age, and old age.[60] Likewise Augustine frequently alludes to the six ages of humanity's labor.[61] In support of this view, he repeatedly appeals to the six days of
creation:

> Sacred scripture commends its perfection to us above all in
> declaring that God completed his works in six days, and that on
> the sixth day man was made to the image of God. And in the sixth
> age of the human race the Son of God came and was made the Son
> of man in order to refashion us to the image of God. That is the
> age we are now in, whether we allot the ages 1,000 years each,
> or whether we search the divine writings for certain memorable
> and outstanding turning points . . . the sixth began with the birth
> of the Lord, and still continues to the unknown end of time.[62]

Yet Augustine endeavors to separate the six-age schema from attempts to predict the end, insisting that the end cannot be known.[63]
Although we are in the sixth and final age of the world, the world's
old age can last as long as all the other ages put together—just as the
old age of an individual man. Thus Augustine insists that we cannot
say how many generations the sixth age will include.[64] Although hop-
ing that the Lord is soon to return and the end is soon to come, Augustine is unwilling to affirm that that is the case; he is equally unwilling
to affirm that the Lord's coming will be long delayed.[65] "But the one
who admits that he does not know which of these views is true hopes
for the one, is resigned to the other, is wrong in neither of them."[66] So

he advises, "Let us watch and pray because this life is short and uncertain and we do not know the time when the Lord will come."[67]

On the morning of the seventh age, according to Augustine, Jesus will come again in glory and the saints will rest from their labors.[68] Just as God rested on the seventh day of creation, so too the saints will have their rest in the seventh age.[69] This seventh day "will be our Sabbath, whose end will not be an evening."[70] Asserting that the seventh age will not end is another way to exclude millenarianism. Quodvultdeus inherits this theological development from Augustine; he too spurns millenarianism, associates the seventh age with the resurrection, and holds that the seventh age, like the seventh day of creation, has no end.[71] Yet Quodvultdeus clearly believes that the date of the end can be derived from scripture, and in this he quite deliberately parts from Augustine.

In sum, second- and third-century authors who lived through times of persecution, such as Hippolytus, Tertullian, Cyprian, and Lactantius, were much concerned with eschatological questions and they often expected a millennium of earthly reign to follow the close of the sixth age. Apocalyptic scriptural interpretations became less important in the fourth and early fifth centuries, as demonstrated here by Augustine. Theologians of that period did not form their views under the looming threat of violent persecution.[72] Quodvultdeus benefits from this development; he clearly is not a millenarian. However, having experienced the fall of Carthage and the persecution of African Catholics by the Vandals, Quodvultdeus considers the church and the Empire to be far less secure than they seemed to the previous few generations of Christians. Thus, he revives the earlier tradition of reflecting upon apocalyptic scriptural passages, as well as the earlier belief that the end can be dated by determining when the final thousand-year age of the world began. In short, Quodvultdeus re-appropriates the apocalyptic import from which his recent predecessors—especially Augustine—attempted to free the ages of the world tradition.

Conclusion

Quodvultdeus believes the world is in its sixth and final age, following a common interpretation of the six days of creation evident in pre-Constantinian authors such as Hippolytus, Tertullian, and Lactantius. Quodvultdeus also adheres to an ancient, pre-Constantinian tradition that interprets the thing holding back Antichrist in 2 Thessalonians 2 as Rome. Since Antichrist will wield world-wide political power, Rome must be removed before his advent. In the light of the reversal of order and the persecution that accompanied the Vandal invasion of Africa, Quodvultdeus believes that Rome is at its end. Hence, he critically re-appropriates the reflections of those who suffered under the pagan empire in an attempt to interpret the signs of his own times from scripture. He does so in the light of theological developments after Constantine—above all those spearheaded by Augustine—which he similarly approaches selectively. The result is an apocalyptic theology firmly rooted in scripture that gives meaning to the political and religious turmoil experienced by Roman African Christians in the mid-fifth century.

Notes

[1]"Christianus nullius est hostis, nedum imperatoris, quem sciens a deo suo constitui necesse est, ut et ipsum diligat et revereatur et honoret et salvum velit cum toto Romano imperio, quousque saeculum stabit; tamdiu enim stabit." Tertullianus, *Ad Scapulam* 2.6, in CSEL 76:10.

[2]"Videte igitur, ne ille regna dispenset, cuius est et orbis qui regnatur, et homo ipse qui regnat; ne ille uices dominationum temporibus in saeculo ordinarit, qui ante omne tempus fuit, qui saeculum corpus temporum fecit." Tertullianus, *Apologeticum* 26.1, in CCSL 1:138.

[3]"precantes sumus semper pro omnibus imperatoribus, uitam illis prolixam, imperium securum, domum tutam, exercitus fortes, senatum fidelem, populum probum, orbem quietum, quaecumque hominis et Caesaris uota sunt. Haec ab alio orare non possum, quam a quo me scio consecuturum, quoniam et ipse est, qui solus praestat." Tertullianus, *Apologeticum* 30.4-5, in CCSL 1:141.

[4]Tertullianus, *Apologeticum* 32.1, in CCSL 1:142-3, trans. Rudolph Arbesmann, Emily Joseph Daly, and Edwin A. Quain, *Tertullian: Apologetical Works and Minucius Felix Octavius*, The Fathers of the Church, vol. 10 (New York: Fathers of the Church, 1950), 88.

[5]"*Ne quis uos seducat ullo modo, quoniam nisi ueniat abscessio primo,* huius utique regni, *et reueletur delinquentiae homo,* id est antichristus, filius perditionis." Tertullianus, *De resurrectione mortuorum* 24.14, in CCSL 2:952. I have corrected an error in the versification of the volume.

[6]For examples among the Greeks consider the following: "*Only he who now letteth will let, until he be taken out of the way,* that is, when the Roman empire is taken out of the way, then he [Antichrist] shall come. And naturally. For as long as the fear of this empire lasts, no one will willingly be subject to him. . . ." John Chrysostom, "Homily IV on 2 Thessalonians," in trans. *The Homilies of S. John*

Chrysostom Archbishop of Constantinople on the Epistles of St. Paul the Apostle
(Oxford: John Henry Parker, 1843), 492. Chrysostom mentions that some interpret
the thing restraining as the Holy Spirit, but he prefers the interpretation that says it
is the Roman Empire. See also Cyril of Jerusalem's *Catechetical Lectures* 15.12,
cited in translation in Peter Gorday, ed., *Colossians, 1-2 Thessalonians, 1-2 Timothy, Titus, Philemon*, Ancient Christian Commentary on Scripture: New Testament, vol. 9, ed. Thomas C. Oden (Downers Grove, Ill.: InterVarsity Press, 2000).
This interpretation may accord with the intention of the letter's author. For a summary of the diverse contemporary opinions on the *katechon* of 2 Thessalonians
2:7, see Frank Witt Hughes, "Early Christian Rhetoric and 2 Thessalonians," *Journal
for the Study of the New Testament*, Supplement Series 30 (1989): 59-60.

[7]"tempus et signa adventus domini designavit, quia non prius veniet dominus,
quam regni Romani defectio fiat et [ante] appareat Antichristus, qui interficiet
sanctos, reddita Romanis libertate, sub suo tamen nomine." Ambrosiastrus, *Ad
Thesalonicenses secunda* 2.4.2., in CSEL 81.3:239; "quamdiu steterit regnum
Romanorum (Romanum); hoc est quod dixit: donec de medio fiat." Ambrosiastrus,
Ad Thesalonicenses secunda 2.7, in CSEL 81.3:240.

[8]"Hoc est quod dicit: 'cum Romanum,' inquit, 'cessauerit imperium,' et sic, ut
Danihel propheta ait, 'in x fuerit regna diuisum, tunc antichristus surget.'" *Pelagi
expositiones xiii epistularum Pauli interpolationes*, in *Pelagius's Expositions of
Thirteen Epistles of St. Paul*, vol. 2, *Pseudo-Jerome Interpolations*, ed. Alexander
Souter (New York: Cambridge University Press, 1931), 63.

[9]Paula Fredriksen Landes, "Tyconius and the End of the World," *Revue des
Études Augustiniennes* 28 (1982): 71.

[10]Lactantius, *Divinarum institutionum* 7.25, in CSEL 19:664-5, trans. McDonald,
534.

[11]Tertullianus, *Adversus Marcionem* V.16, in CSEL 47:630-1; cf. Tertullianus,
De resurrectione mortuorum 24.12, in CCSL 2:952; Jaroslav Pelikan, *The Excel-
lent Empire: The Fall of Rome and the Triumph of the Church* (San Francisco:
Harper & Row, 1987), 46.

[12]"qui tenebat, de medio fit, et non intellegimus adpropinquare antichristum,
quem dominus Iesus interficiet spiritu oris sui." Jerome goes on to list the disasters
the Roman Empire had recently suffered at the hands of barbarian peoples.
Hieronymus, *Epistula* 123.15, in CSEL 56.1:91; the empire will only be destroyed
at the end of the world. "Ergo dicamus quod omnes scriptores ecclesiastici
tradiderunt: in consummatione mundi, quando regnum destruendum est
Romanorum, decem futuros reges qui orbem romanum inter se diuidant, et
undecimum surrectum esse paruulum regem qui tres reges de decem regibus
superaturus sit." *In Danielem* 2.7.8, in CCSL 75A:844. Commenting on 2
Thessalonians 2, Jerome writes: "nisi, inquit, ante Romanum imperium fuerit
desolatum et antichristus praecesserit, Christus non ueniet, qui ideo ita uenturus
est, ut antichristum destruat." *Epistula* 121.11, in CSEL 56.1:53-4. Appealing again
to 2 Thessalonians 2:7, Jerome makes the same point in *In Hieremiam* 5.27.4
(25:26c), in CCSL 74:246. Jerome also appropriates the traditional designation of

the fourth beast in Daniel 7:7 as the Roman Empire. *In Danielem* 2.7.7a, in CCSL 75A:842. See O'Connell, *The Eschatology of Saint Jerome* (Mundelein, Ill.: Apud aedes seminarii Sanctae Mariae ad Lacam, 1948), 26-7.

[13]"in una urbe totus orbis interiit." Hieronymus, *In Hiezechielem* prol., in CCSL 75:3.

[14]"*Tantum qui modo tenet teneat, donec de medio fiat,* non absurde de ipso Romano imperio creditur dictum, tamquam dictum sit: 'Tantum qui modo imperat imperet, donec de medio fiat', id est de medio tollatur." Augustinus, *De civitate Dei* 20.19, in CCSL 48:732.

[15]Augustinus, *Sermo* 105.7.9, in PL 38:622, trans. Edmund Hill, *Sermons III.4 (94A-147A) on the New Testament,* by Augustine, The Works of Saint Augustine, vol. 3, no. 4 (Brooklyn, N.Y.: New City Press, 1992), 93.

[16]"Ceolum et terra transibunt: quid ergo mirum, si aliquando finis est civitati?" Augustinus, *Sermo* 81.9, in PL 38:505. My translation.

[17]Quodvultdeus, *Liber promissionum et praedictorum Dei* [henceforth *Liber*] D.4.6 and D.7.14, in SC 102:598 and 616.

[18]*Liber* D.8 (in SC 102:616) is entitled "Praedictio implenda de X regibus quos Antichristus inueniet."

[19]*Liber* D.8.16, in SC 102:618.

[20]*Liber* D.7.13-14, in SC 102:612-6.

[21]"Exeunt enim hi qui non fastus eius sed humilem uiam Christum sequuntur, qui non rapinam sed misericordiam diligunt." Notice the present tenses. *Liber* D.7.14, in SC 102:614.

[22]"Testatur et Paulus dicens: Tantum qui modo tenet, teneat donec de medio fiat; et tunc reuelabitur iniquus quem dominus Iesus interficiet spiritu oris sui." *Liber* D.7.14, in SC 102:616. All translations from the *Liber* are my own.

[23]"Notandum sane post bestiam haec omnia esse uentura, id est sublato regno in quo mulier sedet *ebria sanctorum sanguine*: Quae nos credentes posteris uidenda relinquimus." *Liber* D.9.17, in SC 102:620-2.

[24]"Ergo, in quantum datur aestimatio, aut priores reges memorat qui truculentiores fuerunt in religione Christiana, aut ex decem, tribus exstinctis, VII futuros qui et ipsi saeuiant in ecclesiam. Omnes sane haereticos Arrianos uult intellegi cum dicit: Hi aduersus agnum pugnabunt et agnus unicet eos. Pugnant enim exsufflando et rebaptizando membra agni quae iam Christus suo sanguine sacrauerat." *Liber* D.8.16, in SC 102:618.

[25]Quodvultdeus, *De tempore barbarico II* 14.4-7, in CCSL 60:486; Victor Vitensis, *Historia persecutionis africanae provinciae* 1.21, 1.33, 3.45, 3.48, in CSEL 7:10, 15, 94, 95-6.

[26]In two suspiciously similar passages, anonymous authors use numerology to prove that "Gensericus" is the Gothic name for Antichrist, since the Greek letters in the name add up to 666. *Liber Genealogus* 618, in MGHaa 9:195; Victorinus Petavionensis, *Commentarii in Apocalypsin, recensio Hieronymi una cum posteriorum additamentis* 13 and 17.3, in CSEL 49:127.

[27]*Liber* D.5.7, in SC 102:600.

[28]"partim fictiles ultimum Romanum uidelicet." *Liber* II.34.74, in SC 102:462.

[29]"Senarius uero numerus hoc continet quod sexta die formatus est homo et sexta aetate saeculi ad redemptionem mundi hominem susceperit Verbum Dei…" *Liber* I.7.11, in SC 101:176; "Finis igitur diluuii sexcentesimo et primo anno Noe terminatus finem mundi significat post sex, ut dictum est, aetates saeculi et breue Antichristi spatium." *Liber* I.7.13, in SC 101:182. "Et noster Ioseph Christus dominus mundo per septenarium numerum currenti in finem tale consilium dedit." *Liber* I.29.41, in SC 101:240; see also *Liber* D.13.22, in SC 102:632-4.

[30]Hippolytus, *In Danielem* 4.23, in SC 14:306-9. Hippolytus also sees Mary as a symbol of Noah's ark, and the measurements of the ark as representing fifty-five hundred years. *In Danielem* 4.24, in SC 14:308-11; Gustave Bardy, introduction in SC 14:50.

[31]Hippolytus, *In Danielem* 4.24, in SC 14:310-1.

[32]Nor can the end come before the Gospel is preached to all the nations (Mt 24:14). Hippolytus, *In Danielem* 4.17, in SC 14:296-7; Bardy, SC 14:36. On the reasoning behind Hippolytus' calculation, see David Dunbar, "The Delay of the Parousia in Hippolytus," *Vigiliae Christianae* 37 (1983): 313-27; Richard Landes, "Lest the Millennium Be Fulfilled: Apocalyptic Expectations and the Pattern of Western Chronography, 100-800 CE," in *The Use and Abuse of Eschatology in the Middle Ages*, ed. Werner Verbeke, Daniel Verhelst and Andries Welkenhuysen (Leuven: Leuven University Press, 1988), 147-8.

[33]"nam et confitemur in terra nobis regnum promissum, sed ante caelum, sed alio statu, utpote post resurrectionem in mille annos in ciuitate diuini operis Hierusalem caelo delatam, quam et apostolus matrem nostram sursum designat." Tertullianus, *Adversus Marcionem* 3.24, in CSEL 47:419. "nos enim promo ad caelestia inuitamur, cum a saeculo auellimur, et ita postea inuenimur etiam terrena consecuturi." Ibid., 420. This same notion is also found in Irenaeus, who argues at length and cites many biblical passages to prove that the righteous will enjoy an earthly rule for a period. *Contra haereses* 5.32-35, in PG 7:1210-21.

[34]"post cuius mille annos, intra quam aetatem concluditur sanctorum resurrectio promeritis maturius uil tardius resurgentium, tunc, et mundi destructione et iudicii conflagratione commissa…" Tertullianus, *Adversus Marcionem* 3.24, in CSEL 47:420. For other examples of millenarianism, see Commodianus, *Instructiones* 1.44, in CCSL 128:37-8; Victorinus Petavionensis, *Tractatus de fabrica mundi* 6, in CSEL 49:6.

[35]"sic septem fratres martyrio cohaerentes, ut primi in dispositione diuina septem dies annorum septem milia continentes." Cyprianus, *Ad Fortunatum* 11, in CSEL 3.1:337-8.

[36]Auguste Luneau, *L'Histoire du salut chez les pères de l'Église: la doctrine des ages du monde* (Paris: Beauchesne, 1964), 219.

[37]"primo in loco scire debes senuisse iam mundum, non illis uiribus stare quibus prius steterat nec uigore et robore ipso ualere quo ante praeualebat." *Ad Demetrianum* 3.4-5, in CCSL 3A:36-7; "Mundus ecce nutat et labitur et ruinam sui non iam senectute rerum sed fine testatur." *De mortalitate* 25, in CCSL 3A:30;

Epistula 58.2, in CSEL 3.2:657-8; *Epistula* 67.7, in CSEL 3.2:741.

[38]"sex milia annorum iam paene conplentur, ex quo hominem diabolus inpugnat." Cyprianus, *Ad Fortunatum* praef.2, in CSEL 3.1:317. "in fine adque in consummatione mundi antichristi tempus infestum adpropinquare iam coepit." Ibid., praef.1, in CSEL 3.1:317.

[39]"Sex dies sunt mundi aetas, id est sex milia annorum." Tyconius, *Liber regularum* 5, ed. and trans. William S. Babcock, *Tyconius: The Book of Rules* (Atlanta: Scholars Press, 1989), 90-1.

[40]As McGinn points out, "the doctrine of the world ages cannot be considered apart from the . . . thousand-year kingdom of Revelation 20:4-6." Bernard McGinn, *Visions of the End: Apocalyptic Traditions in the Middle Ages* (New York: Columbia University Press, 1998), 17. The classical studies on this topic are Léon Gry, *Le millénarisme dans ses origines et son développement* (Paris: Alphonse Picard, 1904), and Jean Daniélou, "La typologie millénariste de la semaine," *Vigiliae Christianae* 2 (1948): 1-16.

[41]On this terminology, see Augustinus, *De civitate Dei* 20.7, in CCSL 48:709.

[42]"The seventh and final book of this work—later summarized in chapters 64-8 of his *Epitome*—is Lactantius' vivid and detailed presentation of Christian apocalyptic expectations: a systematic synthesis of earlier Latin eschatological speculation, the Asian millenarian tradition, and a wide range of ancient philosophical and literary speculations on the afterlife." Brian Daley, *The Hope of the Early Church: A Handbook of Patristic Eschatology* (Cambridge: Cambridge University Press, 1991), 67.

[43]Lactantius, *Divinarum institutionum* 7.14, in CSEL 19:629-30, trans. Mary Francis McDonald, *The Divine Institutes* (Washington, DC: The Catholic University of America Press, 1964), 510.

[44]Lactantius, *Divinarum institutionum* 7.24, in CSEL 19:665-6.

[45]Lactantius, *Divinarum institutionum* 7.26, in CSEL 19:665, trans. McDonald, 535.

[46]For a summary of the millennial kingdom according to Lactantius, see Daley, *The Hope of the Early Church*, 68.

[47]Lactantius, *Divinarum institutionum* 7.25, in CSEL 19:664, trans. McDonald, 534.

[48]Mary Francis McDonald, "Introduction," *The Divine Institutes*, by Lactantius (Washington, DC: The Catholic University of America Press, 1964), 8.

[49]*De cursu temporum*, also known as *De mundi duratione*, is thought to have been written by Hilarianus, bishop of Timida Regia in Proconsular Africa. Daley, *The Hope of the Early Church*, 127.

[50]According to Hilarianus, the world is to end after six thousand years. Only four hundred seventy years of the last thousand remain after the passion of Christ. "Ergo a passione domini Christi, ex quo tempore in se fide credentibus resurrectionem pollicitus est dei filius, anni conpleantur necesse est CCCCLXX, ut concludatur summa VI milium annorum. Septimo et millesimo anno incipiente fide uera credentes liberabuntur e mundo: tunc enim erit resurrectio prima om-

nium sanctorum. De CCCC uero et LXX annis a passionem domini in consolatu Caesari et Attici (397) die VIII. Kl. Abrilis anni transierunt CCCLXVIIII. Restant itaque anni CI, ut consummentur anni VI." Quintus Julius Hilarianus, *De cursu temporum* (or *De mundi duratione*) 17, ed. Carolus Frick, *Chronica minora* (Leipzig: B. G. Teubneri, 1892), 171, also in PL 13:1105a.

[51]He seems to place the incarnation at year 5,500 after creation, although the figure is not explicit. Sulpicius Severus, *Chronica* 2.27, in CSEL 1:82.

[52]"quod nonulli sic accipiunt, ut sex annorum milia constituant uelut unum diem eumque in partes uelut horas duodecim partiantur, ut sic quingentos annos postremos hora uideatur habere postrema; in quibus annis iam Iohannes, inquiunt, loquebatur, quando nouissimam horam esse dicebat." Augustinus, *Epistula* 199. 6.17, in CSEL 57:258, cf. ibid., 7.20, in CSEL 57:260.

[53]"His consulibus ignari praesumptores ferunt Antechristum nasciturum. . . . Alii delirantes hoc consule dicunt Antecristum nasciturum." *Paschale Campanum*, in MGHaa 9:746-7; on this text see Bernard McGinn, *Antichrist: Two Thousand Years of Human Fascination with Evil* (San Francisco: Harper Collins, 1994), 77, and Fabio Troncarelli, "Il consolato dell'Antichristo," *Studi Medievali*, 3rd series, 30 (1989): 567-92.

[54]"aut *ab exitu sermonis* quando Danihelo LXX hebdomadae taxatae sunt futurae usque ad Christum ducem. Nam tunc esse bellum factum Michael et angeli eius ut pugnarent cum dracone, et Danihelo angelus ostendit dicens missum se esse ut pugnaret cum principe regni Persarum: Et non est, ait, qui me adiuuet nisi Michael princeps uester. In quo bello diabolus uictus, praecipitatus et uinctus est: sicut idem prophetae in initio, ita Iohanni in fine temporis ostensum est: ut illi CCCXC anni et isti qui excurrunt ab aduentu saluatoris usque in solutionem eiusdem diaboli concludant mille annos in quibus ligatus est diabolus *ne ultra seduceret nationes,* quas antea deceperat in idolatriis." *Liber* D.4.6, in SC 102:598.

[55]Hieronymus, *In Danielem* 3.9.24, in CCSL 75A:876-7; "Labore ingenioque magno beatae memoriae Hieronymus per supputationes annorum regum Babyloniae LXX ebdomadas usque ad nostri redemptoris natiuitatem Christi domini annos CCCCXC perduxit." *Liber* II.35.79, in SC 102:474.

[56]Hervé Inglebert, "Un exemple historiographique au Ve siècle: la conception de l'histoire chez Quodvultdeus de Carthage et ses relations avec la *Cité de Dieu,*" *Revue des Études Augustiniennes* 37 (1991): 316-27. Much of the argument in this paragraph is drawn from Inglebert, although I have not followed him in all details.

[57]Avihu Zakai and Anya Mali, "Time, History and Eschatology: Ecclesiastical History from Eusebius to Augustine," *The Journal of Religious History* 17 (1993): 405ff.

[58]"Qui mille annorum in terra Iudaea regnum Christi recipiunt, Iudaei uidelicet et nostri iudaizantes. . . ." Hieronymus, *In Hieremiam prophetam* 6.29, in CSEL 59:410. For a recent discussion of texts in which Jerome condemns millenarianism and connects it with Judaizers in the Christian community, see Hillel I. Newman, "Jerome's Judaizers," *Journal of Early Christian Studies* 9:4 (2001): 421-52. Origen also attacked such millenarians for interpreting scripture "in a Jewish sense." Daley,

The Hope of the Early Church, 49. Such views of the millennium were indeed rooted in Jewish traditions; see Louis A. Brighton, *Revelation* (St. Louis: Concordia Publishing House, 1999), 534-6, and Jean Daniélou, *The Theology of Jewish Christianity*, trans. John A. Baker (Chicago: The Henry Regnery Company, 1964), 377ff. "Sed Matthaeus et Marcus post dies sex adsumtos hos esse memorarunt. De quo possemus dicere post sex milia annorum—*mille* enim *anni in conspectu dei tamquam dies una*—, sed plures quam sex milia conputantur anni et malumus sex dies per symbolum intellegere, quod sex diebus mundi opera sunt creata, ut per tempus opera, per opera mundum intellegamus. Et ideo mundi temporibus inpletis resurrectio futura monstratur aut quia is qui supra mundum ascenderit et huius saeculi momenta transcenderit uelut in sublimi locatus futurae resurrectionis fructum exspectabit aeternum." Ambrosius Mediolanensis, *Expositio euangelii secundum Lucam* 7.7, in CCSL 14:217; see also ibid., 10.10, in CCSL 14:348; *De bono mortis* 10.46, in CSEL 32.1:742.

[59]The heretical Cerinthiani, Augustine writes, "Mille quoque annos post resurrectionem in terreno regno Christi, secundum carnales ventris et libidinis voluptates, futuros fabulantur: unde etiam Chiliastae sunt appellati." Augustinus, *De haeresibus* 8, in PL 42:27; see also *De civitate Dei* 20.7, in CCSL 48:709; Russell J. De Simone, "The Baptismal and Christological Catechesis of Quodvultdeus," *Augustinianum* 25 (1985): 266-7.

[60]"Nam sexta aetas senectus est, quoniam prima infantia, secunda pueritia, tertia adolescentia, quarta iuuentus, quinta grauitas. Veteris itaque hominis uita, quae secundum carnem temporali conditione peragitur, sexta aetate tamquam senectute concluditur." Augustinus, *De diversis quaestionibus octoginta tribus* 64.2, in CCSL 44A:137-8; *De Genesi contra Manichaeos* 1.23.35-41, in CSEL 91:104-11.

[61]*Contra Faustum Manichaeum* 12.18, in CSEL 25:346-7; *Tractatus in Iohannis evangelium* 9.6, in CCSL 26:93-4. For an evaluation of the theological value of Augustine's six-age schema, see Olivier Rousseau, "La typologie augustinienne de l'hexaemeron et la théologie du temps," in *Festgabe Joseph Lortz*, ed. E. Iserloh and P. Manns (Mainz: Baden-Baden, 1957), 47-58.

[62]*De Trinitate* 4.4.7, ed. Giuseppe Beschin, *La Trinità*, by Saint'Agostino (Rome: Città Nuova Editrice, 1973), 188, trans. Edmund Hill, *The Trinity*, by Augustine, The Works of Saint Augustine, vol. 1, no. 5 (Brooklyn: New City Press, 1991), 158. For other places where Augustine describes the seven ages, see *De catechizandis rudibus* 22.39, in CCSL 46:163; *De diversis quaestionibus octoginta tribus* 58.2, in CCSL 44A:106; *Contra Faustum Manichaeum* 12.8, in CSEL 25:336; *De civitate Dei* 22.30, in CCSL 48:865-6; "quinta ab hac transmigratione usque ad uirginis partum, sexta inde usque in huius saeculi finem." *Quaestionum in Heptateuchum* 7.48.26, in CCSL 33:372.

[63]Stephen D. O'Leary, *Arguing the Apocalypse: A Theory of Millennial Rhetoric* (New York: Oxford University Press, 1994), 73-5.

[64]"Nam cum a sexagesimo anno senectus dicatur incipere, et possit humana uita usque ad centum viginti annos peruenire, manifestum est solam senectutem posse tam longam esse quam omnes priores aetates. Aetas igitur ultima generis humani,

quae incipit a domini aduentu usque ad finem saeculi, quibus generationibus computetur incertum est." Augustinus, *De diversis quaestionibus octoginta tribus* 58.2, in CCSL 44A:107. Augustine also speaks from time to time about a new youth given to the world in this sixth age—perhaps one could refer to it as a second wind: "Ipse ad senem hominem venit, qui mundum veterem invenit. Ergo si mundum veterem invenit, audiat mundus: Cantate Domino canticum novum; cantate Domino, omnis terra. Destruatur vetustas, novitas surgat." *Sermo* 163.4, in PL 38:891; "erat utique Christus in ipsius mundi senectute venturus. Venit cum omnia veterascerent, et novum te fecit." *Sermo* 81.8, in PL 38:504; "In ista tamen aetate tam quam in senectute veteris hominis homo novus nascitur qui iam spiritaliter vivit." *De Genesi contra Manichaeos* 1.23.40, in CSEL 91:108.

[65]Daley, *The Hope of the Early Church*, 134.

[66]Augustinus, *Epistula* 199.54, in CSEL 57:291-2, trans. Wilfrid Parsons, *Saint Augustine: Letters*, vol. 4, *(165-203)*, The Fathers of the Church, vol. 30 (New York: The Fathers of the Church, 1955), 400-1.

[67]Augustinus, *Epistula* 199.53, in CSEL 57:290, trans. Parsons, 399.

[68]Augustinus, *De Genesi contra Manichaeos* 1.23.41, in CSEL 91:110.

[69]"septima aetate tamquam septimo die requieturus est in sanctis suis." *De catechizandis rudibus* 17.28, in CCSL 46:152.

[70]Augustinus, *De civitate Dei* 22.30, in CCSL 48:866, trans. Bettenson, 1091. In earlier days Augustine himself was a millenarian. At that point he seems to have distinguished the eight day of "Sabbath" rest from the seventh age—the age of earthly rule for the saints. Luneau, *L'Histoire du salut*, 325; Daley, *The Hope of the Early Church*, 133.

[71]"usque in mane quod uesperum non habebit, id est usque in resurrectionem." *Liber* I.37.53, in SC 101:272.

[72]"La situation de l'Église est meilleure, mais aussi la réflexion théologique a progressé." Luneau, *L'Histoire du salut*, 282.

SCRIPTURE AND
SYSTEMATIC THEOLOGY

What Does Systematic Theology Say to New Testament Interpretation?

John Topel

Recently Joel Green and Max Turner pointed out that while many works ask "What effects should biblical texts produce in theology?" no contemporary work asks the obverse question, "What effects should [systematic] theology produce in biblical interpretation?"[1] What these evangelical exegetes ask resounds in this Roman Catholic exegete. I think that the next breakthrough in exegetical and hermeneutical methodology will come from those who consciously read the text with theological eyes.

On what in interpretation, however, can I ground this intuition? The whole contemporary movement from an exclusive reliance on the historical-critical method and the investigation of a fixed authorial intent seems to move readers in this larger direction. Emphasis on the unconscious or preconscious moves of the author in structuralist exegesis, emphasis on the imaginative depths of metaphor in parable interpretation, employment of the whole panoply of literary criticism in narrative analysis—all of these open up biblical interpretation to the engagement of the whole person with the text. Particularly important is the recent exegetical emphasis on reader-response criticism, in which the reader utilizes his or her own manifold of literary, historical, social scientific skills to fill the gaps left by the author. Then if the interpreter who reads the text also has some of the conceptual skills of a systematic theologian, how can the interpreter avoid drawing on these as he or she fills in the gaps left by the author in the text?

A biblical interpreter who has read Paul's texts on justification by faith, considered the history of interpretations of the passages, consulted the dialectic of different understandings of the human person and of human authenticity, and who, in a defining moment, decides on a synthetic position to explain his or her faith experience can now read the texts in a new and more illuminating way. Indeed, recent hermeneutical theory that stresses the importance of the author's and the reader's underlying world-view in the fusion of their two horizons vindicates this more conceptual approach to the text.

What is the interpreter's way forward, however, to this presumably enriched understanding of the text? Bernard Lonergan's scheme of functional specialties in theology offers a method whereby the exegete can relate his narrative, symbolic, descriptive mode of understanding to the more theoretic explanation of the systematic theologian. This paper discusses Lonergan's view of these specialties, isolates the specialties most important to the exegetical-hermeneutical/systematic dialogue, and tries to propose some ways of understanding a theological interpretation of the Bible in general and the New Testament in particular. It should be noted that the method of interpretation being proposed is only one of many methods available to a variety of readers, all of whom are diverse themselves in their approach to the Bible.

The Bases of Lonergan's Method

Of all the great twentieth-century theologians, none seems less interested in doctrinal theology than Bernard Lonergan. Lonergan's starting point and consuming interest was in an analysis of the sad state of the world in respect to the problem of evil.[2] He thought that under God's healing and cooperating grace human intelligence could analyze what caused human systems to pervert authentic human creativity.

This could not be the task of one person or of one discipline. Rather, Lonergan embraced the specialization of contemporary human learning as the way to more profound analysis of an ever more complex world. In order for these specialized disciplines to bear on a common problem, however, they needed some agreed-upon framework in which they could collaborate. Lonergan began by providing the method for such collaboration between artists and politicians, theoretical astrophysicists and economists. He judged that such an agreed-upon framework must take its stand on ways of knowing common to all arts and sciences, upon an invariant structure that would inescapably be exercised in every discipline.

Insight

Lonergan arrived at the position that all human knowing, from common sense to the most theoretical exercise, rises from *experience* to *understanding* to *judgment*. Thus "all knowing" exemplifies what one takes as a given in the scientific method, where attention to and assembling of data leads to hypothesis, which is then tested by experiments and so developed into a theory. Once verified by replication through further experiments, it becomes a law.[3] If anyone would deny this explanation of the invariant structure of human knowing, she would have to do so by: 1) attending to the evidence (seeing, hearing, smelling, touching, tasting); 2) inquiring, imagining, understanding, and conceptualizing in a different way and; 3) weighting the evidence, testing the hypothesis, and arriving at a more adequate formulation of the data—all of which verifies the invariant structure to which Lonergan points. Since each stage of the knowing process drives a person on to the next stage by an inherent eros of the mind, knowing is a continual process of self-transcendence.

Method in Theology

Between the completion of *Insight* (1956), and the publication of *Method* (1972),[4] Lonergan expanded his cognitional analysis into an intentionality analysis. The first three steps of human knowing (*experience*, *understanding*, and *judgment*) were now seen to terminate in a fourth step, *decision*, in which one evaluates what one has discovered in thought, decides how to actualize this good, and acts to effect it. Human self-transcendence, then, finds fulfillment not only in thought, but also more properly in constituting oneself and one's world in action. In this development, Lonergan's thought opens up not simply to the world of value, but to loving and being in love, as these are found in emotions and expressed by image and symbol. Intellectual conversion is intimately related to moral, psychic, and religious conversion.[5] And so Lonergan arrives at these transcendental precepts for human authenticity: be attentive, be intelligent, be rational (by which he means critical), be responsible.

One last element is necessary to understand Lonergan's use of functional specialties in theology. The history of theology reveals that theologizing occurs in two basic phases. The first phase is "the way of discovery" that deals with things that are prior in one's experience. Here one listens to the Word, assimilates tradition, and so encounters the past historical development of Christian thought. This is mediating theology, which tells what the Bible and the Councils, as well as Augustine, Aquinas, Luther, and Rahner had to say about God and the economy of salvation. If one listens to the past, however, then one must also take a stand toward the future. This stand toward the future sets the stage for the second phase, the "way of exposition."

The "way of exposition" creatively synthesizes things that are prior in themselves, and that evoke one's interaction with such things. This is mediated theology in which the tradition's findings confront the problems of today. Frederick Crowe clarifies the distinction by an example:

> ... in trinitarian theology, the order of analysis is from the missions of Son and Spirit in the New Testament, first to their consubstantiality with the Father, then to the distinction of the Three by mutually opposed relations, and finally to the processions understood through the psychological analogy. ... The synthetic order of Thomas Aquinas moves in exactly the opposite direction, beginning with the processions, moving to the relations, then to the persons, and so to the missions of Son and Spirit.[6]

The example shows that the way of exposition not only explains more clearly and profoundly the nature of reality, but also explains its order.

The Functional Specialties

Having discussed the two guiding principles of Lonergan's functional specialties, these specialties are now outlined in detail.

The Way of Discovery

Research. At the level of experience, research assembles and "makes available the data relevant to theological investigation. ... It locates, excavates, and maps ancient cities ... deciphers unknown scripts and languages ... collects manuscripts and prepares critical editions of texts ... compiles dictionaries and encyclopedias" (*Method*, 127). One needs to note, however, that missing from this level is the cultural contexts of the researcher.

Interpretation. This functional specialty understands the meaning of a text in its proper historical situation and literary context, in accord with its proper mode and level of thought and expression. It attends to the circumstances and intention of the writer, and to the text's surplus of meaning to be derived from structuralist analysis and reader response criticism.

History. This specialty judges and settles some matters of fact, but it really sets forth what was going forward in a given era or country. As a theological specialty, it deals principally with "the doctrinal history of Christian theology with its antecedents and consequents in the cultural and institutional histories of the Christian religion . . ."(128). An interpreter would lay out who Mark envisioned Jesus to be for his early Christian community, or John for his. These very diverse and highly contested images of Jesus inevitably, however, provoke the question, "Which was the Jesus of history?" This is not an issue settled by the interpreter; rather, it becomes the domain of the historical Jesus critic operating as an historical theologian.

Dialectic. This specialty involves the appreciative and critical evaluation of what one has arrived at in the three prior specialties. Theological dialectic investigates the concrete, dynamic, and contradictory conflicts in Christian movements to arrive at a comprehensive viewpoint from which to understand the character, the oppositions, and the relations of their conflicting viewpoint. Such comparative study goes beyond the facts to the reasons for the conflict, to eliminate superfluous oppositions, and to discover where differences are irreducible, where they are complementary, and where they seem to be successive stages in a single process of development.

If the encounter is real, it will lead to conversion (not a theological specialty but an event), in which one not only moves to a higher horizon, but also actually achieves an about-face, a repudiation of the limiting and misleading features of one's previous horizon. Such a conversion for Lonergan can be intellectual, moral, or religious. Intellectual conversion means taking the critical realist position on knowing sketched at the beginning of this study. It moves beyond naïve realist, empiricist, and idealist theories of knowledge based on "taking a look," to an objective grasp of reality as that which can be reasonably affirmed. Moral conversion changes the criterion of one's choices from satisfactions to values. One moves beyond an egoistic calculation of pleasure and pain to an option for the truly good which serves to advance one's own authenticity and the common good of society. "Religious conversion is being grasped by ultimate concern. It is otherworldly falling in love" (240) in an unrestricted manner, creating a dynamic state prior to, and the principle of, subsequent acts. For Christians, religious conversion is God's love flooding into one's heart through the Holy Spirit. This replacement of the heart of stone by the heart of flesh, then, becomes effective in good works through human freedom.[7] This self-transcending conversion then enables one to take a position on the conflicting perceptions and values of the dialectic, and thus rise to a beginning synthesis of the tradition that can be explained in a deductive line of descent.

The Way of Exposition

Foundations. This specialty puts into themes the new horizon embedded in conversion, expresses its new worldview, and consequently takes sides for a particular option exposed in the conflicts of dialectic. The fact that religious or intellectual conversion occurs does not mean, however, that the conflicts discovered in dialectic will be resolved. The new horizon will be expressed differently by different theologians, depending on their differentiation of consciousness. Basically, there are four different realms of meaning, those of common sense, of theory, of interiority, and of transcendence.[8] These can be combined in multiple ways, and each theologian conceives and expresses his horizon according to the modes of differentiation of her consciousness. For Lonergan, the source of basic reconciliation and clarification of dialectic's welter of doctrines is interiorly and religiously differentiated consciousness.

The reality to be expressed in terms of one's culture is nevertheless transcultural, since God's gift of his love (Rom. 5:5) occurs in all peoples of all times and places. What is needed to express this is a method which is also transcultural, which Lonergan identifies as the transcendental method outlined in *Insight* and *Method.*[9] From this base, Lonergan thinks foundations will derive its general categories from analysis of the authenticity or unauthenticity of humans with respect to the transcendental imperatives, and its special categories from the authenticity or unauthenticity of Christians' love of God. One could justifiably wonder, however, if, in fact, Lonergan's method is truly expressed transculturally.

In short, it appears that where dialectic uncovers contradictory positions, Lonergan would ascribe this to a lack of conversion in one or more levels, and particularly to a failure to achieve interiorly and religiously differentiated consciousness. Where dialectic uncovers oppositions that may be complementary, Lonergan would ascribe this to a plurality of differentiations of consciousness or diversity in the special categories used to articulate theological assertions that may be enriching.

Doctrines. In this specialty, one uses foundations to select doctrines from among the multiple choices presented by dialectic. Doctrines express the converted theologian's foundational principles in judgments of fact and judgments of value and deal with truths of doctrinal theology as well as truths of moral and pastoral theology.[10] Doctrines, insofar as they are based on authentic conversion, have a normative function, eliciting authenticity from the unconverted. Such doctrines will be expressed in different terms, depending on the range of differentiations of consciousness, from common sense to interiority, and according to the corresponding stages of cultural development of those articulating the doctrines and those receiving them.

Because church dogmas express a fuller understanding not of data, but of a truth, it is always the same truth that is being understood. Thus dogmas are permanent in their meaning, even if their expression is historically conditioned by the development of culture to which successive expressions belong. An exact grasp of another's mentality is possible only if one attains the same differentiation and lack of differentiation. But since no one is obliged, simply because of his or her faith, to attain a fuller differentiation of consciousness, and anyone may strive to express his or her faith in the manner appropriate to his or her differentiation of consciousness, there results an irreducible pluralism in the expression of doctrines. To this pluralism of individual expression in the same culture must be added the cultural pluralism that arises from so many different cultural contexts. Because it is the doctrinal theologian's responsibility to mediate these different levels of expression, the doctrinal theologian has the requisite autonomy to do so in a way that respects the enriching pluralism of such diverse expressions. A key question now becomes, "Can the doctrinal theologian accomplish such a task?"

Systematics. This specialty promotes an understanding of the realities affirmed in doctrines. It does not add a further proof of doctrines by theological reasoning; rather it attempts "to work out appropriate systems of conceptualization, to remove apparent inconsistencies, to . . . grasp . . . spiritual matters both from their own inner coherence and from the analogies offered by more familiar human experience" (132). Most important, it aims at an understanding of doctrines in terms that can communicate with the culture in which one is living. Today "problems are so numerous that many do not know what to believe. . . . They know what church doctrines are, but they want to know what church doctrines could possibly mean" (345), and systematics tries to answer this question. Understandings that speak to our culture must arise from historical development, be in dialogue with scientific understanding and the scholarship of social sciences, and be founded on the interiority of the human spirit in its process of self-transcendence through knowing and loving. Probably Lonergan's best example of this is his transposing of salvation in Christ from the Pauline and medieval notions of redemption, satisfaction, and atonement into a contemporary understanding of the overcoming of sin and death by the just and mysterious law of the cross.

Communications. Through this specialty, theology communicates to the world the reality of God as the solution to the problem of evil, and also challenges all humans to redemptive action in the world.[11] Communications passes on to the next generation the achievements of past and present generations, which, in turn, become the data for research for the next. The concrete context for theological communications is one's religious community in the world. The church is a community to serve the whole human community in overcoming our human biases and the alienation they engender by preaching and living Jesus' forgiving and redemptive message. Communicating the Christian message is to lead others to share in one's cognitive, constitutive, and effective meaning. Since this goal of healing is worldwide, the Christian message is to be preached to all cultures and to every development of consciousness. Thus communications must engage in interdisciplinary relations with the arts, with natural and human sciences, with philosophy and world religions, and it must make full and proper use of the diverse media of communication.

In conclusion, whether Lonergan's method will achieve the same normative value in theology as his cognitional analysis can for philosophy can be determined only by its fruitfulness for a generation of theological inquirers. It does, however, have one advantage for those reading this volume: by distinguishing the different specialties, Lonergan allows readers to explore the relationship between exegesis and theology. Furthermore, his definition of method itself as "a normative pattern of recurrent and related operations yielding cumulative and progressive results" offers some support for my hypothesis that the speculative theologian can contribute to the interpretation of the text. What follows next is a discussion of a text aimed at testing the hypothesis.

A Systematic Reading of Paul's Justification by Faith

One engaged in New Testament interpretation would use the first two specialties, *research* and *interpretation*. Through these two functional specialties, the interpreter studies the data assembled by field workers in archaeology, cultural anthropology, and ancient languages and literature and comes to an understanding of the history and thought worlds of first-century Jews and Gentile Christians so as to understand the world behind the text. The diachronic methods of analysis, namely text, source, form, and redaction criticism, aid the interpreter in understanding the text's layers of meaning. The synchronic methods of rhetorical and literary criticism complement the diachronic methods. The use of semiotic, structuralist, and reader-response criticism leads to an understanding of the text's surplus of meaning that speaks to the world in front of the text. These methods operate in what Lonergan calls the common-sense level of meaning. Many interpreters also investigate their own interpretative pre-suppositions through the hermeneutics of the later Heidegger, Gadamer, and Ricoeur, and some interpreters are more influenced by their own confessional background than by the use of hermeneutics.

Hence, I come to the interpretation of Romans with some understanding of the role of law in Jewish religious experience, whether that be the Pharisees' strict interpretation or the covenantal nomism represented by Psalm 1. I come with an understanding of the meanings of *sedeqah* and δικαιοσυνη. I come with some knowledge not only of Paul's upbringing as a Pharisee, but also of his unexpected gift of the risen Christ's revelation of the mystery of salvation and his summons to apostleship. I am aware of his tumultuous struggle with the Judaizers of Galatia, and I understand Paul when he says "I am not ashamed of the gospel; it is the power of God for the salvation of everyone who believes" (Rom. 1:16).

Paul's whole rhetorical structure in Romans 1-8 demonstrates that humans are justified freely by faith in God's love in Jesus. Paul documents the impotence of the law to save (Rom. 1-3), and shows through Abraham's experience in the Hebrew Testament that YHWH saved through faith (Rom. 4). Paul describes this as the righteousness of God now made manifest apart from the law through faith in Jesus Christ for all who believe (3:21-22, 28); humans beings are justified freely by God's grace through Jesus, which excludes human boasting over its achievement (3:21, 23). Paul later roots this justification in God's unconditional love, "because the love of God has been poured out into our hearts through the Holy Spirit that has been given to us. For Christ, while we were still helpless yet died . . . for the ungodly" (5:5-6). Thus, the law has no positive role in leading one to salvation; in Romans 7 Paul allows it only the negative value of pointing to the sins from which a person needs deliverance. It is no wonder that Paul's Jewish Christian adversaries considered his doctrine as leading to antinomian license (3:5-8; 6:1, 15).

As is usually the case when one uses literary language and symbols to express one's thought, there are some elements of Paul's thought in Romans that are, if not contradictory, at least contrary, to his doctrine. Paul asserts that "those who observe the law will be justified" (Rom. 2:13), that "circumcision has value if you observe the law" (Rom. 2:25), and that "the Gentiles who . . . by nature observe the prescriptions of the law" can escape on judgment day (Rom. 2:14-16). There are even texts in which good works make one acceptable to God (Rom. 2:6-10; 14:10-12). In short, Paul operates out of "a key motif in the symbolic universe of apocalyptic Judaism . . . [and] fully embraces the principle of justification according to one's works."[12] Although Paul's main argument in Romans surely is that justification is by faith, there are enough contrary statements to provoke controversy throughout the history of Christian theology.

The third functional specialty, *history*, investigates what actually went forward in history. In Pelagius, and even more in his disciple Caelestius, the doctrine of salvation by the works of a naturally good human will found a hearing in North Africa. There it provoked a determined response from Augustine, who continued the thinking of

Cyprian of Carthage that all humans had inherited original sin, that the *massa peccati* was damned, and that only a pre-destined remnant would be saved by faith and baptism. Augustine's polemical and rhetorical style is Christianity's most forceful defense of the universality of sin and of the necessity of grace flowing from divine predestination to heal the will and enable it even to delight in the good. In one place (*The Soul and Its Origin*, IV, 11, 16), his emphasis on the absolute necessity of grace seems to have led him to assert a double predestination as the only way to account for both salvation and condemnation—a position with its own contrary in 1 Tim. 2:4, where God wills all to be saved.

In this debate lay the roots of controversy throughout the history of Christian theology—the (so-called) semi-Pelagians vs. the Council of Orange; Luther vs. Trent on the importance of works; the Dominicans vs. the Jesuits on human freedom and God's grace; Karl Barth vs. the liberal Protestants—all the way to the concord on justification by faith between the Lutherans and Catholics in 1998.

The fourth specialty that offers insight into the interpretative process is *dialectic*. The persistence of the aforesaid debate demands some understanding of the principles at work in the opposed positions. The Reformation may provide the clearest example. Against various abuses of the sixteenth-century church and in reaction to all his futile attempts to prepare himself for the gift of grace, Luther articulated the Augustinian theology of justification by faith. In his religious experience, even in his moments of deeply experienced grace, he was aware not only of his unworthiness before God, but also of his concupiscence. Since he identified concupiscence with sin, he described Christians as "*simul justus et peccator*." If one interprets Genesis 3 as a "fall from grace," as Luther does, then it would follow that after the fall, the human will was bound and humans really could do nothing toward their own salvation. Justification, as Paul saw, could be only a pure gift of God, who, because of the merits of Christ's passion, death and resurrection, forgives sins without any merit on the part of humans. Further, since they are always sinners, no act of theirs subsequent to justification could be in any way meritorious for their final salvation.

Although he rejected its preoccupation with logical distinctions and its emphasis on the autonomy of the will, Luther was influenced by his education in nominalist philosophy and theology. Because there were no natures of things to be understood, Luther thought in personalist categories. Because he was not a systematic theologian but a rhetorician, he expressed himself in different metaphors at different times. Thus, for Luther, as sinners we must be the object of God's wrath, but the word of God (about our being justified by faith in Christ) "renders us certain that God has put away all wrath and hatred towards us." Luther paints the imputation of justification as follows:

> . . . because I am covered under the shadow of Christ's wings, as is the chicken under the wings of the hen, . . . God covers and pardons the remnant of sin in me. . . . So we shroud ourselves under the covering of Christ's flesh . . . flying unto Christ our mediator and reconciler. . . . When we believe this, God winks at the remnants of sin yet sticking in our flesh, and so covers them, as if they were no sin. (*1535 Commentary on the Epistle to the Galatians* 3:6)[13]

Such descriptions of "imputed justification" are balanced by other expressions that describe the subsequent sanctification of the justified as a reception of Christ's spirit, which works a real change in Christian character and action. The more forceful expressions are, however, the ones that Melancthon built into a doctrine of forensic justification; they were later condemned by the Council of Trent.

The Council Fathers, on the other hand, were educated in the remnants of a realistic scholastic philosophy based on Aristotelian categories of nature. For them, human nature was severely damaged, not vitiated, by original sin. They distinguished sin from concupiscence, which is the natural rebellion of the lower principles against the higher in a complex nature. They recognized grace as necessary to heal the breach sin creates between God and man (*gratia sanans*), and also necessary if the creature is to attain to the supernatural end (the beatific vision) to which she is called (*gratia elevans*). In one process of justification and sanctification, grace is conceived as a quality given to the soul that transforms persons into children of God, participators of the divine nature. Those who work out of this transformed (supernatural) state cooperate with God and so, always under God's prevenient influence, can merit their salvation.

Therefore the Tridentine bishops, understanding justification as a changed ontological state in Christians, could make no sense out of *simul justus et peccator*, and so they took Luther's strong language on imputed justification as the merely forensic justification that some Lutheran texts suggested. On the surface, they had no problem with justification by faith, which they freely agreed was right there in St. Paul (*Decree on Justification*, DS 1521, 1525). They believed that Christians were justified on no merit of their own, but entirely on God's initiative through the merits of Christ's obedience in his passion, death, and resurrection. Their problem was that Luther's interpretation of Paul seemed to leave the justified Christian enslaved to sin, and so they thought there was no real sanctification of the justified Christian. They declared heretical a theology that denied the real sanctification of the justified Christians, denied free will, and made no place for the Christians' own contributions to their salvation through the exercise of their own free will in works done under the power of God's grace (DS 1532, 1535). For their part, Lutheran theologians have always been suspicious that Catholic theologians, by not distinguishing adequately between justification and sanctification, have bootlegged some meriting of salvation into their doctrine of justification itself.[14]

The biblical interpreter now recognizes that in the dialectic the two positions are not contradictory. Both agree that justification occurs freely, entirely by God's grace, through the merits of Jesus' suffering, death, and resurrection. At the root of the controversy is not a question of interpretation, nor even a question of common-sense literary language against the technical language of systematic theology. Instead, we are dealing with a dispute between a realist position on knowing and the nominalist counter position on knowing.[15] Where the nominalist sees impotence, the realist sees both the possibility and the necessity of the graced human will to "work out its salvation with fear and trembling" (Phil. 2:11).

At this impasse, the interpreter, whether Catholic, Lutheran, or Calvinist, realizes that a new horizon is necessary. Thus, the *conversion* specialty comes to the fore. Such a conversion always begins from where the person already is, and may push one only to a deeper and quite different apprehension of one's previous orientation; however, it may effect a breakthrough in which one must change one's scale of values and even previous confessional commitments.

The biblical interpreter understands from the dialectic of the opposed positions that most Christian theologians agree on the following points: 1) human beings can do nothing to merit either forgiveness of sins or the life of intimacy to which they are called in Christ;

2) their access to these (their justification) is not through works but solely through faith in God's unconditional love granted through the passion, death, and resurrection of his son, Jesus Christ; and 3) this justification means the forgiveness of sins and a sanctification of the Christian's person and subsequent works. In dispute are questions of the nature of sin, how justification and sanctification occur, and how important for justification itself are the subsequently graced acts of the justified Christian. Thus, by and large, the dialectic has revealed among interpreters of justification by faith not contradictions, but considerable agreement. The disagreements may be due to different technical levels of expression or to different stages of development in various interpreters.

Theological method is concerned with the intellectual conversion of the interpreter.[16] This intellectual conversion constitutes a new horizon in which God and humans are seen not as opponents locked in a struggle of wills; rather, they are as lovers seeking the good of the Other in a process of continual self-transcendence. In order for God to be omnipotent, it is not necessary for humans to be impotent. In this new horizon the divine emerges as pure Love, without any hatred or disgust, and the human emerges as one whose purified desires give momentum and weight to one's actions transformed in Christ. The interpreter fully attends to the radical nature of the transformation that has occurred through God's justifying grace, both healing and elevating the Christian.[17] This vision, then, leads one to the next specialty, foundations.

Foundations helps one to take a stand among the various inchoate explanations advanced in the history of the dialectic. With respect to the discussion at hand, the foundation would take its stand in Luther's insight that all the initiative is with God and that only believing in God's gracious love in the life, death, and resurrection of Jesus allows God's justifying action to occur efficaciously and yet freely without any merit of one's own. It would also take its stand in Augustine's teaching that God's grace is both initiating and cooperating with human freedom so that the Christian really does works that bring the reward of God's favorable judgment.[18] The new position, then, affirms both the divine transcendence and the power of God's love to transform and recreate the human heart as that of a child of God.

A new horizon has now emerged that will affect all realms of theology. For this study, however, the discussion must be limited to a brief sketch of those elements that bear on 1) the primary data on justification by faith in Paul and the rest of the New Testament, and 2) the consensus that has arisen from the dialectical development of Christian theology on justification.

The first element is the *doctrine of God*. God is understood as pure love, and so Luther's talk about God's wrath and hatred toward us may be effective rhetoric, but cannot be a correct understanding of God's relation to the sinner. Further, this absolute love cannot be reconciled with any doctrine of double predestination. Not only can it not be reconciled with the Pauline school's insistence on the universal salvific will of God (1 Tim. 2:4), nor with Paul's own insistence that God is not partial (Rom. 2:11; Gal. 2:6), but it cannot be reconciled with the understanding of God as pure love. The solution to the problem of evil in the world is this God who summons humans to enter freely into God's plan of salvation and empowers them to live the demanding ethic of self-transcending love.

The second element, *Christian anthropology*, will accept the truth of Luther's *simul justus et peccator*. The justified Christian will still find himself in the position of Paul's divided man (Rom. 7:15-25), capable of living virtuously or of sinning. This formula cannot, however, be understood in terms of a forensic justification, in which a person remains merely a sinner whose sins are overlooked. To be preferred are those texts of Luther and Trent that speak of a real sanctification, a change in the Christian, a healing by which one passes from the state of *non posse non peccare* to a state of *posse non peccare*. Even more, human persons will be seen as summoned by God from the first moments of their existence to an intimacy with the Trinity, which is their historical vocation. This summons is itself grace, an expression of God's unconditional love, and it expects not only a response that is first and foremost faith in God's unconditional love, but also cooperation with God in Christ's healing grace in the world.

The third element is *moral theology*. There is, then, a Christian ethics that begins from the point of graced summons that then considers all human ethical striving as a response to God's gracious initiative. Each human person experiences, in his or her thirst for self-transcendence in knowing and loving, a call to a dreaded holiness to which he or she can and must respond.

The fourth element is *christology and soteriology*. In the aforesaid view of the world, the saving grace of Christ extends backward to creation in the divine Word and forward to its graced consummation in Christ. This grace is everywhere the grace of Jesus Christ poured out by the Holy Spirit that is given to humankind (Rom. 5:5); it is enacted through the necessary and immutable law of the cross that leads to resurrection, not only for Jesus, but for all those who experience death in his way.

Such a complex of doctrines demands a view of the human person that can resolve the antinomies of the dialectic, which involves the fifth element, *systematics*. The Christian must be the subject of more than a moment-to-moment existential authenticity. Rather, there must be a profound and stable healing of her interior constitution whereby the Christian becomes a participator of the divine nature (2 Pet. 1:4). This graced person is the subject of a miraculous interchange of initiatives that, always under God's gracious power, nevertheless preserves the autonomy and freedom of the human person. Such a systematic view will also require a consonant psychology of grace and congruent political and economic theories, expressed with the power of imagination and emotion by artists and poets. This collaborative enterprise is, in Lonergan's terms, a cosmopolis (*Insight*, 238-242).

The Systematic Interpreter's Reading of Paul on Justification

The interpreter who has worked his or her way through these theological specialties, or has attended to those who have, can now read the text in a richer way. A caveat: I am not saying that the systematician can read the author's intent better than can the biblical interpreter. The biblical interpreter, operating within the functional specialty of interpretation, can best assess what Paul may have said and intended. What interpretation seeks is what the *text*, with its manifold of opposing statements, may suggest as a whole, with consideration given to the genuine diversity of readership. Paul may have had a conscious way of resolving the dialectical antinomies of his text, but he did not state it. More likely, he had a subconscious worldview in which these oppositions held together, and his preconscious artistic expression left these statements in a tension that he could not have resolved consciously.

The biblical interpreter who reads the text in light of a systematic theology may fill in the gaps that Paul left in the text. The interpreter can now see that there are not two contrary sets of texts in Paul, one that speaks of justification by faith and another that speaks of justification by works. Rather he sees Paul as insisting on a justification by faith that is absolutely prior to and (as *unconditional* love) independent of any human works or merits, yet that does not deny, but rather augments the importance of works in the saving process. The interpreter sees that Paul, as a first-century Jew, could have hardly conceived of a justification in which the human free will was of no use.[19] Further, the interpreter sees from his or her own position in foundations that both God's absolutely free gift of justification of the sinner and the graced freedom of the will to respond must be safeguarded in any process of justification that can be called human. Consequently, the interpreter reads the two sets of texts as being complementary rather than contradictory or even contrary.

From this synthesis, the biblical interpreter fills in the gaps in Paul's expression, so that the text teaches the following points:

1. The initiative in justification is entirely with God, whose love predestines (Rom. 8:28-30) and makes effective the divine summons to discipleship in faith (Rom. 6:4, 12-14).

2. This love is unconditional, coming to humans while they are sinners (Rom. 5:6, 8, 10), and so humans can do absolutely nothing to merit it (Rom. 4:4) but must accept it as the pure gift of God (Rom. 3:24; 5:15).

3. Consequently, the law is of no value in preparing persons for justification (Rom. 3:21-22, 28), nor do the works of the law contribute in any way to one's being justified (Rom. 7:4).

4. What humans can do, under the initiative of God's grace, is surrender in faith to the unconditional love of God expressed in the death and resurrection of Jesus as the only true ground of being in relationship with the true God (Rom. 1:17; 3:22, 25, 28; 4:3, 22-24).

5. And, at the same time, the love of the Holy Spirit that floods the Christian heart (Rom. 5:5) turns it from a heart of stone into a heart of flesh, prompt in discipleship to live the authentic human life of the Master (Rom. 6:12-14; 12:9-21).

6. These works are the graced work of the sanctifying Spirit, and so there is no boasting (Rom. 3:27). These works do not cause, but manifest the presence of justification and the sanctifying Spirit.

7. These works are necessary for God's righteousness to be present in the kingdom and its righteousness. The whole point of the Pauline parenesis in Romans 12-14 is to overcome evil with good (Rom. 12:21).

Christians living out Christ's necessary and immutable law of the cross are God's solution to the problem of evil in the world.

8. Ultimately, humanity is justified by faith and judged on the basis of its works (Rom. 2:6-10,13, 14-16, 25; 14:10-12), for only through human action in the Spirit of Christ has God chosen to bring about the salvation of the world.

Conclusion

This study demonstrates how at least one systematic theologian might read Paul's text more richly and deeply. Whether it is a right reading of the text is not to be judged so much by biblical interpreters, or other theologians, but rather by the experience of the church. If this meaning is communicated, preached, and made effective in symbol and ritual, and is found to issue in the sanctity of the community, then it will become the experience of the next generation of the church, who, in turn, will interpret it, have their history of formulating it, appropriate it dialectically, and so come to a conversion that passes through foundations and doctrines to be systematically appropriated and communicated as the completion of the hermeneutical cycle and the beginning of the new one.

Notes

[1]*Between Two Horizons: Spanning New Testament Studies & Systematic Theology* (Grand Rapids: Eerdmans, 2000), 1-2. The authors allude to work by Robert Wall, Francis Watson, Colin Gunton, and Stephen Fowl, but their work usually relates scripture to biblical theology or canon criticism rather than to systematic theology. In the interests of brevity, I omit a bibliography for biblical methods and content and secondary literature on Lonergan. Since parts III and IV are a sketch of what would take a book to document, I omit a bibliography there as well.

[2]His earliest interests in the philosophy of culture and history (with special emphasis on Hegel and Marx) and the economic theories that underlie the great depression perdured to the end of his life. The starting point of his *magnum opus*, *Insight*, was Chapter Seven, on how common-sense biases produce the cycles of decline.

[3]This pattern is verified in all branches of knowing in the first ten chapters of *Insight: A Study of Human Understanding* (New York: Philosophical Library, 1958). "Cognitional Structure," *Continuum* 2 (1964): 530-542, reprinted in F. Crowe, ed., *Collection: Papers by Bernard Lonergan, S. J.* (New York: Herder & Herder, 1967), 221-239, gives the argument in a somewhat simplified and much briefer form.

[4]*Method in Theology* (New York: Herder & Herder, 1972). Henceforth all numbers in parentheses refer to page numbers in *Method*.

[5]Most often, intellectual conversion to an accurate position on knowing is the most subtle and difficult, usually coming after religious or moral conversion. For psychic conversion, see Robert Doran*, Subject and Psyche: Ricoeur, Jung, and the Search for Foundations* (Washington: University Press of America, 1977).

[6]Frederick E. Crowe, *Lonergan* (Collegeville: Liturgical Press, 1992), 85.

[7]Since all three conversions are modes of self-transcendence, they can be related to one another through Karl Rahner's notion of sublation (*Horer des Wortes* [Munich: Kösel, 1963], 40). Thus, moral conversion sublates the intellectual commitment to the one value, truth, to commitment to values generally. Religious conversion sublates moral conversion to an unrestricted personal surrender to the transcendent love that grasps one totally. Lonergan cautions, however, that this is not the usual temporal sequence. Rather, there is first God's gift of his love, which then reveals values in their splendor, and so leads to believing the truths of one's tradition as the seeds of intellectual conversion.

[8]Actually, Lonergan adds the realms of scholarship and art, and there are more, whenever a specialized language, distinct mode of apprehension, and group of its practitioners occur (272).

[9]Lonergan is not naïve: he recognizes that in both the grasp of God's love and the use of the transcendental method cultural and developmental issues restrict the transcultural reality being described.

[10]Lonergan distinguishes between doctrines as revealed truths, church dogmas, doctrines of theological schools, and the methodological doctrines of those operating on the level of interiority exercised in the functional specialties (295-298).

[11]To be noted is that the problem of evil has a myriad of faces in need of further clarification and discussion that go beyond the present scope of this study.

[12]Brendan Byrne, *Romans* (Collegeville: The Liturgical Press, 1996) 89; cf. 2 Cor. 5:10; 9:6; 11:15; Gal. 6:7.

[13]This more graphic translation is taken from P. S. Watson, *A Commentary on St. Paul's Epistle to the Galatians* as found in John Dillenberger, *Martin Luther* (Garden City, N.J.: Doubleday Anchor, 1961), 129.

[14]David Yeago, "Lutheran-Roman Catholic Consensus on Justification: The Theological Achievement of the Joint Declaration," *Pro Ecclesia* 7 (1998): 449-470, esp. 451-453.

[15]Erwin Iserloh, the first Catholic theologian to undertake a sympathetic understanding of Luther's theology, remarks that the difference between the bishops at Trent and Luther was not the question of justification by faith, nor even the sinfulness of the church. It was Luther's nominalist understanding of the human person and its capabilities.

[16]It may be that moral and religious conversion precede, accompany, or follow upon this intellectual conversion. If the exegete experiences moral conversion, she finds herself more deeply committed to the values that lead to an authentically ethical human life, and finds more ease and joy in living the life of Jesus and his

commands. If she experiences religious conversion, she finds herself falling in love with God as the unconditioned infinite lover of herself and of everything in the cosmos. This God she accesses only in faith, and in that faith she finds the unconditional love that evokes faith and causes it to grow in all aspects of her life.

[17]From this perspective, it is Luther's lack of a psychic conversion that could have liberated him from the tyrannical father and his lack of intellectual conversion dealing with real change in his nature that kept his authentic religious conversion from its full expression in his theology.

[18]*De gratia et libero arbitrio*, #27-33, PL 44, columns 897-901.

[19]The whole of the biblical tradition, from Genesis to Wisdom, presumes and depends on the human capacity to respond freely in faith and in works of justice to God's summons to the covenant, to the precepts of the various law codes, and to the prophetic urgings of the Word of God. This emphasis becomes all the more important in the apocalyptic Judaism in which Paul was steeped.

Balthasar's Theodramatic Hermeneutics: Trinitarian and Ecclesial Dimensions of Scriptural Interpretation

Jason Bourgeois

Hans Urs von Balthasar developed a unique style of biblical interpretation. This paper will discuss four elements of his scriptural hermeneutics, a topic that offers glimpses of his fundamental theology and his ecclesiology as well. The first element of Balthasar's hermeneutics is *aesthetics*. Balthasar's aesthetic approach to scriptural interpretation stands in contrast with the commonly employed historical-critical method, which he found to be potentially limiting. The second element is *theodrama*. In Balthasar's notion of theodramatic hermeneutics, the interpreter is already participating in the very salvation history that is being interpreted. The third and fourth elements of Balthasar's hermeneutics involve the Trinitarian and ecclesial dimensions of interpretation; that is, he focuses especially on the role of the Holy Spirit and the church in the life of the interpreter.[1]

Contrast between Aesthetic and Historical-Critical Approaches to Interpreting Scripture

Both Balthasar and Hans-Georg Gadamer share the conviction that if one distances oneself from the object of interpretation, one will not be able to perceive the truth of that object. This is so because there is no such thing as a neutral standpoint for interpretation, and also because the goal of interpretation is the *appropriation* of the truth of a text into one's concrete situation. On this premise, both authors emphasize aesthetics as a proper mode of describing the task of interpretation, for we cannot remain neutral or distanced in the face of beauty. Rather, we are receptive to it and are transformed by it. Balthasar, in particular, will contrast an aesthetic approach to interpreting scripture with the more methodical and distanced approach of historical-critical methods.

He addresses this contrast in the very first pages of *The Glory of the Lord*. For Balthasar,

> . . . since the exact sciences no longer have any time to spare for [beauty] (nor does theology, in so far as it increasingly strives to follow the method of the exact sciences and to envelop itself in their atmosphere), precisely for this reason is it perhaps time to break through *this* kind of exactness, which can only pertain to one particular sector of reality, in order to bring the truth of the whole again into view—truth as a transcendental property of Being, truth which is no abstraction, rather the living bond between God and the world.[2]

Here he expresses a concern that the scientific method does not comprehend the whole of the subject matter that is explored by theology (or indeed by most other disciplines). He also finds that its theory of truth is entirely ineffective in dealing with the subject matter of Being, God, and God's relationship to the world (expressed in revelation). Rather, Truth is discovered through a response to the beautiful that involves the whole person and not merely a detached intellect. For Balthasar, this entails an active receptivity toward the truth of revelation, that is, an attitude of faith.

Balthasar continues by contrasting two ways of understanding and interpreting revelation, namely "seeing the form" and the historical-critical method. For Balthasar, an awareness of the whole is necessary for the interpretation of any beautiful form, including that of Christian revelation. This awareness of the whole is often impaired by the analysis of parts that occurs in a historical approach to scriptural texts. Balthasar expresses this succinctly when he says that "if form is broken down into subdivisions and auxiliary parts for the sake of explanation, this is unfortunately a sign that the true form has not been perceived as such at all." For Balthasar, this is often the case in analyses of scripture based on the historical development of texts.[3]

Balthasar expresses his conviction that the fullness of the Christian faith cannot be explained by a layer-based approach to scriptures, given that the earliest layer is the most authentic while each subsequent layer deviates further and further from the historical truth about Jesus. Rather, for him "the fact that research demonstrates that a given redaction belongs to an older layer of composition does not mean that preference should automatically be given [to] that redaction."[4] Furthermore, it is not through historical reconstruction but through *faith* that the full truth of the gospels can be discerned. For Balthasar, the historical-critical method leaves one "with the problem of explaining how so slight a kernel could become such a full-powered and seamless form as is the Christ of the Gospels."[5]

Indeed, it takes the "eyes of faith" to discern the full form of Christ, and this is the perspective from which the New Testament writers composed their texts. The historical development of the text is less important because the inspiration of the Spirit continually influenced the text until it reached its final form:

[O]nly the final result of the historical developments which lie behind a text—a history never to be adequately reconstructed— may be said to be inspired, not the bits and scraps which philological analysis thinks it can tear loose from the finished totality in order, as it were, to steal up to the form from behind in the hope of enticing it to betray its mystery by exposing its development.[6]

In fact, for Balthasar, the form of this revelation of Christ and his relationship to salvation history is more central even than the texts themselves that mediate that revelation. For Balthasar, "Scripture is not the Word itself, but rather the Spirit's testimony concerning the Word."[7] What is most important for him are the actual events themselves and their significance for human salvation. Scripture itself belongs to the larger totality of the revelation of God to the world expressed through creation, incarnation, and redemption. This larger totality is, in fact, the form of revelation, which is not wholly text-based. As Balthasar says, "[e]ven Scripture is not an isolated book, but rather is embedded in the context of everything created, established and effected by Christ. . . . Only in this context is the form of Scripture perceivable."[8]

Therefore, the interpretation of scripture cannot be carried out in isolation from the full context of the Christian faith, a context that is not merely an idea or set of ideas but involves a lived understanding of God's relationship to human beings and to the world. For Balthasar, this relationship is a totality that can ultimately be understood only by an awareness of the whole, namely, seeing the form, and not by a reduction of the whole to its various parts that represent the layers of historical development that have been combined over time to form the completed texts of scripture.

Theodramatic Hermeneutics:
The Participation of the Interpreter in Salvation History

The aesthetic style of hermeneutics involves receptive engagement with the truth being revealed through the text. For Balthasar, hermeneutics has a theodramatic dimension as well; that is, his hermeneutics involves an awareness of the *situatedness of the interpreter of divine revelation* within salvation history. Again, like Gadamer, he rejects the idea that an interpreter can take a viewpoint "over and above history." In Balthasar's theodramatic approach to hermeneutics, the interpreter of divine revelation is participating in the drama of divine revelation itself, through her place in its history. The interpretation of revelation is thus a dialogue between the human being and God across time, whose subject matter is that selfsame relationship between human beings and God.

For Balthasar,

All theology is an interpretation of divine revelation. Thus, in its totality, it can only be hermeneutics. But, *in revealing himself in Jesus Christ, God interprets himself—and this must involve his giving an interpretation, in broad outline and in detail, of his plan for the world—and this too is hermeneutics.* [This] hermeneutics, however, cannot seal itself off and ignore man's freedom and his free understanding . . . God does not play the world drama all on his own; he makes room for man to join in the acting.[9]

This passage makes it clear that for Balthasar the task of theology is eminently hermeneutical. First, it is the task of understanding revelation. Second, revelation itself is God's *self-interpretative* communication to us in such a way that we can understand it. In other words,

God's revelation to us is already "translated" by God, as it were, into a humanly understandable mode. The incarnation is the culmination of this communication, complemented in our present situation by the mediation of the Spirit within the context of the church.

It is also clear that the hermeneutics of theology is a complex dialogue between the free, self-revealing God and the free human interpreter. God has, in a sense, the greater role in this dialogue, being both the initiating partner and also the subject matter of the dialogue. Yet this dialogue is engaged in for the benefit of the human being, who becomes more aware of the necessary role of God in the process of human history, both collectively and for individual human beings. For Balthasar, the encounter with the infinite freedom of God the revealer does not stifle the finite freedom of the human interpreter but rather brings it to its fulfillment.[10]

It should be apparent that for Balthasar hermeneutics is a discipline that involves an awareness of being situated within a grand historical plan in the relationship between God and the human being. As present-day interpreters of revelation, we are situated in a particular stage of salvation history, what others have termed the "already but not yet" stage. This stage is one in which Christ has already come and reconciled the world to himself. It remains for us to appropriate this salvation within the context of grace and the church. This is the great "theodrama" that reaches its culmination in the "not yet" stage of eschatological fulfillment.

Hence, theodramatic hermeneutics involves discerning, with the help of the Holy Spirit and in the context of the church, who Christ is and what this means for us in terms of salvation. The interpreter of scripture is not distanced but existentially involved in what is being interpreted. For this reason, the interpreter cannot bracket faith or the content of faith. In fact, the very act of interpreting will be described in terms of this faith. Hermeneutics for Balthasar is explicitly Trinitarian and ecclesial; in other words, Balthasar understands the act of interpretation to take place within the context of an interpersonal relationship with the Trinity and within the social setting of the church.

The Trinitarian Dimensions of Interpretation

Balthasar's hermeneutics acquire a Trinitarian dimension through his understanding of the Word and the Spirit in the process of interpreting revelation. The Word (Christ) is interpreted in light of the Holy Spirit by both the scriptural authors and subsequent scriptural interpreters.

The main goal of the interpretation of the New Testament is the discernment of who Christ is and what he has done for humanity. As discussed above, it is Balthasar's view that a merely historical-critical analysis of the identity of Christ cannot do justice to the full aesthetic and religious dimensions that came to light through the reflections of the apostles and evangelists (and which have not yet been exhausted, even after several christological councils and centuries of theological debate). An analysis of the New Testament will not truly have "perceived the form" for Balthasar without an awareness of the Trinitarian dimensions of Christ's own life. In particular, Christ's role as the Word of God and his link with the role of the Holy Spirit are crucial to Balthasar's interpretation of the New Testament. The action of the Spirit is necessary in order to aid the interpreter herself to see the form. This is based on the idea, as mentioned above, that God already "interprets himself" for us in his self-revelation.

Thus, for Balthasar the Word is contained in history and reveals itself progressively through history. The entire Old Testament is a proleptic, historical movement toward the incarnation. For this reason, Balthasar is sympathetic to a typological, neo-patristic style of interpreting the Old Testament. Furthermore, the Word incarnate in Christ is not revealed in the New Testament as a static entity, such that one need only consult the fixed meaning of the text in order to discern who Christ is. For Balthasar,

> According to this view of things, hermeneutics would limit itself to establishing as securely as possible the meaning found in the document; it would then go on to confront the meaning, thus attained, with the contemporary understanding of existence and critically assess the former by the latter or vice versa.[11]

Rather than this fixed view of the meaning of the New Testament, Balthasar views the Word as *always acting* in history, such that there is a continual unfolding of the interpretation of who Christ is. In this sense revelation was not "closed" with the completion of the New Testament, but rather "the meaning of Scripture (where it is in process of development) journeys *along with* history."[12] Scripture is not simply an objective and dispassionate account of what happened but is rather "part of the drama itself, moving along with it."[13]

In addition, the continual, developing presence of the Word is, as it were, mediated throughout history through the Holy Spirit.[14] This assertion requires an awareness that Jesus (the Word of God) and the Holy Spirit have always been intimately linked. For Balthasar, the Holy Spirit enabled the disciples to perceive the full form of Christ and continues to enable Christians to "see the form" today. Thus, based on the Trinitarian link between Word (Jesus) and Spirit, the presence of the Holy Spirit enables one to perceive the full identity of Jesus in the New Testament. In a short article titled "God Is His Own Exegete," Balthasar explicates the link between the Holy Spirit and the interpreter of scripture, saying that human beings cannot "understand [God's] self-interpretation [in Christ] . . . before the Holy Spirit has been sent to them and has settled in their hearts."[15] The Spirit is the necessary link between God and human beings in understanding his self-revelation, for

> Were God not his own interpreter, man, who certainly knows that he is a creature and that there is a Lord who is his origin and end . . . would never ascertain what "the inner life of God" is. Only the Spirit of God is able to fathom that. But precisely this Spirit is given to us "to teach us to understand the gifts that he has given us."[16]

For Balthasar, the Holy Spirit is necessary to perceive this self-revelation rightly. Thus, any correct interpretation of the New Testament will require the actual grace of the Holy Spirit in the life of the interpreter. In this way, scriptural hermeneutics and theodramatic participation are interdependent.

The Ecclesial Dimension of the Interpretation of Revelation

Finally, the fourth dimension of Balthasar's hermeneutics is the ecclesial dimension: interpretation is conducted within the life of the church. This touches upon the question of temporal development in the interpretation of revelation. How do we discern what is permanent and what is time-bound (and changeable) within divine revelation? When dealing with this question, Balthasar places the emphasis on faith. The faith that comes from the Holy Spirit is seen as necessary in order to discern which elements of revelation are permanent and which are time-bound in such a way as to be dispensable. When there is a lack of faith-based perception, "there will be a tendency to concentrate on the secondary, time-bound elements within a particular horizon of understanding and to elevate them into primary ones; thus they will seem to be *untranslatable* and will have to be abandoned."[17]

Balthasar's primary example of this tendency is the project of demythologization, which finds such doctrines as the Virgin Birth as "untranslatable" into a contemporary mindset and so abandons such doctrines in favor of a more palatable explanation. As can be expected from his aesthetic emphasis on the uniqueness of the Christian form (the concrete universal), Balthasar rejects the idea that these particulars of Christian revelation are secondary and thus able to be discarded. Rather "God was able to express a uniquely divine element of this unique drama [through such doctrines], something that cannot be replaced by the categories of the universally human and the existential."[18]

Balthasar sees two possible solutions to the problem of demythologization, which results from the conflict between a contemporary mindset and some of the traditional doctrines of faith. The first solution is to regard the doctrine in question as not "outdated" but rather an integral aspect of the faith, without which the faith would not hold the same meaning in its totality. Such is the case with Balthasar's own evaluation of the Virgin Birth, which he regards as essential to the incarnation. The second solution is to regard the doctrine in question as having been "expressed in an obsolete terminology or conceptual world," with the understanding that the doctrine was "intending to express *greater and different things* than can be contained in the limited concepts of the period."[19] Balthasar's example of this is the imminent expectation of the end of the world expressed in the synoptic gospels or the Pauline epistles.

Balthasar counsels extreme caution when placing doctrines in the second category and attempting to explain what the doctrine "really meant." In attempting such an explanation, one must be careful to make judgments in light of the whole Christian form of revelation, perceived with the help of the Holy Spirit. In Balthasar's words: "this spiritual judgment has regard to a *totality* or *fullness* which the believer can discern through the Holy Spirit, at least to the extent that, while he can never attain an overview of it, he can detect every *sub-*

stantial omission from it as a violation of the law as the whole."[20]

For Balthasar, the principle remains that if a "re-interpretation" results in the omission of an integral doctrine of the faith (such as, for example, the resurrection of Christ), then it has not been done in light of the form. One final question remains: namely, how to mediate the decision of what is and is not an integral doctrine within a faith community. This is where, for Balthasar, the teaching office of the church enters the hermeneutical debate.

Balthasar believes that the teaching office of the church is an essential element in theological hermeneutics. He claims that although "the individual endowed with faith is . . . given a faculty enabling him to discern this totality [of the form of revelation],"[21] there is the possibility of a great divergence of opinion among individuals on various issues (some of which are essential to the faith and some of which are not). In light of this possibility, it is "necessary for the entire community of the Church to be equipped with a special organ to serve as a regulatory principle for maintaining the integrity of revelation; its function is to indicate any serious interference with the *balance* of the Church's organism, any loss of substance or weight."[22]

The role of the teaching office is to weigh the individual judgments of those engaged in the task of re-interpreting revelation from a contemporary standpoint and to make decisions about whether or not such judgments damage the integrity of revelation as a whole. The tension that this role can create between theologians and the magisterium is well known, but for Balthasar this is a necessary component of any attempt to mediate between contemporary and traditional understandings of the faith. The magisterium has the function of deciding which doctrines themselves are essential to the faith (such as Balthasar's example of the Virgin Birth) and also of deciding whether a theological "translation" from one cultural language to another has left out something significant.

Conclusion

Balthasar's style of interpreting scripture is much broader than that of the historical-critical methods. It presupposes aesthetic engagement and existential participation in the truths being interpreted. The interpreter is in dialogue with God about God's self-revelation, and such a dialogue requires receptivity in faith. Balthasar's style has Trinitarian and ecclesial dimensions: it presupposes that the grace of the Holy Spirit is necessary for correct interpretation, and it requires a relationship with the church, whose teaching office judges what elements of revelation are essential to the faith, such that the faith is altered if they are omitted or interpreted in another way. Balthasar's style of scriptural interpretation rests on a phenomenology of the interpreter as a person of faith and a participant in salvation history, in communion with the Trinity and the church.

Notes

[1]This paper derives from a chapter of my dissertation, "The Aesthetic Hermeneutics of Hans-Georg Gadamer and Hans Urs von Balthasar: A Comparative Analysis."

[2]Hans Urs von Balthasar, *The Glory of the Lord*, vol. 1, *Seeing the Form*, trans. Erasmo Leiva-Merikakis, ed. J. Fessio and J. Riches (San Francisco: Ignatius Press, 1982). Hereafter cited as *GL* I.

[3]*GL* I, 26. Balthasar was never opposed to limited use of historical-critical method to help understand the text at hand and, in fact, he used it himself at times. But he opposed the reduction of meaning in scripture to historical-critical interpretations alone, because they did not take into account the role of the Holy Spirit.

[4]*GL* I, 542.

[5]*GL* I, 486-487.

[6]*GL* I, 31.

[7]*GL* I, 31.

[8]*GL* I, 32.

[9]Hans Urs von Balthasar, *Theo-Drama: Theological Dramatic Theory*, vol. 2, *The Dramatis Personae: Man in God*, trans. Graham Harrison (San Francisco: Ignatius Press, 1990), 91 (emphasis mine). Hereafter cited as *TD* 2.

[10]This is the theme of a long reflection in *TD* 2, 189-334.

[11]*TD* 2, 103.

[12]*TD* 2, 105.

[13]*TD* 2, 112.

[14]To use Gadamer's language, one could say that the Holy Spirit in a sense effects a "fusion of horizons" between Christ and the interpreter.

[15]Hans Urs von Balthasar, "God Is His Own Exegete," trans. Stephen Wentworth Arndt, *Communio* 4 (Winter 1986): 280-287, at 284.

[16]Ibid., 287.

[17]*TD* 2, 96. Emphasis mine.

[18]*TD* 2, 97.

[19]*TD* 2, 98.

[20]*TD* 2, 99-100. Emphasis mine.

[21]*TD* 2, 100.

[22]*TD* 2, 100.

"O Caesarea Philippi":
On Starting Christology in the Right Place

Terrence W. Tilley

O Caesarea Philippi: to accept condemnation of the Way as its
*   fulfillment,*
its definition, to accept this both when it is chosen and when it is
*   realized.*

—Dag Hammarskjöld[1]

Many christological investigations take Jesus' question at Caesarea Philippi as the place to start christology. The ATLA Database brings up some two dozen items with "Who do you say that I am?" (Mk. 8:29 and parallels) in the title. The pericope in which Jesus asks his disciples "the christological question" and Peter answers it "correctly" remains the jumping-off point for much contemporary christological work.

However, authors often then spring quickly from that place to hurry along and answer their (not Jesus') christological questions and develop their christological theories (not answers) using whatever historical, philosophical, or other methodologies they find compelling. The thesis of this paper is that if we would tarry with Jesus and his disciples at Caesarea Philippi a bit longer, we could get our christologies off to a better start. To make this point, it first argues where *not* to start christology. More positively, it argues that christology is a task that can only be done as a constituent of discipleship; this argument is developed in a second section examining the Caesarea Philippi scene and its significance for christology. In fact, I take the Caesarea Philippi scene as the type for christological work. If typological interpretation of scripture be grounds for criminal charges among scripture scholars, then the author gladly pleads "guilty as charged." Third, the paper sketches what a christology based in the practice of discipleship will look like.

On Starting Christology by Lingering in the Right Place

The main point of this section is to clear the ground for an argument that christology properly begins as a constituent of discipleship.[2] This appears a difficult argument to make because many who do christology seem to avoid issues regarding discipleship completely and/or seek other sources for christology.[3] Indeed, few authors tarry at Caesarea Philippi; few seem to think that discipleship is relevant to the christological task.

In avoiding or ignoring discipleship, scholars develop six places to dig foundations for christology: phenomenology, history, the titles of Jesus, biblical portraits of Jesus, the christological councils, or "experience." I will argue that christologists should not begin their work in any of those places.

First, some argue for a more "neutral" approach to starting christology than most theologians would accept by utilizing phenomenology. For them, discipleship is irrelevant. Leander Keck, for example, writes:

> "Christology" is a comprehensive term for the statement of the identity and significance of Jesus. Although the vast preponderance of such statements occur in Christian contexts, this phenomenological definition recognizes that christological statements are implied whenever Jesus' identity and significance are expressed, be it "religious genius" or avatar.[4]

Keck is surely correct to imply that "phenomenological" approaches to the identity and significance of Jesus of Nazareth are possible and important. After all, one can study Mohammed or Thomas Jefferson or Florence Nightingale "phenomenologically" without being a follower or disciple of any of them. But notably, there is no such field of study as Mohammedology or Jeffersonology or Nightingaleology. At root, christology is a *theological* discipline, even if Jesus can and should be studied in non-theological ways. Hence, the term "christology" ought to be reserved for reflections done out of faithful discipleship because questions of "identity" and "significance" are always questions that arise from and require answers for audiences: to whom is he identified and for whom is he significant? Christology is, *pace* Keck's attempt to broaden it to a form of Jesusology, a properly theological discipline; Jesus is first significant for and needs first to be identified clearly for Christians. This is not to deny the significance of non-theological investigations of Jesus or explorations of the impact of Christianity on world cultures or on individuals who are not Christian. But then Jesus has no significance and does not need to be identified except as a constituent of an enduring social movement, Christianity. Investigating such impact is the study of the significance not of Jesus but of Christianity that has spread the good news.

To begin with discipleship, however, does not preclude contributions from those who would not identify themselves as disciples of Jesus or Christians, for they bring perspectives that can often correct disciples' biases and get committed Christians to rethink their presuppositions. However such work may contribute to christology or help us to understand others' christology, it is not *doing* christology. Other work on Jesus is of a different genre from that of christology. In taking this position, I am in basic agreement with Edward Schillebeeckx, whom Keck takes as his foil for his own work.[5] In sum, while "neutral" phenomenological investigations can contribute to christology, there is no reason to think that phenomenology can provide a foundation for a properly theological christology.

A second set of seemingly "neutral" approaches would ground christology in and through history. However, such approaches are rarely, if ever, neutral. Moreover, they are often confused. Van A. Harvey noted a specific confusion some thirty-five years ago. There is a profound ambiguity in the terms "the Jesus of history" or "the historical Jesus." Sometimes they refer to "the *actual* Jesus" and sometimes to "the Jesus that is *now recoverable by historical means.*"[6] This confusion continues in the contemporary quest for the historical Jesus.[7] Marcus Borg, for example, prefers not to talk of the "historical Jesus/ Christ of faith" dichotomy, but of the "*pre-Easter Jesus* and *the post-Easter Jesus.*" But then notice his explication of his preferred term: "By *the pre-Easter Jesus*, I mean, of course, Jesus as a figure of history before his death."[8] Yet, in the next chapter he claims, "In this chapter, I will introduce you to the pre-Easter Jesus."[9] Is this "figure" one "meets" created by Borg the historian? Or is it the actual man? Borg's claims throughout are remarkably ambiguous on this issue; what he presents, of course, is a historical reconstruction, but readers are led to think they meet the actual man, long concealed by the ecclesiastical and academic establishments. Perhaps Borg is not being deceptive here, but his audience can clearly conflate *his* "pre-Easter Jesus" with the "actual Jesus."

This specific confusion about the meaning of "the historical Jesus" and christology is one instance of a more general confusion about history and theology. This confusion is found in many theologians' works. One such instance is found in Paul Tillich's *Systematic Theology*. Tillich claims, "The event on which Christianity is based . . . is *given* in history."[10] However, Tillich's use of "history" is ambiguous. He does not always clearly distinguish between "events that occurred" and "the results of historical investigation." That there would be no such thing as Christianity or a church had there not been Jesus and his disciples is an unexceptionable point; theologians and historians must presume this as much as particle physicists must presume that mathematics applies to reality. But these are not the foundations of those disciplines, but the presumptions necessary even to engage in practicing them. The existence of Jesus or of the church are hardly the deliverances of the discipline of history. Just as one has to presume that there is/was a historical reality called "church" to do ecclesiology, so one has to presume that there is/was a historical person called Jesus to do christology. It is, of course, theoretically possible that historical investigations will upset those presumptions about historical actualities, just as some criminal trials defeat the presumption of innocence accorded the defendant. If that were to happen, then disciplines such as christology and ecclesiology could no longer be properly theological disciplines.

But then Tillich also found that history, in the sense of the results of historical investigation, was a source for theology. In so doing, he lamented the "unbridged gap" between a thoroughly and unrestrictedly historical-critical biblical theology and a devotional-interpretive biblical theology.[11] Van Harvey later pointed out that the gap between the disciplines of historical-critical and devotional-interpretive theological approaches was not merely unbridged, but practically unbridgeable. The different canons of relevance and evidence held by critical historians and believers following a devotional-interpretive approach suggest that a theoretical solution to the problem of the relations between unrestricted historical investigation and devotional, or committed theological, study may be impossible.[12]

Moreover, if historical work were an irreducible source for christology, our christology would have to change with every new investigation of "the historical Jesus." The Jesus sculpted by the historians out of the rough clay of the New Testament is too malleable to be a constitutive source or norm for any credible or reliable christology. Even if historical events and actions are the necessary basis for Christianity, it is difficult to see how historical reconstruction can be a ground for theology. Historians can inform theologians. They can present theologians with data to be analyzed theologically. Whatever role historical investigation plays—and I think it a large one—the results of historical investigation do not provide a foundation for christology. The mere presumption of Jesus' existence as an important historical figure is not stout enough to provide a grounding for christological claims. In short, christologists should not ground their work on the results of historical investigations.[13]

A third approach is to focus on the titles attributed to the actual Jesus as the place to begin christology.[14] My argument in the next section that this approach does not work for the title "Christ" can be generalized to show that titles alone are too indeterminate in meaning to be the place to begin, much less ground, christology, but I will not do that work in this paper.

A fourth location for founding christology is some specific biblical portrait of Christ.[15] The Johannine or the synoptic portraits of Jesus, for example, have often functioned as *de facto* norms for christology. Any christology that contravened these portraits was suspect, at best. In a variant form of this approach, Schubert Ogden has argued that the New Testament contains both more primitive or spontaneous christological witness and more deliberate and developed christological reflection about Jesus.[16] The former, as more primitive, is to be the norm for christological work. Ogden does not claim that the primitive christological witness is an irreducible source for christology. In that sense, he avoids attempts to provide data that will ground christology. However, by making the primitive witness in fact the *norma normans* by which all christological work must be judged, he canonizes one portrait that theologians and historians might debate as a *de facto* theological absolute, not as a foundation from which one must build, but as a test all must pass.

But why canonize this specific portrait as a test? First, it is not clear that the distinction between witness and reflection will carry the weight Ogden requires of it. For Ogden, reflective christology alone raises questions of the "truth" of christology. But, then, why should one accept the earliest, primitive interpretations of Jesus as normative for all others if their truth is not a factor? Just as the first interpretation of the U.S. Constitution cannot serve as a norm for present interpretations, why should the first interpretation of Jesus serve as a norm for all others?[17] Second, even if the distinction between witness and reflection can be stabilized, historians will continue to engage in quests for the primitive witness as much as in quests for the historical Jesus. Ogden's norm is subject to the vagaries of historical investigation. Can such a fragile norm carry the weight of being that to which all christology must conform? Third, Ogden's criterion of truth as "credible to human existence as judged by common experience and reason"[18] is not tenable. There is no such thing as "common" human experience and reason sufficiently robust to warrant such credibility, unless one takes Richard Rorty's anti-realist position that construes truth as the fit between a proposition and what others who have a "common human experience" in a linguistic community accept.[19] In sum, attempting to absolutize a norm or standard for christology is as fraught with problems as attempting to find an irreducible source for christology.

Analogous criticisms apply to others who would lift up one segment of the New Testament or one portrait in the Christian tradition as the final norm, source, or foundation for christology. Neither the primitive witness, the synoptic portrait(s), the reflective christologies, nor the Johannine portrait(s) can provide a norm for all other christologies. Arguments for warranting one's choice of one over the others are susceptible to arguments like those mounted against Ogden's preferred norm.

A fifth approach is to take the christologies of the great councils of the fourth and fifth centuries as the place from which to begin. However, as many have pointed out, the christological settlements reached at Nicea and Chalcedon are more guides to what to avoid in doing christology than guides for theologians in constructing substantive christologies. As William P. Loewe put it, Chalcedon's affirmation "does not satisfy the tendency to want to be able to imagine how one and the same can possess two natures, nor does it offer an explanation. Rather it presents the dogma of the hypostatic union as a restatement of the mystery of God's graciousness brought about and made known through Jesus."[20] The councils present us with propositions or rules that govern christology, not with developed christologies.[21] As I have argued elsewhere, propositional theology is not sufficient to carry the substance of faith[22] and rules alone are not sufficient to shape a tradition.[23] Christologists should not start their journeys of theological construction in Nicea and Chalcedon, as these do not ground christology; but orthodox theologians will need to visit these places along the way.[24]

Finally, experience is proposed as a foundation for theology in general and christology in particular. Especially in the modern era, "experience" has served in various ways as a "source for" or "norm of" theology. George P. Schner has noted that "experience" is constructed (thus not "atomistic" or "incorrigible"), has an intentional object, is derivative from other sources and is dialectical, involving self and other(s).[25] However one uses "experience" in theology (Schner found a number of uses), it cannot bear the weight of being a "foundation" or "source" for theological work. In one specific sense, an individual's or community's experience may be the occasion upon which theological and christological reflection arise, but in this usage "experience" is typically a generic placeholder term for other more precise terms (such as "suffered," "had an insight," "were challenged to rethink," and so forth).[26] While Schner noted that the theologian cannot neglect the appeal to experience, such an appeal cannot be to experience as a ground or source or norm sufficient for theology, but, at best, an invitation to consider what we have obscured, erased, or overlooked in our theological constructions.[27]

Paul Tillich argued that experience is a "medium through which the objective sources are received."[28] My experience is not a source, but a product. It may be an integration and a shaping of what comes to me from many sources, but it cannot be a source for theology. Nor can my experience or the experience of a group to which I belong be a defining norm for christology. While all theology may be local, theology must strive to present what is universal. Although any theology that denies or diminishes "our" experience is inadequate, any claim that "our" experience is the norm (rather than a necessary component of a norm for theology) for theological constructions falls into the trap noted in the previous paragraphs: on what grounds is "your" experience and not "ours" the final and absolute arbiter?

Tillich claimed, correctly in my view, that the basis of Christianity "is not derived from experience. . . ."[29] A theology based only on experience would be, in Tillich's terms, an "illusion."[30] An individual's or community's experience of Jesus or the salvation God brings in and through him is not a foundation or source of theology. Rather, the "intentional object" of such experience, namely, what the experience is "of" and the conditions that generate that experience, are more important.

Christologists should not ground their work in phenomenology, history, titles, biblical portraits of Jesus, the councils, or experience, though each of these can trigger the christological imagination and all can be constituents of their christological constructions. What all these approaches have in common is that they are forms of foundationalism. Each seeks to find an "irreducible" source or norm, that is, a source behind which we cannot get or a concrete norm by which all christologies are to be measured. While at first glance, "norms" don't seem to be foundational, they do in fact canonize one part of the tradition. That part of the tradition is claimed to be the source for the absolute norm. Hence, even those who try to avoid foundationalism directly bring it in "by the back door" because an irreducible source, like the "primitive witness" Ogden valorizes, is the foundation of the norm, even if it is not the foundation for all christology.

The quest for such an irreducible source, that is, a foundation, uses the term "source" in a specific way. The debate whether scripture and tradition were the sources for revelation at Trent and Vatican II is one example of this use. Like Trent, Vatican II refused the term "source" to either scripture or tradition, but allowed it to God, the divine "wellspring."[31] Another example can be found in Tillich's theology, as noted above. A third example can be found in scholarship on the "historical Jesus" that uses a criterion of multiple attestation not to the gospels, but to the sources (insofar as they are irreducible to other sources) to support the historical reliability of items in texts. The argument made here is that all of the candidates for "irreducible sources" do not succeed in being such sources. This does not mean that they cannot be "sources" for christology in another sense, that is, as "constituents" and even "negative norms" for christological construction. But they cannot serve as foundations.

My negative point, I think, is now obvious: I am denying that the quest for a firm foundation, an irreducible source, can be successful for christology. This quest for such a ground strikes me as a confusion that plagues these approaches to christology, despite the contributions that each makes and the insights we can harvest from them.

So where is the right starting place? My answer is that a proper appreciation of the Caesarea Philippi scene clearly shows the starting point and the structure of christology.

Understanding Caesarea Philippi

Many scholars have noted that this scene marks a turning point in the Gospel of Mark.[32] It is a point at which many find that the gospel "breaks." For a typical example, consider Richard Longenecker's comments on Mark:

> The first half of his Gospel is concerned with the question of the identity of Jesus, and concludes with the affirmation of Peter: "You are the Christ!" (8:29). The second half spells out the nature of Jesus' ministry as being that of a suffering Messiah and concludes with the acclamation of the Roman centurion, "Surely this man was the Son of God" (15:39).[33]

There are textual and literary reasons for making the claim that the gospel breaks in the middle of the scene. First, it is is clear that the story in Mark's text is a composite. The incidents narrated as occurring at Caesarea Philippi are of different literary forms. The first plot item is Jesus' question that leads to Peter's confession. This unit is, in Bultmann's view, an incomplete legend in the Markan version, "completed" by the redactor of Mark with a passion prediction, and the rejection of Peter.[34] The second item is Jesus' command to silence, an expression of the "messianic secret." The third twist in the plot is Jesus' teaching that the son of man will suffer and die,[35] which leads to Peter's remonstrance. The fourth move is Jesus rebuking Peter as "Satan" for his error. The fifth is the call to discipleship (to the multitude as well as the disciples).[36] However many units of material are incorporated into the scene, it is a composite given its present form either by the Markan editor or by a source used in composing the gospel.[37]

Second, it seems that the scene is a transition. The "messianic secret" proclaimed by Peter is seen as a climax to the narrative so far, and the tone seems to change with the first passion prediction immediately thereafter. That Peter's confession (8:29) is halfway between the narrator's proclamation of Jesus as the Son of God (1:1) and the Gentile centurion's recognition of Jesus as Son of God (15:39) suggests, as Longenecker and others have written, that this is part of the rhythm of Mark's story.

Yet these reasons to see this scene as split between two "acts" in Mark's gospel are not convincing. First, even if the pericope is woven by Mark into a whole and does not accurately report a specific historical event, this says nothing about the historicity of the particular units Mark utilized in his construction. Pheme Perkins has argued that each of the units in the story—the Petrine confession, Jesus' silence, the passion prediction, the rebuke of Peter, and the call to discipleship—can reasonably be viewed as reflecting actual events, even if their literary form has been shaped over time.[38] Placing the elements together in one scene, a visit to one specific town, may well be Mark's contribution. But an argument that the scene as a whole is a literary creation of the Markan redactor (an argument that seems conclusive) cannot sustain a claim that none of the individual elements woven together in the scene is historical or based in historical events. Such claims would require further arguments (which do not seem convincing), as Perkins notes.

Second, the scene does not mark the end of an identity story and the beginning of a mission story.[39] Longenecker's point suggests that we can separate a story of Jesus' identity from that of his ministry. To be blunt, that separation is as artificial as the separation of soteriology from christology, a separation that I do not think can be found in the Markan text, but is rather an imposition on it. The Gospel of Mark is too complex, with too many crisscrossing themes and concerns, to support such a simple, dual-movement central structure. There are numerous other patterns in the narrative that suggest that this "simple" structure is unwarranted.[40] Because this division of the gospel does violence to the literary integrity of the scene, seems anachronistic in its conceptual assumptions, and is not the only option, I find that there is good reason not to accept the proposal to divide the gospel of Mark in the middle of the Caesarea Philippi scene. While there are literary and textual reasons that support this approach, there are better reasons, adduced above, for not accepting it.

If we take the scene as a purposively constructed whole, how can we construe the scene as showing the structure of christological reflection? First, Elizabeth Struthers Malbon and M. Eugene Boring, among others, provide an insight. They take Mark's christology as fundamentally narrative. In the context of an article undermining numerous anachronistic questions being asked of the Gospel of Mark, Boring put the point as follows:

> . . . Mark struggles with a variety of traditional christological material that he wishes to adopt and adapt in a variety of ways. . . . Mark himself wants to hold more than one view in tension, and has devised a narrative means of doing so. . . .
>
> The narrative genre chosen/devised by Mark must be given full due in discussions of his Christology. The differences between narrative and discursive language, the capacity of narrative to hold together contrary perspectives in tension, and the limitation of narrative in necessarily delineating its content in a diachronic mode must be taken into account in assessing Mark's Christology.[41]

I am in agreement with Struthers Malbon and Boring that narrative is key to Markan christology in general. But I also want to suggest that a narrative approach is key to understanding the Caesarea Philippi scene in particular.

Second, the Caesarea Philippi scene makes sense as a scene if it is taken in this narrative context. As Boring suggests for the gospel in general, this scene in particular is constructed as a way of holding together diverse christologies—*and in so doing, also pointing out a profound christological error.* Certainly, the "messiah" and "son of man" titular christologies jostle each other in the narrrative and are united by it. But that is a side issue. Peter's error is not in using two different titles for Christ. Stanley Hauerwas identified the error in precise terms: "Jesus thus rebukes Peter, who learned *the name*, but *not* the story that determines the meaning of the name."[42]

When we take christological assertions as propositions whose meaning can be determined without attending to their context and their use— a use often made clear only in stories—we make what we can now label "Peter's error." We get the title right, but the story wrong; we call Jesus "messiah," but we imagine the messiah so mistakenly that we *really* miss the point. If we get the title right, but the story wrong, we really get the whole thing wrong.[43] The principle is that if a key concept is contextualized in two stories that give the concept different uses, then the concept also will have different meanings or significances.[44] In the Caesarea Philippi scene, the character Jesus rebuking the character Peter can be construed as making just this point: "You're in the wrong story, Peter; if you don't get your story straightened out, you are a Satan." Narrative is not merely a device for reconciling competing views or holding together contrary perspectives. Boring goes this far. Properly understanding a narrative can also provide a place from which errors can be seen and rectified; Jesus' act in the scene exemplifies this point.

The point of the scene is that Mark is telling his hearers that the story of the triumphant Davidic messiah is the wrong story. Peter is perhaps commended for getting the title right (especially in the Matthean version [16:17]—remember it took an act of God to get Peter to see the truth in Matthew's version[45]), and then rebuked violently for getting the story wrong. The new story of messiahship or of the son of man coming on the clouds is that of the suffering and dying messiah, the suffering and dying son of man. To construe the messiahship of Jesus as a classic political triumph is an error. To understand Mark's narrative christology, then, one must understand the importance of its narrative, both the overall narrative and the stories that are nested within the gospel, especially the nutshell christology of Caesarea Philippi.

Third, Hauerwas claims that the story is really about discipleship. Mark's gospel was probably meant to be heard rather than read. It is more a drama or a saga performed to involve and shape the hearers into disciples or to shape and reshape their understanding of what discipleship entails.[46] David Rhoads and Donald Michie say that their study "suggests that the overall narrative leads the reader to see the hidden rule of God in Jesus and to follow him."[47] In constructing a world in which the characters in the gospel are so often blind to the acts of God and fearful because they cannot recognize the events as part of God's reign in and through Jesus, the author's rhetoric seeks to enlighten and comfort the blind and bewildered hearers of the gospel.[48]

But this enlightenment is not sweet and easy. Discipleship has a cost. The author leads the hearer to abandon the desire to save oneself and to "identify and align with the hero Jesus, to want to be as courageous as he is, and to want to have such faith in God's salvation as to relinquish one's own life in spite of one's fears and desires."[49] To become an authentic disciple, then, is to undertake the journey whose path is so economically narrated in the Caesarea Philippi scene: to recognize Jesus as the expected messiah, to hear the shocking story of what messiahship really is, to reject it, to be rebuked, and to learn the shape of authentic discipleship—a discipleship in which even the first-called were afraid, but were able to share the story with us.

In short, the Caesarea Philippi scene narrates and thus links both the essence of christology and the essence of discipleship. Boring claims, "For Mark, to tell the story of *Jesus* is to talk about *God*; the *one* God. Thus to dispute whether the Markan narrative is theocentric or Christocentric is a misplaced question."[50] Boring is correct so far as he goes. But Mark is not merely talking about God; Mark tells the story of God-with-us and our-being-with-God. For Mark, christology *is* soteriology. To be saved is to be one of the disciples. Disciples are saved by a specific faith. They are saved from fear of the worldly powers and for life in God's reign. In Mark, it is not merely that Jesus is inseparable from God. In Mark, discipleship and christology are also inseparable. In sum, discipleship shows what christology concretely means, while christology says what discipleship truly is.

The Pericope and Christology

Understood this way, the pericope shows us how to begin christology in the right place: that christology begins in the lively ("life-shaped") religious imaginations of disciples. I am making a radical claim here. I have claimed earlier that neither scripture nor tradition nor experience is a foundation of christology.[51] They are, of course, vehicles for and constituents of christology. I am claiming that the disciples' imagination[52] is the (proximate) source for christology; as an "imagination" it may not be irreducible and is certainly not a foundation for christology. I show the significance of this point by tarrying a bit longer at Caesarea Philippi and examining the shape of this pericope.

First, the questions arise. In this case, they are raised by Jesus and addressed to the disciples.[53] He initially asks who οἱ ἄνθρωποι (the people) say he is. The response is imaginative. The people imagine him as the deceased John the Baptist, Elijah, or one of the prophets.

He is imagined (by the folk or by the disciples faced with a tough question) either *to be* or *to be like* a figure they know. To answer the question, the people have to typologize or analogize. They don't say, "Mary and Joe's son, a sometime carpenter from Nazareth." They don't come up with "dumb answers" that avoid the serious identity question. They use their imaginations to provide answers of significance— whether the disciples report or make up their responses to Jesus. Jesus then asks who do "you" say that I am. Once again, the answer is imaginative. Peter, perhaps as spokesperson for all disciples, imagines Jesus as ὁ χριστός, the "Christ," the anointed one, the messiah. Peter analogizes or typologizes to give his answer (even if it takes an act of God, as Matthew has it, to get Peter's imagination moving). Again, the prototypical disciple offers an imaginative answer, not a literal or stupid one.

The answers to both questions are imaginative. They utilize culturally available categories and concepts. But then they extend these concepts to a new instance, in this case the "instance" of Jesus. The culturally given concepts are not the source of these christologies. The disciples' experiences of Jesus are not the source of these christologies. Experiences and conditioned concepts are stimuli for and constituents of the christological claim. The answers they give utilize these concepts and reflect on experiences. But the claims are propositions. They are imaginative inventions, constructions that the respondents "think up" in order to answer the questions. This is the exercise of the disciples' christological imagination.

Second, Jesus begins to teach them.[54] His teaching them about the suffering son of man is a corrective to their christological imaginations. Unlike foundational sources, which must be simply "taken as given," the deliveries of the disciples' imagination are always corrigible. Rhetorically, Mark's Jesus is correcting the imagination of all the disciples. That christologies arise from the disciples' imaginations is not a criticism, but an identification of their actual non-foundational source.[55] What flaws such imaginatively generated claims is that they are uncritical or mis-imagined. Jesus' teaching is a corrective: "You think the messiah is a political victor. Think again. *Here* is how to imagine the anointed one of God."

Third, Peter remonstrates with him. This prototypical disciple refuses to accept the teaching of Jesus that will discipline his imagination. Peter remains attached to his own imagination, his own imaginative christology. His mind is shaped by the people, not God. He is stubborn. He refuses to give up or modify the product he has imagined into existence, the imagination that Jesus is the Davidic kingly messiah who will overthrow the reign of Rome and initiate the reign of God. This stubbornness gets Jesus to "cursing" Peter as "Satan." But what Jesus adds to explain this is crucial: Peter, as the RSV familiarly has it, is "not on the side of God, but of men." This is about as strong a curse as calling him "Satan," especially if Boring is correct in saying that the story of Jesus is the story of God.[56]

But what the RSV obscures (though the NRSV, the JB and the Douay Rheims do not) is that what Jesus in Mark says is that Peter does not have a mind for (οὐ φρονεῖς)[57] the things of God, or the way he thinks (JB) is not of God, or, as I would prefer, his practical wisdom is not of God's things, but of "humans'" (τὰ τοῦ Θεοῦ ἀλλὰ τὰ τῶν ἀνθρώπων).[58] Jesus in Mark accuses Peter and all the disciples who follow him of not so much a failure of imagination as a level of arrogance that leads to a profound failure, that is, the failure to have one's own wisdom disciplined by God's wisdom. This is a failure of their practical wisdom, their mind, of a creative imagination gone wild.[59] The problem is a failure of discipline; dare I say, "a failure in discipleship"?

Well, where do we find the discipline to be formed in the mind of God, in God's imagination? That is the fourth point. Peter got slammed directly by Jesus in the Gospel of Mark. But remembering that christology is theology in Mark and that Mark is a gospel to be heard, we can say that Mark then gives the answer for all the disciples: we must allow our imaginations to be formed by the story Mark tells us. This is the story of taking up the cross and following Jesus, the story of the Christ, and the story of discipleship. The text alone, of course, cannot be a source of christology. Rather, hearing how to live in and how to live out the story is the way in which our christological imaginations are disciplined. Like Peter in the story, having been rebuked for our attachment to human wisdom, we can learn divine wisdom from the story of the suffering son of man and his disciples. When we remember how to tell and live his story as our story and our story as his, our imagination, so prone to being undisciplined, becomes the imagination of discipleship.[60]

In short, when we tarry at Caesarea Philippi, we find that christologies begin in disciples' imaginations; that these imaginations can go wrong and require correction; and that when our imaginations are properly disciplined, we as disciples will get the story right.[61]

Within the Gospel of Mark, of course, Jesus corrects Peter directly. But the rhetoric of Mark suggests two possible imaginative understandings for disciples when Jesus has gone to the Father. First, a typological understanding: that Peter is our antitype in discipleship, that we fit in the story like Peter does, that we need to hear the proclamation of the good news in order to have our imaginations disciplined by the very word of God. Second, an analogical understanding: that we, the hearers of Mark's Gospel, can have our imaginations disciplined by the stories, such as the Gospel of Mark, that carry and are carried by and told in the community of disciples, the ongoing body of Christ, just as Peter in Mark had his imagination corrected by the Christ, the one who is recognized even by the Gentile who says "Truly, this was the Son of God." In both cases, we must not only exercise our christological imaginations, but we can do so well only if we are conformed in discipleship, a discipleship that allows our imaginations to be shaped and disciplined by those who carry on the story of the son of God. In short, my claim is that when we tarry at Caesarea Philippi, we see that christology is an enterprise of the imagination of disciples to be corrected by the community of disciples who carry on as Christ's body in the world. There is no foundational source nor irreducible norm beyond the ongoing practice of discipleship.

Toward a Christology Based in Discipleship

If this paper has successfully argued that christologists need to begin their work as disciples in Caesarea Philippi, then where might we go from that place?

First, I think we can come to see similar patterns in at least some other New Testament christologies. The kenosis hymn in Philippians 2:6-11, for example, does not tell a story whose main or only point is pre-existence. Its practical point is to show that to which the disciples must shape their minds (φρονεῖτε): the kenotic Christ. Perhaps it corrects or inoculates imaginations that might begin with Christ's divine status or exalted destiny and remain there, drawing inferences about the disciples' status above the fray. While I am not in a position to claim that all New Testament christology accords with this insight, it certainly fits some key instances: Discipleship shows what christology concretely means and christology says what discipleship truly is.

Second, I think we can then write the history of christology differently, in a sense "from below," from the community, not from the episcopal and theological elites alone. Theory dominates the history of christology; I am suggesting a history in which the images the ongoing community of disciples constructs for Jesus are at the center. The community—through its practices, creeds, and symbols—does not provide irreducible sources for christology, but constituents of and correctives to the christological imaginations through time.[62] When the martyrs saw Jesus as a martyr, or the monks as a master in asceticism, or the revolutionaries as an activist,[63] they were exercising their christological imaginations. Insofar as their images of Jesus were well disciplined, they were and are appropriate for the Christian community. The point of credal symbols, professional theological debate, and historical investigation is not to *do* christology, but to provide constituents and correctives for the lively imaginations of who He is and what it means to be His disciple. Such a perspective "from below" reveals a christological tradition that is contextual and plural, multiple but not "relativist."

Third, there are as many images of Jesus as there are types of disciples. These images are the sources for our christologies. A christology truly "from the people" must understand how these images are shaped and normed. In doing so, we can, I believe, unknot some terribly tangled contemporary christological issues (like the necessity of Christ and the church for salvation). This may lead to bold claims about some strands of contemporary christology conforming more to minds formed not by God, but by "man."

In sum, this project begun in the company of the disciples at Caesarea Philippi reconceives the place of christology in the life of faith. This approach thus moves theory, phenomenology, history, scripture, symbol and dogma, and experience to their appropriate places: stimulating and restraining disciples' imaginations. This non-foundationalist approach to christology argues that there is no place other than the place of the disciple from which to begin to do christology. There is no norm, source, or foundation of christology available apart from the practices[64] of discipleship, those faithful and imaginative responses to God's grace. As theology is not the substance of Christianity, so theology does not carry the substance of christology. Theory disciplines and criticizes disciples' lives and imaginations. It is a constituent of discipleship; but christology and discipleship are practical correlatives.

The present paper has explored what it could mean for christologists to begin their christologies in the way Mark's Caesarea Philippi scene represents the tradition as starting: in the disciples' imaginations, as voiced by that prototypical disciple, Peter. If correct, then discipleship, practice, narrative, and imagination are primary. Theory, history, symbol, and dogma are to this primary christology as literary criticism is to literature and rules are to performance. Because we who try to do christology too often proceed assuming a very different structure to theological work than the one advocated here, we do not achieve a christology that is useful for Christian practice, the real life of faith. If our tarrying with Jesus, Peter and the disciples at Caesarea Philippi has been instructive, we can be happy to leave Caesarea Philippi remembering the scriptural lessons we learned there in order to develop a "practical" christology that is rooted not in some irreducible sources but in the imaginations of faithful disciples like that of our antitype, the always fallen, always raised, Peter.

Notes

[1] Dag Hammarskjöld, *Markings*, trans. W. H. Auden (London: Faber and Faber, 1966 [1964]), 50. Thanks for help in preparing this paper to Susan Perry, my research assistant Kevin Feltz, and to colleagues Maureen Tilley, James Heft, S.M., Sandra Yocum Mize, Dennis Doyle, Una Cadegan, Michael H. Barnes, and M. Therese Lysaught for their critical readings of earlier versions of this paper. I especially thank Stanley Hauerwas for the insight that stimulated this project (see note 32 below); for a quarter century he has challenged theologians in the mainstream churches to think more creatively about Jesus, the church, and ethics. We are all in his debt, a debt on which this paper seeks to make a very small payment.

[2] The present approach has similarities to that of Sandra M. Schneiders, *The Revelatory Text: Interpreting the New Testament as Sacred Scripture* (San Francisco: HarperSanFrancisco, 1991), especially 60-61, where Schneiders highlights the necessity of faith for an adequate interpretation of the text as Scripture.

[3] For example, Elizabeth Struthers Malbon, in an article of fewer than thirteen pages on Markan christology, quickly turns to the christologies in and of Mark as "titular" christology, "enacted" christology, "deflected" christology, "refracted" christology, and "reflected" christology. Discipleship is not on her radar screen, though it is central to Mark's Gospel and his christology (as I will argue below). Her concerns are literary. Yet the fact that Jesus in Mark addresses his question to

disciples is treated as if it were irrelevant to this piece of literature. See Elizabeth Struthers Malbon, "The Christology of Mark's Gospel: Narrative Christology and the Markan Jesus," *Who Do You Say That I Am? Essays on Christology in Honor of Jack Dean Kingsbury*, ed. Mark Allan Powell and David R. Bauer (Louisville: Westminster/John Knox, 1999), 33-46. Struthers Malbon's essay is a fine categorization of Markan christologies but does not really address the "christological question."

[4]Leander Keck, "Toward the Renewal of New Testament Christology," in *From Jesus to John: Essays on Jesus and New Testament Christology in Honour of Marinus de Jonge*, Journal for the Study of the New Testament Supplement Series 84, ed. Martinus C. De Boer (Sheffield: JSOT Press, 1993), 322. Keck's repeated use of "statement" unfortunately seems to blind him to the fact that most Christian assertions in christology are "confessions," or "witness," or "theological claims." Christological utterances are not primarily "neutral" statements, but much richer assertive speech acts.

[5]See Edward Schillebeeckx, *Jesus: An Experiment in Christology* (New York: Seabury, 1979), 545-50.

[6]Van A. Harvey, *The Historian and the Believer* (New York: Macmillan, 1966), 268; emphasis added.

[7]Discussions of the "historical Jesus" are legion. I find the modest claims summarized by Norman Perrin and Dennis Duling (*The New Testament: An Introduction,* Second Edition [New York: Harcourt Brace Jovanovich, 1982], 411-412), and E. P. Sanders (*The Historical Figure of Jesus* [London: Penguin, 1993; paperback edition, 1995], 280-81), to exhaust what is historically warrantable with some level of reliability about Jesus. In my judgment, the works produced by members of the Jesus Seminar (M. Borg, J. D. Crossan, R. Funk) are profoundly flawed in ways described by Luke Timothy Johnson, *The Real Jesus* (San Francisco: Harper, 1997). Johnson's criticisms are often overstated for rhetorical effect, but they do effectively show the flimsiness of the methodologies the Jesus Seminar scholars use. John P. Meier, "The Present State of the 'Third Quest' for the Historical Jesus: Loss and Gain," *Biblica* 80/4 (1999): 459-486, offers nuanced responses to the most recent work, especially an emphasis on Jesus' Jewishness and his miracles. For an attempt to base christology in a theological appropriation of the historical evidence, see Roger N. Haight, *Jesus Symbol of God* (Maryknoll: Orbis Books, 1998); for one criticism of Haight's use of history, see Terrence W. Tilley, "The Historical Fact of the Resurrection," *Theology and the Social Sciences*, The 45th Annual Volume of the College Theology Society, ed. Michael H. Barnes (Maryknoll: Orbis Books, 2001), 88-110.

[8]Marcus Borg, *Meeting Jesus Again for the First Time: The Historical Jesus and the Heart of Contemporary Faith* (San Francisco: HarperSanFrancisco, 1994).

[9]Borg, *Meeting Jesus Again*, 20.

[10]Paul Tillich, *Systematic Theology* I (Chicago: University of Chicago Press, 1951), 42.

[11]Tillich, *Systematic Theology* I, 36.

[12]See Harvey, *The Historian and the Believer.*

[13]One could say similar things about naive approaches to tradition. For contemporary theologies of tradition, see Terrence W. Tilley, *Inventing Catholic Tradition* (Maryknoll: Orbis Books, 2000) and John E. Thiel, *Senses of Tradition* (New York: Oxford University Press, 2000). Both authors call for far more fluid understandings of tradition than those used by most theologians who make tradition a norm and/or source for theology. Tillich also made room for specific ecclesial traditions as legitimate sources for denominational theologies. However, if tradition is the historical sediment of ongoing Christian experience, then an analogous conclusion must be drawn with regard to tradition: it is part of the data to be explored and evaluated, not the foundation on which theologies can be built or an independent source to be correlated with present questions.

[14]For discussions of "titular" christology, see, *inter alia*, James D. G. Dunn, *Christology in the Making* (Philadelphia: Westminster, 1980), especially 12-77; idem, *The Evidence for Jesus* (Philadelphia: Westminster, 1985), especially 30-52.

[15]See, *inter alia*, the essays in *Jesus of Nazareth: Lord and Christ: Essays on the Historical Jesus and New Testament Christology*, ed. Joel B. Green and Max Turner (Grand Rapids: Eerdmans, 1994) for a useful survey and criticism of the New Testament and subsequent portraits. I don't find that these essays, however, set up "one" *norma normans* as Schubert Ogden's work does.

[16]Schubert M. Ogden, *The Point of Christology* (New York: Harper and Row, 1982), 2.

[17]For a similar criticism, see Francis Schüssler Fiorenza, "Reflective Christology," *Cross Currents* 32/3 (Fall 1982): 374.

[18]Ogden, *The Point of Christology*, 4.

[19]For Rorty's position, see *Philosophy and the Mirror of Nature* (Princeton: Princeton University Press, 1979); for a criticism and alternative account of truth criteria in light of contemporary work in epistemology, see Tilley, *Inventing Catholic Tradition*, 156-170.

[20]William P. Loewe, *The College Student's Introduction to Christology* (Collegeville: Liturgical Press, 1996), 188-201; quotation at 201. Conciliar christology is rarely the focus of christological construction as it was in some Catholic christology before Vatican II. Despite its modest title, Loewe's work is a significant contribution to understanding the issues in christology.

[21]See Loewe, *College Student's Introduction*, 194.

[22]Terrence W. Tilley (*Story Theology* [Wilmington: Michael Glazier, 1985], 11-16) contrasts theologies that make narratives central with those that are proposition-centered.

[23]Tilley, *Inventing Catholic Tradition*, 88-101.

[24]The argument mounted against Ogden also could apply *mutatis mutandis* to the councils—why privilege this one point in the process? However, I do not say that a christologist should ignore either Ogden's "earliest strata" or the conciliar developments, but merely that these cannot be the sources or foundations for

christology. Moreover, *how* the conciliar definitions are to be normative and how they are to be applied is a matter of dispute, even among orthodox theologians. While I do not want to minimize the conciliar contributions and insights, they were developed as responses to controversies. As such, their strength is their saying what orthodox theologians cannot properly say. But how to use their complex terminology, formed in a language and culture that is not our own, is a much more difficult issue. Because these are *quaestiones disputatae*, the councils' ability to function as more positive norms is minimal, at best.

²⁵See George P. Schner, S.J., "The Appeal to Experience," *Theological Studies* 53/1 (March 1992): 46-49.

²⁶Nonetheless, this does not imply that experience is in some way not "direct." Although my experience is constructed, intentional, derivative, dialectical, and shaped by practice, when I report "I hear the organist playing the 'Triumphal March' from Aida" that is not the report of some "indirect" or "mediated" experience as some use these terms. Categories like "direct/indirect" or "mediated/immediate" seem rhetorically to function defensively, to seek to isolate some form of experience (e.g., sense experience, mystical experience) from further analysis. William P. Alston, *Perceiving God: The Epistemology of Religious Experience* (Ithaca: Cornell University Press, 1991) goes far to "locate" experience as a component of religious practice and belief in general and theology in particular.

²⁷Schner, "The Appeal to Experience," 59.

²⁸Tillich, *Systematic Theology* I, 46.

²⁹Ibid., 42.

³⁰Ibid. Because experience can be a beginning point for theological work does not imply that it is a source for theology, even if it occasions theological reflection and education—as a *datum* it is to be analyzed, not merely accepted. Even the data of the New Testament require examination to understand the event on which Christianity is based.

This position seems to contrast with that of many feminist, liberal, and third-world theologians, who treat experience as a source for theology. For instance, Ada María Isasi-Díaz writes, "the fact that the great majority of Hispanics relate very little to Jesus is . . . glossed over [by some Hispanic theologians]. This results, therefore, in a 'new' emphasis on Jesus but never in new questions about Jesus or about how Jesus has been used by theologians and those with power in the churches to oppress and marginalize Hispanic Women.

"*Mujerista* theology, on the other hand, using the lived-experience of Hispanic Women as its main source, pushes out the old parameters and insists on new questions" (*En la Lucha/In the Stuggle* [Minneapolis: Fortress, 1993], 74). However, experience as described by Isasi-Díaz is not a source in the sense used here, but the crucial condition in which a theology based in *praxis* can develop (cf. Isasi-Díaz, 167ff). What Isasi-Díaz calls a "referent" (168) is more a "source" for her theology in the present use of "source." The experienced conditions of oppression provide a stimulus and opportunity for theological work and suggest, as Isasi-Díaz rightly notes, new questions; but mute experience does not provide the questions or the answers to them; articulate theological work is required. Yet I would add that any theological work that demeans or diminishes the experience that Isasi-Díaz points out would be seriously flawed.

[31]*Dei Verbum*, §9; also see §7 and the editors' commentary in *The Documents of Vatican II*, ed. Walter M. Abbott, S.J. (New York: Guild Press, American Press, Association Press, 1966), 115, footnote 15.

[32]See, *inter alia*, Jack Dean Kingsbury, *The Christology of Mark's Gospel* (Philadelphia: Fortress Press, 1983); Robert C. Tannehill, "The Gospel of Mark as Narrative Christology," *Semeia* 16 (1979): 57-95; David Rhoads and Donald Michie, *Mark as Story: An Introduction to the Narrative of a Gospel* (Philadelphia: Fortress Press, 1982), 125; Stanley Hauerwas, "Jesus: The Story of the Kingdom," *A Community of Character* (Notre Dame: University of Notre Dame Press, 1981), 46-49.

[33]Richard N. Longenecker, "The Foundational Conviction of New Testament Christology: The Obedience/Faithfulness/Sonship of Christ," in Green and Turner, *Jesus of Nazareth: Lord and Christ*, 484. Dennis E. Nineham, *The Gospel of St. Mark* (Hammondsworth, Middlesex: Penguin, 1969 [1963]) connects 8:27ff to the second half of the gospel (223) but treats the scene as a whole, rather than breaking it up into individual components as most commentaries do (223-232). William L. Lane, *The Gospel According to Mark* (Grand Rapids: Eerdmans, 1974) splits the gospel between 8:30 and 8:31 (292).

[34]Rudolf Bultmann, *The History of the Synoptic Tradition,* rev. ed., trans. John Marsh (New York: Harper & Row, 1968), 257-59, 431. Bultmann rejects views that treat the Caesarea Philippi pericope as unified and historical, e.g. Cullmann's view, which is characterized by Bultmann as a "psychologizing interpretation." That the story is composite cannot *ipso facto* exclude the possibility of traces of actual events remaining in the text (as Bultmann seems to think). But the implication is to see in the composite story a point composed by the redactor from and for the community.

[35]The reference to the Resurrection at this point is so out of place that it must be at minimum a formulaic insertion into the text. It may also be, as many have suggested (e.g., Bultmann, *History of the Synoptic Tradition*, 258), an indicator that the concept "suffering son of man" narrated here in Mark for the first time is a post-Resurrection invention (Bultmann suggests other indicators as well, but they are not entirely persuasive). As I both incline to accept the point of view that it is possible, but not certain, that the actual Jesus referred to himself as "the son of man" in a messianic sense (and, if so, probably in an apocalyptic sense) and find no reason to think that he was not astute enough to discern the various authorities' opposition to him, I also incline to the view that the insertion of the reference to the Resurrection is merely formulaic, a result of transmission of the text. Hence, I find it possible that the "pre-Easter Jesus" could have referred to himself as a suffering son of man. I would concede that the *use* Mark makes of the "suffering son of man" is to inform and comfort an audience of disciples of Jesus long after the Resurrection. I just am not convinced that this late *use* of the concept is necessarily

the *original locus* of the concept, that is, a pure Markan invention. This extends my argument in *Story Theology*, 118-121, 136-143; also see Dunn, *Christology in the Making*, 65-97.

36The prediction that some will not see death before the kingdom comes in power in 9:1 is another preexisting element, rhetorically connected with the call to discipleship. However, if the comments about the use of ἀνΘρώπος below (see note 58) are accurate, then this verse would be something of an afterthought to the Caesarea Philippi scene added by the redactor.

37One ironic move in Mark's narrative is the juxtaposition of this scene with the next pericope, the Transfiguration. Peter is one of the three who "see" Jesus' significance—although there has been no "reconciliation" between Jesus and the humiliated Peter.

38Pheme Perkins, *Peter: Apostle for the Whole Church* (Columbia: University of South Carolina Press, 1994), 29-31. Raymond E. Brown, *An Introduction to New Testament Christology* (New York: Paulist Press, 1994) suggests that the scene might not be unhistorical ("If we were to judge that the confession itself is not implausible historically . . ." [75]). Yet Brown writes in the subjunctive in the context of answering the question whether Jesus affirmed himself to be the Messiah, so it is not clear whether he would find the scene as a whole historically accurate.

39Frank Matera, "The Incomprehension of the Disciples and Peter's Confession (Mark 6, 14-18, 30)," *Biblica* 70/2 (1989): 153-172, argues that Peter's confession makes narrative sense in continuity with the preceding miracle: as the blind man's eyes are opened by Jesus at Bethsaida, so are Peter's eyes opened. However, Peter's eyes are *not* opened in the confession, but only in the correction of his imagination later in the scene. Matera presumes that getting the title right is sufficient; obviously, this essay argues quite otherwise.

40For example, Elizabeth Struthers Malbon finds different breaks in the narrative: Because the cure of a blind man in 8:22-26 occurs at Bethsaida, the deflected goal of Jesus' and the disciples' journey that began with the lake crossing in 6:45, she finds this "completes" a cycle and that 8:27 begins another one—perhaps one framed by the second cure of a blind man at 10:46-52 which is the end of another aspect of Jesus ministry, for in 11:1 Jesus is getting closer to Jerusalem. See Elizabeth Struthers Malbon, "'Reflected Christology': An Aspect of Narrative 'Christology' in the Gospel of Mark," *Perspectives in Religious Studies* 26 (1999): 137. Robert R. Beck finds a nest of plot lines overlapping in multiple ways. See his *Nonviolent Story: Narrative Conflict Resolution in the Gospel of Mark* (Maryknoll: Orbis Books, 1996), 39-62.

41M. Eugene Boring, "Markan Christology: God-Language for Jesus?" *New Testament Studies* 49 (1999): 471; also see the previously cited articles of Struthers Malbon.

42Stanley Hauerwas, "Jesus: The Story of the Kingdom," 48. In a meeting devoted to the relationship of theology and scripture, I hope it is not unfair to point out that this interesting move regarding the meaning of this pericope—one that shows how its parts fit together and how it exemplifies the narrative character of Markan christology—seems to have been totally ignored as a possibility by scripture scholars. I came across no references to Hauerwas or to his insight in any of the fairly extensive material I reviewed in preparation for this paper.

[43]Of course, this point is not ignored by scripture scholars and historians (for example, see Boring, "Markan Christology," 470-71), but all too often it is so muted that it becomes irrelevant. It is now commonplace that titles like "son of God" and "son of man" do not mean the same thing for Mark and the fathers of Nicea, but when we look at narratives that give meaning to these specific terms, there may also be continuities that concentration on "influences" (e.g., Hellenistic philosophy, the loss of Jewish intellectual roots, etc.) may obscure.

[44]The stories that contextualize "son of God" in the New Testament make this clear. In most of them, the story is that God made a human being God's son; in John and possibly the hymns, the story is that God made God's son a human. See Tilley, *Story Theology*, 121-26.

[45]Interestingly, Bultmann thought this part of the original legend; see *The History of the Synoptic Tradition*, 258-59.

[46]See Rhoads and Michie, *Mark as Story*, 143, citing Thomas E. Boomershine, "Mark, the Story-teller: A Rhetorical-Critical Investigation of Mark's Passion and Resurrection Narrative" (Ph.D. dissertation, Union Theological Seminary, New York, 1974), 7-9; idem, "Oral Tradition and Mark" (Society of Biblical Literature, Markan Seminar Papers, 1979), and Werner Kelber, "Mark and Orality," *Semeia* 16 (1979): 7-55. With appropriate cuts of duplicated material, the gospel can be performed as a dramatic reading in about two hours.

[47]Rhoads and Michie, *Mark as Story*, 137.

[48]Compare Rhoads and Michie, *Mark as Story*, 138. In addition to the motifs of the messianic secret and the disciples' blindness, the motif of fear is important in the gospel. While Jesus was at home (1-4), his actions evoked amazement and opposition. As he begins to teach away from home, the storm enables him to oppose fear and faith (δειλοί Ὑφῦ πιστιν; 4:40). And at the end the disciples maintain silence at the empty tomb not to keep the messianic secret, but because "they were afraid" (ἐφοβοῦντο γάρ; 16:8).

[49]Rhoads and Michie, *Mark as Story*, 139.

[50]Boring, "Markan Christology," 471.

[51]Hence I would agree with a remark made by David Kelsey in *The Uses of Scripture in Recent Theology* (Philadelphia: Westminster, 1976), that "at the root of a theological position there is an imaginative act . . ." (163). I would also agree with his overall thesis: "In short: Our analysis suggests that it is the *patterns* in scripture, not its 'content,' that makes it 'normative' for theology" (193).

[52]The use of "imagination" is not an appeal to a "faculty," but to the practice exemplified by those who have the virtue of φρονησίς, "practical wisdom." Those who have this virtue, the φρονίμοι, have the ability to imagine how standards, rules, or universals apply in specific situations. In Aristotle's *Nichomachean Ethics*, this is the virtue that bridges intellectual and moral virtues, the practical (but

not theoretical) capstone of the mind (see 1140a: 24-28). To exercise the imagination, in this sense, is for someone with practical wisdom to see how concepts, rules, or standards apply. To exercise the christological imagination is for someone who is a disciple (or trying to be one) to see how concepts like "messiah" or "Christ" apply to Jesus whose disciple one is and in whom one has faith.

A case study of one form of such an imaginative practice in a specific religious cultural context (for Aristotle's account was also specific to an androcentric, slaveholding culture even if its basic insights can be extended to other contexts) can be found especially in chapters three through five of Robert A. Orsi, *Thank You, St. Jude: Women's Devotion to the Patron Saint of Hopeless Causes* (New Haven: Yale University Press, 1996), 70-184. Some would find this a questionable exercise of practical wisdom, but the problems with the St. Jude devotion were not with the women who were devoted or even the highly fictionalized saint to whom they were devoted, but the social, economic and religious contexts that made this devotion one that "fit" (and still "fits") for the devout. Orsi clearly criticizes the trivialization of the practice which, for some, simply "masked what was in fact a deeply passive and alienated experience of reality" (197). Yet in theological terms foreign to Orsi's work, Jude was an occasion of grace for many of the devout (see 198). The devout were "disciples" of Jude as a proximate occasion of the salvation Christ brought. They exercised an imagination analogous to the christological imagination, even if it is a practically, psychologically or theologically flawed exercise.

[53]At other points in the gospels Jesus' identity is questioned by the Nazarenes, the Sanhedrin, Pilate, and Herod, and answered by various voices, from a Roman centurion to a heavenly voice.

[54]I omit the element of the injunction to keep the "messianic secret" because it is a *leitmotif* utilized throughout the gospel and seems not especially significant for the meaning of the present scene.

[55]Consider the following dialogue from scene one of George Bernard Shaw's *Saint Joan:*

JOAN. I hear voices telling me what to do. They come from God.

ROBERT [DE BAUDRICORT]. They come from your imagination.

JOAN. Of course. That is how the messages of God come to us.

[BERTRAND DE] POULENGEY. Checkmate.

(Bernard Shaw, *Saint Joan: A Chronicle* and *The Apple Cart: A Political Extravaganza* [London: Constable and Company, 1949 {1924}], 66). While I am in great sympathy with Joan's position, Poulengey's response is too facile.

[56]Boring, "Markan Christology," 471. Also see Raymond E. Brown, Karl P. Donfried, and John Reumann, eds., *Peter in the New Testament: A Collaborative Assessment by Protestant and Roman Catholic Scholars* (Minneapolis: Augsburg, and New York: Paulist, 1963), 69.

[57]The verb φρονέω that is used here (a unique use in the synoptics, save for the parallel in Matthew, but not in Luke) has a curious history. In the Septuagint, it is found almost exclusively in Wisdom Literature. In the New Testament, it is used either to indicate a way of understanding that is reprobated (when it is used with

οὐ) or to indicate a way of understanding that is supported, given that there are other "live options," mentioned either explicitly (as here) or implicitly, as in Philippians 2:5, typically translated, "Let the same mind be in you that was in Christ Jesus" (NRSV). This latter exhortation implies that other minds have been or might be "in" the addressees. The kenosis hymn follows immediately, evidently as part of the same sentence. Here again is the connection of φρονέω to discipleship. To have the "mind" of Jesus is to conform one's understanding in practice to Jesus—*given that other options are possible*. Other uses are similarly suggestive.

As I will suggest below, soteriology in practice, namely, discipleship—being conformed to Christ—and christology are inseparable. The curious use of φρονέω— apparently only when multiple life-patterns options are available—seems to differ from classic uses of the verb, and of the noun connected with it, practical wisdom, φρονησίς. Connecting this concept with extra-scriptural uses goes beyond the work of the present paper by far. However, it should be noted that G. W. H. Lampe, ed., *A Patristic Greek Lexicon* (Oxford: Clarendon Press, 1982 [1961]) 1490-1491, does not list the verb, so evidently he thinks its meaning in the Fathers is no different from its use in classical Greek.

[58]Rather than connecting Peter's confession with the incredulity of the disciples, as Matera does (see note 39), one could as well construe the repeated uses of ἀνθρώπος in the pericope as a leitmotif in contrast to Peter and the disciples, or even as an *inclusio* device in 8:27 and 8:38.

[59]For contemporary work on the virtue of φρονησίς, see Terrence W. Tilley, *The Wisdom of Religious Commitment* (Washington, D.C.: Georgetown University Press, 1995), especially chapters four and five. The point Orsi made about the trivialization of some women's use of Jude in their devotion (see note 52) is, in my terms, an exercise of practical wisdom at the most minimal level or a failure to exercise practical wisdom at all.

[60]I owe the reminder concerning the healing power of memory to Dermot Lane. In this sense, one way that "history" relates to "theology" is that it is a discipline that helps us to remember and thus to heal and be healed.

[61]This is *not* to say that there is "one way" to get the story right. In future work, I will argue that there are properly multiple, even strongly contrasting ways, to "get it right." One theoretical source for this argument is Isaiah Berlin's acceptance of pluralism in the moral life while rejecting relativism. The history of Christianity provides numerous, perhaps incompatible, perhaps incommensurable, practical illustrations of ways of being disciples of Christ, as well as practical illustrations of what a life that fails to be conformed to Christ looks like.

[62]I intentionally avoid the term "norms" for christology. If there is an overarching norm, it is carrying on faithful discipleship. But what criteria or other standards indicate to what extent we meet that norm and what role our christologies play in it are topics that will have to emerge as the research develops. "Normativity" in practice is a very difficult issue that I hope to treat as this project develops. One crucial problem is that normativity is often connected with theoretical understandings that are "foundationally realist," a position I have rejected (see *Inventing Catholic Tradition*, 162-67).

[63]For these and other imaginations, see William A. Clebsch, *Christianity in European History* (New York: Oxford University Press, 1979); Lawrence S. Cunningham, *The Catholic Heritage* (New York: Crossroad, 1983); Jaroslav Pelikan, *Jesus through the Centuries* (New Haven: Yale University Press, 1985), not to mention the works of the members of the Jesus Seminar.

[64]"Practice" is a term of art. See Tilley, *Inventing Catholic Tradition*, 50-61 *et passim*, for the significance of a "practical" approach to theology.

SCRIPTURE AND LITURGICAL-PASTORAL THEOLOGY

Conflicting Messages?
The Sunday Lectionaries and
Official Church Teachings

Regina A. Boisclair

Biblical scholarship has enriched every theological discipline for the past half-century, but its findings have only a limited effect on the beliefs of the average Christian. Christians are less likely to be influenced by academic theology than by what they experience in public worship. The dictum *"lex orandi, lex credendi"* is a reminder that it is very important to consider how the scriptures are incorporated in Sunday worship.

For Catholics and many other Christians, the most explicit and sustained experiences of scripture in Sunday worship are the pericopes selected from the Bible and assigned to specific occasions in the church's calendar by a lectionary. Lectionaries determine what worshipping assemblies affirm as "Word of the Lord" or "Gospel." Lectionaries establish a canon within the canon that is the only "Bible" many churchgoing Christians know.[1]

Among the recommendations of the Second Vatican Council was the creation of a new multi-year lectionary for Sundays and Solemnities to replace a one-year lectionary used since 1570. The three-year lectionary promulgated in 1969 became mandatory for use in the Roman Rite worldwide on the First Sunday of Advent in 1971. Significant changes in this new lectionary included some revisions to the church calendar and the collection of three readings and a psalm or canticle for each occasion—including regular readings from the Old Testament and highlighting one synoptic gospel each year.

It is one of the most highly regarded initiatives of Vatican II.

With some changes, the Episcopal and many mainline Protestant churches in the United States quickly adopted the new Catholic lectionary. In fact, some Presbyterians were using a variant of the three-year lectionary even before many Catholics. The modest revision of the 1969 Catholic *ordo* issued in 1981 is now used throughout North America, and other churches have consolidated their denominational variants.[2] Today, the Revised Common and Roman Lectionaries are used throughout the world. These lectionaries are sufficiently similar to be described as "synoptic lectionaries" and studied together. Few of the differences between the Roman and the Revised Common Lectionaries[3] impact on this study and these will be noted.

The three-year Sunday lectionary brought about a new emphasis and interest in scripture among Catholics and has been described as Catholicism's greatest gift to Protestant preaching.[4] Among the guiding principles for the whole reform of the liturgy, including the Catholic lectionary, was the concern expressed by Vatican II in *Sacrosanctum Concilium* that called for liturgy to be "in line with the conditions of modern times."[5] It is therefore appropriate to ask if the selections in these lectionaries consistently communicate an appropriate message to the conditions of our times.

Some scholars have recognized that the contemporary three-year lectionaries include passages that convey premises that have marked and marred Christian history with a teaching of contempt for Jews and Judaism since the second century C.E.[6] These studies tend to state that there is a problem without examples or to illustrate by one or two examples one or two aspects of the problem. None has examined this issue in detail. Although this paper will examine what the Roman and Revised Common Lectionaries communicate about the Pharisees in Matthew's gospel, in order to establish beyond question that there really is a problem, I will first call attention to some of the selections from Acts.

During the Easter season, churchgoing Catholics and other Christians who follow one of the three-year lectionaries hear passages from Acts instead of selections from the Old Testament. One message in several of these readings is that the Jews are responsible for the execution of Jesus. The following table lists these selections and identifies the verses in which the assertion is found.

Roman Lectionary	Revised Common Lectionary
	Baptism of the Lord A Acts 10:34-43 *See Acts 10:39*
Easter ABC Acts 10:34a, 37-43 *See Acts 10:39*	Easter ABC Acts 10:34-43 *See Acts 10:39*
	2 Easter A Acts 2:14a, 22-32 *See Acts 2:23*
3 Easter A Acts 2:14, 22-28 *See Acts 2:23*	3 Easter A Acts 2:14a, 36-41 *See Acts 2:36*
4 Easter A	
Acts 2:14a, 36-41 *See Acts 2:36*	
3 Easter B Acts 3:13-15, 17-19 *See Acts 3:15*	3 Easter B Acts 3:12-19 *See Acts 3:15*
4 Easter B Acts 4:8-12 *See Acts 4:10*	4 Easter B Acts 4:5-12 *See Acts 4:10*
	2 Easter C Acts 5:27-32 *See Acts 5:28, 30*
3 Easter C Acts 5:27b-32, 40b-41 *See Acts 5:28, 30*	

These readings are from speeches attributed to Peter. One is a selection appointed by the Catholic lectionary every year on Easter Sunday; others are provided for the Third Sunday of Easter each year, and others for the Fourth Sunday of Easter in years A and B. The same readings are found in the Revised Common Lectionary, although some are appointed to different Sundays.[7] Since most Catholic dioceses already or will likely soon celebrate the Feast of the Ascension in place of the Seventh Sunday of Easter, the twenty-one Sundays of Easter in the three-year cycle are or will be reduced to eighteen. On ten of these Sundays—over half—the selection from Acts communicates a very serious teaching of contempt and the Easter Season is a context that lends reinforcement to the message.

The idea that Jews are culpable for the death of Jesus is known as "deicide." Pawlikowski states that "probably no other accusation against the Jewish community by the Christian church is responsible for more Jewish suffering throughout history than this charge."[8] While most North American Christians are not consciously anti-Judaic, the idea that the Jews are guilty of deicide lingers in Western culture, popular piety, and even in the minds of preachers who should know better.

Even before the Second Vatican Council issued *Nostra Aetate* in 1965, the Third Assembly of the World Council of Churches identified anti-Semitism as a sin.[9] Since *Nostra Aetate*, numerous other documents issued by the Vatican, the World and National Councils of Churches, and individual Anglican and Protestant churches have repudiated various forms of the traditional Christian teaching of contempt toward Judaism. Over the past four decades, several articles, books, and textbooks have made substantive efforts to change this teaching of contempt. One must wonder, though, how effective these efforts can be, when the idea that the Jews killed Jesus is repeatedly proclaimed and affirmed as the "Word of the Lord."

Church Documents and Lectionaries

Statements from several documents are directly pertinent to lectionaries. In 1968, the Faith and Order Commission of the World Council of Churches issued a report on Christian anti-Semitism. The report included the following suggestion:

We recommend that especially in religious instruction and preaching great care be taken not to picture the Jews in such a way as to foster inadvertently a kind of Christian anti-Semitism. . . . We feel it would help if the churches would re-examine . . . the lessons, hymns and other texts used in worship from the point of view set out in this document.[10]

In 1974, the Vatican Commission on Jewish-Christian Relations issued "Guidelines for the Implementation of *Nostra Aetate*." Using stronger and clearer language than was possible when *Nostra Aetate* was issued, "Guidelines" provided hermeneutical directives for interpreting the conciliar document. One paragraph specifically applied to the new three-year Catholic lectionary:

With respect to the liturgical readings, care will be taken to see that homilies based on them will not distort their meaning, especially when it is a question of passages which seem to show the Jewish people as such in an unfavorable light. . . . Commissions entrusted with the task of liturgical translation will pay particular attention to the way in which they express those phrases and passages which Christians, if not well informed, might misunderstand because of prejudice. Obviously, one cannot alter the text of the Bible. The point is that with a version destined for liturgical use, there should be an overriding preoccupation to bring out explicitly the meaning of a text while taking scriptural studies into account.[11]

The final sentence was followed by this footnote:

Thus the formula "the Jews" in St. John, sometimes according to the context means "the leaders of the Jews" or "the adversaries of Jesus," terms which express better the thought of the evangelist and avoid appearing to arraign the Jewish people as such. Another example is the use of the word "Pharisee" and "Pharisaism" which have taken on a largely pejorative meaning.[12]

While the lion's share of *The Interpretation of the Bible in the Church* issued in 1993 by the Pontifical Biblical Commission describes

the critical methods and hermeneutical strategies of professional exegetes, Part Four is titled "Interpretation of the Bible in the Life of the
Church." The PBC rightly recognized that the Bible is more than a
resource for academic analysis—it is the Word of God that forms and
informs the faith, practices, and experiences of believing Christians.
Part Four concerns "the work of actualizing and inculturating the biblical message, as well as the various uses of the inspired text in liturgy,
in *Lectio Divina*, in pastoral ministry and in the ecumenical movement."[13] Among the specific instructions concerning actualization, the
following statement is significant:

> Particular attention is necessary, according to the spirit of the
> Second Vatican Council (*Nostra Aetate*, 4) to avoid absolutely
> any actualization of certain texts of the New Testament, which
> could provoke or reinforce unfavorable attitudes to the Jewish
> people. The tragic events of the past must, on the contrary, impel
> all to keep unceasingly in mind that, according to the New
> Testament, the Jews remain "beloved" of God, "since the gifts
> and calling of God are irrevocable" (Rom. 11:28-29).[14]

All three documents acknowledge that there are passages in the
New Testament that lend themselves to anti-Judaic premises. All three
recognize that Christians have inherited tendencies toward negative
understandings of Jews and Judaism, much as they "inherited the fur-
nishings in their churches."[15] Both the Faith and Order Report and
"Guidelines" recognize that liturgical readings have an extraordinary
capacity to reinforce anti-Judaic sentiments and presume that problems can be ameliorated by preaching and/or careful translations.
"Guidelines," however, assumes that the selections are cast in stone
and that it would be unthinkable to change them. Thus, it is notewor-
thy that the PBC subtly suggests that changes really should be made to
the lectionary: "The lectionary issued at the direction of the Council
(*Sacrosanctum Concilium*, 35) is meant to allow for a reading of Sacred Scripture that is 'more abundant, more varied and more suitable.'
In its present state, it only partially fulfills this goal."[16]

The Faith and Order report specifically recommends that those liturgical lessons fostering anti-Judaic sentiments be reconsidered. When
the PBC used the words "in its present state," it implied that changes
are desirable but did not specify why any should be made. It is fair to

suggest that "more suitable" readings from sacred scripture could be found and used that would eliminate at least some of the many passages that contradict contemporary efforts to purge anti-Judaic presuppositions from contemporary Christian teaching. Would this not fulfill the Council's charge that liturgy take into account the "conditions of our times"?

Admittedly, the present climate in Rome appears hostile to liturgical changes. *Liturgiam Authenticam*, issued on May 7, 2001, insists that "the delineation of biblical pericopai is to conform entirely to the *Ordo Lectionum Missae*."[17] Mindful, however, that the latest word is rarely the last word, I believe we are in an auspicious interlude that provides a fine opportunity to demonstrate the problems with the three-year *ordo* and to discuss possible resolutions.[18]

It is essential to remember that lectionaries are by their very nature selections. Changing selections is not expurgating the Bible. Changing selections does not change canonical texts. An undue reverence for the passages selected for inclusion in lectionaries gives more authority to a lectionary than is warranted. It is possible and legitimate to consider substituting pericopes that were not included for passages that are now included in the Sunday lectionaries.[19] It is also possible to skip one or more verses—a practice attested in the "Introduction" to the Catholic lectionary, which admits the original compilers eliminated verses that "involve truly difficult issues."[20] This is not an interest in being politically correct; rather, it is an interest in ceasing to pretend that ignoring a problem will make it go away.[21] While it would not be appropriate to purge from the Sunday lectionaries every instance in which Jews are introduced in a negative light, it would be appropriate to eliminate some of the more egregious selections from the liturgical readings. Before this can be attempted, though, it is necessary to have a clear understanding of what selections include problems and then to suggest some criteria to identify when changes should be considered.

Since there are too many issues to explore in a single study and "Guidelines" acknowledged that the term "Pharisee" tends to have pejorative meaning for Christians, this paper is confined to places in which the selections refer to Pharisees. In addition, since Matthew is especially antagonistic toward Pharisees, the present study will also be limited to selections from his gospel. However, it is beneficial to have in mind an understanding of some of the particular features of

Matthew that clarify his complex relationship with and understanding of Pharisees.

Matthew's Gospel

Belief in the resurrection of the dead, forms of piety such as alms-giving, prayer, and fasting, as well as the priority of the command-ment to love God and neighbor are understandings that characterized the Pharisees and continue to be shared by both Jews and Christians.[22] While different scholars locate Matthew's community in different places, most are convinced that the gospel originated in an urban com-munity in or near Galilee, where rabbinical Judaism developed out of Pharisaism. As Alan Segal rightly recognizes, "the ways in which Ju-daism and Christianity evolved were very much affected by the con-flicts between them."[23] With the possible exception of John's gospel, Matthew, more than any other New Testament text, betrays the depth of the internal struggle between the early Jesus movement and emerg-ing Judaism in the last quarter of the first century. There are three features in Matthew's gospel that disclose how deeply Matthew and his community were involved in this struggle with Judaism in general and with the Pharisees in particular.

First, it seems that whoever formulated Matthew was well schooled in the exegetical methods and legal argumentation of the Pharisees. Although Matthew casts his Pharisees into the role of Jesus' principal antagonists, interpretations on the lips of Matthew's Jesus are frequently Pharisaic in form and also often in content. There can be no pretense that the situation portrayed in this gospel goes back to the time of Jesus. During Jesus' lifetime the Pharisees were not as prominent as Matthew suggests. However, during the time when the gospel was formulated, the Pharisees were prominent authorities. Just as every gospel adjusts the memories of Jesus' deeds and teachings as witness to the Risen Lord to a particular community, Matthew also incorpo-rates his community's particular experience of the Pharisees by sharp-ening their role as antagonists in his story of Jesus.

Second, Matthew's polemical language was common to compet-ing groups throughout the late post-exilic period. Matthew and other New Testament authors used this language to distinguish the Jesus movement from other Jewish groups, to defend the legitimacy of their appeal to Israel's ancient traditions, and to explain to their communities why other Jews rejected the gospel. Like the Qumran covenant-ers before him, Matthew expressed his convictions and frustrations in a kind of rhetoric that was acrimonious toward other Jews even before clear boundaries between Judaism and Christianity were es-tablished.

Third, Saldarini notes that internal evidence indicates that Matthew's gospel reached its canonical form after the community had withdrawn or had been expelled from the synagogues.[24] Still, as Kingsbury in-sists, Matthew's community "is best understood as a sect within Juda-ism."[25] E. P. Sanders and Alan Segal describe various ways in which a tension between association and disassociation is found in the gos-pel.[26] The following three examples are especially significant.

First, statements such as Matthew 5:22b, "whoever says to his brother, 'Raqa' will be answerable to the Sanhedrin," or Matthew 5:35, "(do not swear) by Jerusalem, for it is the city of the great king," or Matthew 10:17, "for they will . . . scourge you in their synagogues" only make sense, as Segal observes, "in a community of people who are presumed to be part of the synagogue, under its aegis and subject to its punishments, not outside of it."[27] At the same time, Matthew distinguishes his *ecclesia* from those who do not believe in Jesus by several references to "their" or "your" synagogue (4:23, 9:35, 10:17, 12:9, 13:54, 23:34).

Second, some verses such as 5:18, 23:2 and 23:23 maintain that observance of the law is the ideal and the most appropriate, if not the only, manner of living an authentic Christian life. At the same time, Matthew identifies the manner in which some observe the law as grandiose hypocrisy, as in 6:2, "when you give alms do not blow a trumpet before you as the hypocrites do in the synagogues and in the streets"; in 6:5, "when you pray do not be like the hypocrites, who love to stand and pray in the synagogues and on the street corners"; and throughout chapter 23, where Matthew's Jesus reviles various practices and teachings attributed to the scribes and Pharisees and calls them hypocrites.

Third, in 5:21-48 Jesus intensifies the obligations of Torah to the point of prohibiting what was permitted, as, for example, in 5:31-32: "It is written 'Whoever divorces his wife must give her a bill of di-vorce.' But I say to you whoever divorces his wife . . . causes her to commit adultery and whoever marries a divorced woman commits adultery." At the same time, Matthew's Jesus teaches that following

him supersedes the normal requirements of Torah; for example, in
8:21-22: "Another disciple said to him, 'Lord let me go first and bury
my father.' But Jesus answered him, 'Follow me, and let the dead
bury their dead.' "[28] Matthew does not contrast Christian faith with
Jewish legalism. For Matthew, following Jesus is a hermeneutic principle that calls the *ecclesia* to observe the law with greater sincerity
and intensity.

These forms of internal contradictions were likely derived from
traditions that were formulated at different stages in the life of
Matthew's community, some at a time when the community was part
of the synagogue, others after the community had withdrawn or had
been expelled. Although recognizing the tension in the canonical text
helps to clarify the complexity of this gospel, one must acknowledge
that this tension would be lost in lectionaries, where detached selections are separated one from another, often by several weeks.

Although most Christians are not aware of rhetorical strategies at
all, let alone those of Matthew, it is important to be mindful that Matthew used the exegetical forms of the Pharisees and incorporated typical Jewish polemics. These features of the gospel nuance our understanding of Matthew's presentation of Jesus' opponents. Those who
affirm lectionary selections as "Gospel" in Sunday assemblies will
most likely understand what is proclaimed about these opponents.

Matthew's Pharisees and the Lectionaries

In Matthew, Jesus' opponents are the Pharisees, scribes, Sadducees,
priests, elders, Herodians, and the Council. However, the scribes,
Sadducees, elders, Herodians, and the Council always appear either
with priests or the Pharisees. Thus, all but the Pharisees, who are identified in thirty verses (29 = plural, 1 = singular), and the priests, who
are identified in twenty-four verses, are secondary. Although Matthew assigns to the chief priests the major responsibility for events
that led to Jesus' execution, Matthew also frames his account of the
opposition to Jesus in Jerusalem with two references to Pharisees in
21:45-46 and 27:62.[29] This framing subtly suggests that Pharisees were
active opponents throughout the arrest, trials, and passion of Jesus.

The following chart lists the readings from Matthew in the Roman
and Revised Common Lectionaries that mention Pharisees. The ob-
servations that follow presuppose this chart.

Roman Lectionary	Revised Common Lectionary
2 Advent A Matt. 3:1-12 (Baptist denounces Pharisees)	2 Advent A Matt. 3:1-12
6 in *Anno A* Matt. 5:17-37 (Teaching about Law)	5 Epiphany A Matt. 5:13-20
Palm Sunday A Matt. 26:14-27:66 (Passion Narrative)	
	Holy Saturday ABC
	Matt. 27:57-66 (Request for guard)
10 in *Anno A* Matt. 9:9-13 (Call of Matthew)	Proper 5 A Matt. 9:9-13, 18-25
	Proper 15 A Matt. 15:10-28 (Traditions of the Elders)
29 in *Anno A* Matt. 22:15-21 (Taxes to Caesar)	Proper 24 A Matt. 22:15-22

Roman Lectionary	Revised Common Lectionary
30 in *Anno A* Matt. 22:24-40 (Greatest Commandment)	Proper 25 A Matt. 22:34-46
31 in *Anno A* Matt. 23:1-12 (Denunciation of Pharisees)	Proper 26 A Matt. 23:1-12

Seven readings in the Roman Lectionary introduce Matthew's Pharisees. They are included in nine selections assigned to eleven occasions in the Revised Common Lectionary. It is evident that Pharisees, who are prominent throughout Matthew's gospel, are not as prominent in either lectionary. More verses in the Matthean selections include either the chief priests or high priest, although these opponents appear in only two readings. The Pharisees are the principal antagonists to Jesus in lections from Matthew.

Both lectionaries include the passage in which the Baptist identifies the Pharisees, together with Sadducees, as vipers (3:7). Both include two selections in which Jesus calls his followers to behavior that surpasses that of the scribes and Pharisees (5:20, 23:2). Both have one selection in which the Pharisees question Jesus' disciples concerning his table fellowship (9:11), another in which the Pharisees are said to plot to entrap Jesus (22:15), and one lection in which the Pharisees send one of their scholars to test Jesus' understanding of the law (23:34). Both also include the report that the Pharisees, together with the chief priests, ask Pilate to place a guard on Jesus' body (27:62).

Only the Revised Common Lectionary includes Matthew's account of Jesus questioning the Pharisees concerning their understanding of scripture (22:41), as well as the report that the Pharisees took offense at one of Jesus' responses (15:12). Quantitatively and qualitatively, the Revised Common Lectionary admits more of Matthew's Pharisees than the Roman Lectionary, although neither lectionary identifies the Pharisees often enough for an assembly to hear the full severity of the animosity toward the Pharisees that is found in this gospel.

Most of Matthew's bitter diatribe in chapter 23 in which the Pharisees, together with the scribes, are repeatedly identified as hypocrites (vv. 13, 15, 23, 25, and 29) is not included in either lectionary. Both lectionaries exclude asides where the Pharisees condemn Jesus (9:34 and 12:24). Both omit the instances in 12:2, 12:38, 15:1, 16:1, and 19:3, where Matthew's Pharisees question Jesus. Both leave out Matthew's Jesus' warnings concerning the Pharisees in 16:6 and 16:11, as well as excluding two asides about the Pharisees voiced by the narrator in 12:14 and 16:12, the former being a report that the Pharisees sought to put him to death, and the latter an explanation that Jesus' teaching did not concern the leaven of actual bread but was, rather, a warning against the teachings of the Pharisees.

The most severe reading in both lectionaries is the selection from

Matthew 23:1-12. Since this selection appears at the end of a sequence in which the Pharisees are mentioned three Sundays in a row, this selection is very likely to have a greater impact on worshiping assemblies. The first gospel selection in this three-week sequence reports that the Pharisees "plotted how they might entrap him" (22:15) and the second reports that the Pharisees "gathered together and one of them tested him"(22:34). These two readings convey a negative understanding of the Pharisees, so that when on the following Sunday the gospel reports that Matthew's Jesus instructs his audience not to follow the example of the Pharisees, the worshiping assembly is predisposed to consider the behavior Jesus ascribes to the Pharisees an accurate report. When this reading speaks about phylacteries and tassels (fringes on a tallit [prayer shawl]) that are still used by observant Jews, Christians are encouraged to assume that Jews still normally seek to be exalted in the way Matthew's Jesus challenges his disciples to avoid. Having discussed Matthew's Pharisees and the lectionaries, the next section of this study addresses specifically lectionaries as liturgical collections that have their own contexts.

Liturgical Collections and Contexts

Lectionaries are more than selections. The three selections form a collection and each collection is assigned to a context in the church calendar. Both collections and contexts have the capacity to reinforce understandings advanced by any one selection in a collection. Some of the collections and the contexts of the selections considered in this study call for further consideration.

Matthew 3:1-12 is John the Baptist's denunciation of the scribes and Pharisees as a "brood of vipers" who are convinced that, as descendants of Abraham, they would escape divine retribution. This passage is collected with Isaiah 11:1-11, which declares a descendant of David will effect judgment. In the minds of many preachers, this collection lends itself to the application of an anti-Judaic message. The season of Advent increases the possibility that homilists or those who hear them may contrast Christians, who commemorate Jesus' first coming while awaiting his second, with Jews, who are to be judged for rejecting the Messiah just as the Baptist denounced their ancestors.

With the inclusion of Matthew 9:9-23, both lectionaries provide a story of the Pharisees who question Jesus' behavior. Jesus responds to their question by claiming that mercy not sacrifice is what is pleasing to God. Here, Matthew's Jesus cites Hosea 6:6 and the gospel reading is collected with Hosea 6:4-6. Hosea condemns Ephraim and Judah for inconstancy and an inability to recognize that love for God is more pleasing than sacrifices. While it is clear that the message is intended to challenge Christians, it is very possible that Jesus' critique of the Pharisees may instead be associated with present-day Jews. It is important to recognize that when none of those being challenged in the texts are Christian, it is possible for Christians to distance themselves from those who are challenged in the text.

The Revised Common Lectionary collects Matthew 9:9-23 and Hosea 6:4-6 with Romans 4:13-17. In the gospel, the Pharisees are presented as those for whom the law is integral to their religious identity. As Jesus' opponents, their challenge to his behavior is based on the law. The verses from Romans state that faith rather than observance of the law is the true heritage of Abraham. Thus, this collection presents a Christian teaching that fosters a negative impression of the Pharisees.

The Revised Common Lectionary collects Matthew 5:20, where Jesus asserts that Christian righteousness must surpass that of the Pharisees, with Isaiah 58:1-12, which calls for care of the oppressed. This collection in the Revised Common Lectionary suggests that the Pharisees do not care for the downtrodden. In the Roman Lectionary, the same passage from Matthew is collected with Sirach 15:15-20. The verses in Sirach declare that observance of the commandments is a personal choice and that God never leads individuals to sin. This collection in the Roman Lectionary lends itself to the suggestion that the Pharisees are unrighteous and sinful.

Among the Matthean selections that have been mentioned, Matthew 23:1-12 conveys the most negative impression of the Pharisees among the Matthean selections. This impression is reinforced when both lectionaries collect it with Malachi 1:4b-2:2b, 8-10, which condemns Israel for insincerity and violations of cultic observances. In addition to a collection that links Matthew 23:1-12 with Malachi 1:4b-2b, 8-10, the Revised Common Lectionary also provides Micah 3:5-12 with Matthew 23:1-12 as an alternative collection.[30] Micah 3:5-12 condemns prophets, leaders, and priests who misuse their roles for personal gain. Assemblies who hear Matthew 23:1-12 with Micah 3:5-

12 may associate these unrighteous officials with the Pharisees in the gospel.

While it is clear that the context of Palm Sunday intensifies the negative impression of those Jews who are said to conspire to bring about Jesus' execution, the Pharisees siding with the chief priests and asking Pilate to place a guard on Jesus' body is somewhat incidental.[31] In this reading, the most serious problem is the inclusion of Matthew 27:25 "All the people answered 'His blood be on us and on our children.'" This sorry verse is the most unfortunate statement in the New Testament. It is tragic that it was not omitted from the selection when the lectionary was formulated in 1969. This is one instance that indeed "involve[s] truly difficult issues."[32]

Criteria and Conclusion

Early Christian authors engaged in what James Sanders calls "the canonical process" when they selected and reapplied established traditions of Israel using methods of interpretation and application that they shared with other first-century C.E. Jews.[33] However, it is an oversimplification to declare early Christian texts "Jewish literature" and thereby acquit them from accusations of being anti-Judaic.

Throughout history, the church has highlighted some texts and ignored others, thus continuing this canonical process. "Canons within the canon" have shifted over nineteen centuries to renew and reform Christian witness in different historical contexts. Today, the most significant "canons within the canon" are the three-year Sunday lectionaries since they determine what church-going Christians hear when they worship.

In 1984, Vincent Truijen observed that the selections in the Catholic Sunday lectionary eliminated much of the negative presentation of the Pharisees when compared with the New Testament.[34] In this study I have demonstrated that the selections from Matthew really do not highlight Matthew's polemics pertaining to Pharisees. However, I have also identified how some of the passages included in the selections retain what Sloyan would claim is "a capacity to harm."[35] In view of this, it is now appropriate to propose criteria to identify when a selection or some part of a selection should be reconsidered for inclusion in the Sunday readings.

Some might be initially tempted to suggest eliminating passages or verses that contain a well-established historical inaccuracy, such as those from Acts that assign collective responsibility for Jesus' execution to the Jews. However, contemporary understandings of historical reliability distort the very nature of the gospel as well as its role in the believing community.

While I sense that it would be inappropriate to remove every instance in which Jesus' Jewish opponents are mentioned in the liturgical selections, there are two criteria that I believe would be useful for considering whether or not changing a selection or eliminating a particular verse would be desirable.

The first criterion for exclusion would be to eliminate passages that insult Jewish religious practices. A passage such as Matthew 23:1-12 that ridicules phylacteries and tallits fosters sentiments that discount the sincerity of those who wear them. The second criterion would be to eliminate verses or change passages that reinforce aspects of the church's traditional teaching of contempt toward Jews. Matthew 27:25 should be removed from any liturgical selection and the verses from Acts should be reconsidered. These profess Jewish culpability for the death of Jesus and foster the very tradition church teachings have significantly nuanced.

The decision to change any of the existing readings is not an individual decision. Only a significant consensus among biblical scholars, theologians, and liturgists will assist the Congregation for Divine Worship in determining when there is a serious conflict between official teachings pertaining to Jews and Judaism and what is proclaimed as "Word of the Lord" or "Gospel" in worshiping assemblies. I would invite readers to consider if other selections either introduced in this study or elsewhere in the lectionaries fall into one of these two categories.

There is an unbroken trajectory between the animus of New Testament authors toward Jews who rejected Christian insights in the second half of the first century and the subsequent nineteen centuries of animosity on the part of Christians toward Judaism. New Testament texts embedded with first-century polemical rhetoric became the proof-texts for anti-Judaism. Tragically, Jews suffered because all too often the persecution of Jews was considered an appropriate expression of Christian convictions. Today the same texts—canonized as scripture—are enshrined in the churches as revelation and retain their potential to support anti-Judaism. Liturgical readings that reiterate the traditional teaching of contempt encourage anti-Judaism to smolder in the minds of Christians like an underground fire with a potential to flare up in the future.[36]

Notes

[1]John Reumann, "A History of Lectionaries: From the Synagogue at Nazareth to Post-Vatican II," *Interpretation* 31 (April, 1977): 129. The influence of lectionaries extends beyond the Sunday services. Lectionary readings provide the biblical texts for many textbook catechetical programs, pamphlets for personal devotion, and parochial Bible studies.

[2]Using the new Catholic lectionary, American Presbyterian, Methodist, Lutheran, and Episcopal churches devised their own three-year lectionaries in the 1970s. In 1984 The Consultation on Common Texts issued *The Common Lectionary* (Nashville: Abingdon Press, 1983) that was replaced by *The Revised Common Lectionary* (Nashville: Abingdon Press, 1992) in 1993. Although only Catholic and Episcopal churches are obligated to use a lectionary, a preference for the three-year lectionary is fostered in most mainline Protestant seminaries.

[3]*The Revised Common Lectionary* tends to have longer gospel and psalm selections. However, the most notable difference is that it provides two alternative patterns of Old Testament readings for each week following Trinity Sunday. One option follows the pattern established by the Catholic order where the Old Testament reading corresponds to the gospel; the other follows a pattern of semi-continuous readings from the Old Testament that was developed in *The Common Lectionary.*

[4]John White, *Christian Worship in Transition* (Nashville: Abingdon Press, 1976), 136.

[5]Vatican II, *SC*, 107.

[6]Gerard Sloyan, "The Jews and the New Roman Lectionary," *Face to Face* 2 (1976): 5-8; Eugene Fisher, "The Jewish People in Christian Preaching: A Catholic Perspective" in *The Jewish People in Christian Preaching*, ed. Darrell J. Fasching (New York: Edwin Mellen Press, 1984), 43-4; John T. Pawlikowski and James A. Wilde, eds., *When Catholics Speak about Jews* (Chicago: Liturgical Training Publications, 1987); Eileen Schuller, "Some Criteria for the Choice of Scripture Texts in the Roman Lectionary," in *Shaping English Liturgy: Studies in Honor of Archbishop Denis Hurley*, ed. Peter Finn and James M. Schellman (Washington, D.C.: Pastoral Press, 1990), 402-4; Gail Ramshaw, "The First Testament in the Christian Lectionaries," *Worship* 64 (1990): 494-510; Alan Detscher, "The Second Edition of the Lectionary for Mass," *Liturgy* 90 (1993): 6-7; Howard Clark Kee and Irvin J. Borowsky, eds., *Removing Anti-Judaism from the Pulpit* (New York: Continuum and Philadelphia: American Interfaith Institute, 1996).

[7]In addition, the same assertion is included in a selection in the Revised Common Lectionary on the Sunday that commemorates the Baptism of the Lord in Year A.

[8]John T. Pawlikowski, *What Are They Saying about Christian-Jewish Relations?* (New York: Paulist Press, 1980), 1.

[9]"Resolution on Anti-Semitism," Third Assembly of the World Council of Churches, New Delhi, India, 1961, in *Stepping Stones to Further Jewish-Christian Relations*, ed. Helga Croner (London: Stimulus Books, 1977), 72.

[10]Faith and Order Commission. World Council of Churches, "Report on Anti-Semitism," in Croner, *Stepping Stones*, 84.

[11]"Guidelines" (2), in *In Our Time: The Flowering of Jewish-Catholic Dialogue*, ed. Eugene Fisher and Leon Klenick (New York: Paulist, 1990), 33-34.

[12]Ibid., 34, n.1. It is of interest to note that the word Pharisaism never appears in the New Testament.

[13]Pontifical Biblical Commission, *The Interpretation of the Bible in the Church* (Boston: Pauline Books and Media, 1993), 117.

[14]Ibid., 125.

[15]This especially apt analogy was introduced by Clark M. Williamson and Ronald J. Allen, "Interpreting Difficult Texts," in Kee and Borowsky, *Removing Anti-Judaism from the Pulpit*, 39.

[16]Pontifical Biblical Commission, *The Interpretation of the Bible in the Church*, 125.

[17]Congregation for Divine Worship and the Discipline of the Sacraments, "*Liturgiam Authenticam*: On the Use of Vernacular Languages in the Publication of the Books of the Roman Liturgy" (37), *Origins* 31:2 (May 24, 2001): 23.

[18]Should the Catholic Church make any significant changes to its lectionary, it should be anticipated that similar changes would be made to *The Revised Common Lectionary*. It would be most desirable if both lectionaries were revised together recognizing that each lectionary would have differences regarding other issues.

[19]Approximately 60 percent of each gospel is included in the Catholic *ordo* and 65 percent of each gospel is included in *The Revised Common Lectionary*. The compilers used the findings of source critics to include representative pericopes from each distinguishable ancient tradition (Mark, Q, M, L, and John), although some stories are included from more than one tradition. A careful reconsideration could easily find important pericopes that are not already found in the selections even if the stories are already included from another gospel.

[20]Lectionary, "Introduction," 77.

[21]While much can be done with careful preaching, the pulpit is not a Bible study and the people of God do not affirm homilies as "Word of the Lord" or "Gospel."

[22]Vatican Commission for Religious Relations with the Jews. "Notes on the Correct Way to Present the Jews and Judaism in Preaching and Catechesis in the Roman Catholic Church" (3, 17), in Fisher and Klenick, *In Our Time,* 31.

[23]Alan F. Segal, *Rebecca's Children: Judaism and Christianity in the Roman World* (Cambridge: Harvard University Press, 1986), 141.

[24]Anthony Saldarini, "The Gospel of Matthew and the Jewish Christian Conflict," in *Social History of the Matthean Community: Cross-Disciplinary Approaches*, ed. David L. Bach (Minneapolis: Fortress, 1991), 4.

[25]Jack Dean Kingsbury, "Conclusion: Analysis of a Conversation," in *Social History of the Matthean Community*, 265.

[26]E. P. Sanders, *Jesus and Judaism* (Philadelphia: Fortress, 1985), 245-93 and Segal, *Rebecca's Children*.

[27]Segal, *Rebecca's Children*, xx.

[28]Other instances are found in Matthew 9:12-13 and in 21:31.

[29]Matthew 21:46 reports that Pharisees with the chief priests "tried to arrest him" and 27:62 identifies the Pharisees together with the chief priests who ask Pilate for Jesus' body.

[30]See note 3 above.

[31]The gospel reading is long and often so much is going on during Palm Sunday that it is doubtful if Christian assemblies will really catch this concluding detail.

[32]When the Roman Lectionary was formulated, the full implications of *Nostra Aetate* were not yet recognized. At the time many presumed that the problem was not really in the New Testament but was the fault of past interpretations. Subsequent studies have recognized that there really is a problem in the texts. One suspects that were the compilers devising the lectionary today they would have chosen to skip this verse.

[33]James Sanders, *From Sacred Story to Sacred Text* (Philadelphia: Fortress, 1987).

[34]Vincent Truijen, "Les evangiles de la Messe," *Questions liturgique et paroissiales* 65 (1984): 232.

[35]Sloyan, "The Jews and the New Roman Lectionary," 5.

[36]I acknowledge the assistance of Pamela A. Phillips from Nacogdoches, Texas, who helped me clarify the prose of this paper before publication.

The Choice and Function of Biblical Texts in the Post-Conciliar Rites for the Commendation of the Dying

James M. Donohue

The Rite for the Commendation of the Dying has been revised within the post-conciliar liturgical reform of the rites of the sick, the dying, and burial. The emergence of this reformed rite as it appears in the 1983 *Pastoral Care of the Sick: Rites of Anointing and Viaticum*[1] is the result of the adaptations made to the 1972 *Ordo commendationis morientium*, found in the Latin *editio typica* of *Ordo Unctionis infirmorum eorumque pastoralis curae*,[2] which itself was a revision of the *Ordo commendationis animae*, found in Title V, chapter vi of the 1614 *Rituale Romanum*.[3] This paper will examine the selection and function of the biblical texts in the 1614 *RR* and in the post-conciliar rites and will also investigate the further alterations made by the International Commission on English in the Liturgy (ICEL), which appear in the 1983 *PCS*.

The 1614 *Rituale Romanum*

The 1614 *RR* took shape from the efforts at reform and unity that followed the Council of Trent (1545-1563). Promulgated by the bull *Apostolicae Sedi* on June 17, 1614, the *RR* of Pope Paul V gradually replaced local diocesan rituals and gained an almost universal status, remaining virtually unchanged until the reforms following the Second Vatican Council (1962-1965).

In the 1614 *RR*, the *Ordo commendationis animae* is used after a number of sacramental rites that are devoted to the care of the dying: confession and absolution, viaticum, and extreme unction. Table 1 provides us with an overview of the arrangement of rites for the dying in the 1614 *RR*.

Table 1. The 1614 *RR*'s Arrangement of Rite

Confession and Absolution
Viaticum
Extreme Unction
Commendation of the Dying
Prayers on Expiration
Funeral Rites

Among the rites of the 1614 *RR*, attention should be given to the placement of the commendation rite in relation to viaticum and anointing. In the 1614 *RR*, communion given as viaticum is a distinct rite, separated from the other rites of the dying; it is no longer provided as the immediate preparation for death but is to be used early in the course of grave illness, and perhaps repeated. In addition, the communion rite itself is a penitential rite that emphasizes the forgiveness of sin, deliverance from pain and punishment, and the need for protection against the enemy. These concerns are illustrated in the formula that the 1614 *RR* uses when communicating the dying: "Receive brother, or sister, the food for your journey, the Body of our Lord Jesus Christ. May he keep/preserve you from the wicked enemy, and lead you into everlasting life."[4]

We should also note that the 1614 *RR* provides extreme unction as a sacrament of preparation for the dying, wherein this anointing (*unctio*) would be received by those who seem near death (*in extremis*). Following the administration of extreme unction, a rite whose focus is on the forgiveness of sins, spiritual healing, and protection from the evil one, the 1614 *RR's* commendation rite sought to move the dying person to a deeper personal conversion as assurance of forgiveness of sins, of deliverance from the pains and punishments of hell, and for hope and confidence in everlasting life.

The 1972 *OUI* and the 1983 *PCS*

Approximately three hundred and fifty years after promulgation of the 1614 *RR*, the Second Vatican Council called for a general restoration of the liturgy. *Sacrosanctum Concilium* (Article 74) foresaw separate rites for anointing the sick and for viaticum, as well as a continuous rite wherein a sick person is anointed after celebrating the sacrament of penance and before receiving viaticum.[5] This recommendation of providing rites for both sickness and dying was put into effect by the promulgation of the 1972 *OUI*. In addition, the 1972 Latin *editio typica* retained a chapter on the *Ordo commendationis morientium*, revising the rite found under Title V, chapter vi of the 1614 *RR*.

This Rite for the Commendation of the Dying was prepared and adapted by the International Commission on English in the Liturgy (ICEL) and approved by the National Conference of Catholic Bishops for American use in the 1983 *PCS*, where Part II treats of the Pastoral Care of the Dying. It is within "Part II: Pastoral Care of the Dying" that we find the Rite for the Commendation of the Dying (chapter six), which follows the Celebration of Viaticum (chapter five), and precedes the Prayers for the Dead (chapter seven).

The ritual context of the commendation rite for the dying has changed in the post-conciliar rites, relative to its position among the rites in the 1614 *RR*. We saw that in the 1614 *RR*, the *Ordo commendationis animae* is used after a number of sacramental rites that are devoted to the care of the dying: confession and absolution, viaticum, and extreme unction. In comparison, the commendation rite in the 1972 *OUI* and the 1983 *PCS* follows the sacraments of anointing of the sick and viaticum. Table 2 provides us with an overview of the arrangement of rites for the sick and the dying in the 1972 *OUI* and the 1983 *PCS*.

Table 2. The 1972 *OUI* and the 1983 *PCS*

Anointing of the Sick
Viaticum
Commendation of the Dying
Prayers on Expiration
Prayers after Death

The 1972 *OUI* and the 1983 *PCS* provide a different arrangement of the rites for the dying than the 1614 *RR*. In the first place, while provision is made to celebrate the sacrament of penance before the sacraments of anointing of the sick and viaticum (*OUI*, no. 65 and no. 100; *PCS*, no. 101 and no. 187), the rite itself is reserved to an appendix in the 1983 *PCS*.

Second, following the prescription of *Sacrosanctum Concilium*, no. 73, the sacrament of anointing of the sick in the 1972 *OUI* and the 1983 *PCS* is restored as a sacrament of the sick, administered to the seriously sick, not to those facing imminent death. This is reflected in the arrangement of rites in the 1983 *PCS*, where the sacrament of the anointing of the sick appears in "Part I: Pastoral Care of the Sick" and not in "Part II: Pastoral Care of the Dying." Further, the post-conciliar reforms clearly indicate that if death is imminent, viaticum, rather than anointing, is the sacrament of the dying (*PCS*, no. 174). This stands in sharp contrast with the relationship between the 1614 *RR*'s rites of extreme unction and the commendation of the soul. Following the administration of extreme unction, a rite whose focus is on the forgiveness of sins, spiritual healing, and protection from the evil one, the 1614 commendation rite sought to move the dying person to a deeper personal conversion as assurance for the forgiveness of sins, for deliverance from the pains and punishments of hell, and for hope and confidence in everlasting life.

Third, in contrast to the 1614 *RR*, which provided viaticum early in the course of grave illness, the 1972 *OUI* and the 1983 *PCS* administer viaticum as a rite for the dying that immediately precedes the commendation rite. Again, this is particularly clear in the arrangement of rites in the 1983 *PCS*, where the Celebration of Viaticum is located in Part II, Chapter Five, which immediately precedes the Commendation of the Dying, located in Chapter Six. In addition to retrieving the more ancient pattern of viaticum-commendation,[6] the post-conciliar reforms restore viaticum as a sacrament of passage in the strength of which a person passes through death with Christ, going from this world to the Father in the hope of resurrection (*PCS*, no. 175). No longer a rite of remote preparation for death concerned with readying the dying person for death by providing pardon, absolution, and remission of sins, warding off the power of the enemy, and alleviating the fear of punishment after death with the hope of everlasting life, the post-conciliar rite of viaticum is celebrated as a more proximate rite for the dying and is restored as a rite of passage in which the dying person, united with Christ, is strengthened with the Body and Blood of Christ in the hope of the resurrection (*PCS*, no. 26).

In its new ritual context, the commendation of the dying complements and seeks to sustain what has been realized in the preceding rite of viaticum. In viaticum, the dying person is united with Christ in his passage out of this world to the Father. Now the church, through the prayers and readings of the commendation of the dying, seeks to sustain this union until it is brought to fulfillment after death, assisting the dying person to overcome the natural human fear and anxiety concerning death that increases as the moment of death approaches (*PCS*, no. 212 and no. 215).

Finally, it is important to note that in addition to the changed ritual context of the commendation of the dying, the 1972 and 1983 postconciliar rites have changed the commendation rite itself, relative to its counterpart in the 1614 *RR*. Table 3 provides an overview of the prayer texts and readings in these commendation rites.

Table 3. Changed Commendation Rite

1614 *RR*	1972 *OUI*/1983 *PCS*
	Short biblical formulae
	Biblical readings (not inclusive of the passion and John 17)
Litany of Saints	Litany of Saints
Proficiscere	Proficiscere [Go forth . . .]
Deus misericors	
Commendo te	Commendo te [I commend . . .]
Suscipe Domine	Suscipe Domine [Welcome . . .]
Commendamus tibi	Commendamus tibi [Lord . . .]
Delicta iuventutis	
Devotional Prayers	Salve Regina [Hail, holy . . .]
John 17	
Passion (John)	
Passion Prayer	
Pss. 117[118] and 118[119]	
Prayers addressed to Christ	
Expiration-devotional ejaculations -Subvenite	Expiration-Subvenite [Saints of God . . .]

Selection and Function of Biblical Texts in the 1614 *RR*

Although there are many comments that could be made about the changes in the commendation and devotional prayer texts, we will focus our attention on the biblical selections in these commendation rites. The 1614 *RR's Ordo commendationis animae* contains a liturgical subunit composed of readings from John 17, the passion according to John and the passion prayer, as well as the selection of Psalms 117[118] and 118[119].

Johannine Readings

The 1614 *RR* includes two lengthy readings if the soul continues to labor: John 17:1-26 and John 18-19. These lections are to be read over the dying person by the priest. After the readings from John's gospel, the rubrics suggest that the dying person (or some other person for her) should say the prayer to "our Lord Jesus Christ about each article of his passion." Together with the Johannine readings, this prayer forms a liturgical subunit within the 1614 *RR's* commendation rite.

We find early evidence of the practice of reading the passions of the Lord to the dying in *OR XLIX*. This Roman *ordo*[7] provides us with a continuous rite that outlines the care for the dying person in his final moments through to the preparation, waking, and burial of the body. When the minister sees that the person is approaching the end, he is to be communicated. Then, as this *ordo* indicates, "the passions of the Lord are read facing the body of the sick person, whether presbyter or deacon, until the soul departs from the body."[8] It is unclear from this rubric whether "passions" refers to the different gospel accounts of the passion or to the sufferings of the Lord that each gospel recounts. Whatever the case, *OR XLIX* provides an early witness to the fact that the "passions" were read until the moment of death.

As Frankish practices came to dominate Roman ones, the reading of the passions of the Lord was replaced by other liturgical texts. So, for instance, among the eighth-century Gelasian sacramentaries only the *Autun Sacramentary* includes it, although it reverses the order of the reading of the passions and viaticum, and it specifies that the reading is to be taken from John's Gospel.[9]

The continued practice of reading the passions of the Lord is evidenced largely through monastic rituals and in the Roman liturgy, through the twelfth-century Roman Pontifical, which Michel Andrieu believed was dependent upon *OR XLIX*.[10] The pervasiveness of the Frankish pattern of rites for the dying can be seen, however, in the absence of the reading of the passions in the *Pontifical of the Roman Curia* of the thirteenth century, as well as in the *Franciscan Regula Breviary* of 1260,[11] which drew from and was very influential in disseminating these thirteenth-century curial rites. Despite this influence, however, two very important predecessors to the 1614 *RR*, Alberto Castellano's *Liber Sacerdotalis*[12] and Cardinal Santori's *Rituale Sacramentorum Romanum*,[13] both include readings from the passions of the Lord in their rites for the dying.

The 1614 *RR* specifies the reading of John's account of the passion and indicates that John 17:1-26, Jesus' farewell discourse to his disciples, is to be read before the passion account. John 17:1-26 is a particularly appropriate reading for one who is in the death struggle, for it embraces some pertinent images for the dying person. This Johannine chapter of Jesus' discourse, largely written in the first person, would have helped to enkindle a personal relationship with Jesus as it was read to the dying person. Known as Jesus' "Priestly Prayer," in it Jesus consecrates/sanctifies himself in death to the Father, for his followers: "And for them do I sanctify myself, that they also may be sanctified in truth" (17:19, DV).[14] Given the power over all flesh by God, Jesus prays "that he may give eternal life to all whom thou hast given him" (17:2, DV). Further, Jesus prays that God "shouldst keep them from evil" (17:15, DV) and that his followers "also may be one in us . . . that they may be one, as we also are one" (17:21-22, DV). Finally, in a line that echoes many of the six commendation prayers, Jesus wills that "where I am, they also whom thou hast given me may be with me; that they may see my glory which thou hast given me" (Jn 17:24, DV).

James McPolin summarizes the essential mood of this priestly prayer: "While on his way to his Father, about to offer himself to his Father in the most supreme expression of his love, Jesus intercedes for the disciples as a mediator and requests that they may receive through his death, leading to resurrection and through the gift of the Spirit, this communion of life with himself and his Father."[15] As part of the commendation rite, this is a very effective reading for the dying person. It encourages repentance for sin and increases devotion to Jesus, who has testified to his love and care through the sacrifice of his own life for his friends and through his promise of eternal life after death for all whom the Father has entrusted to him.

By placing the passion narrative alongside John 17:1-26, the dying person would be invited to see the passion itself as Jesus' sacerdotal act.[16] John's account of the passion and death portrays Jesus as having sovereign power over the situation. Jesus is the one who initiates the dialogue in the garden (18:4, 7), has power over those who have come to arrest him (18:6), dominates the conversation with Annas (18:20-23), stresses that Pilate has power over Jesus only because it is given to him from above, and gives over his spirit at death (19:30). In fact, throughout John's gospel Jesus is clear that he is the good shepherd who lays down his life for his friends (10:11, 15) and that no one takes his life from him, but he lays it down on his own accord (10:18). This is a sign of the great love that Jesus has for his friends (15:13). Even in death Jesus is portrayed as triumphant, for this is the moment in which the Father and the Son will be glorified (17:1), the moment in which the Son will pass over to the Father (13:1), the moment in which he will be lifted up on the cross (3:14, 8:28, 12:32).

Dying persons who listened to this account of Jesus' suffering and death would be inspired to have sorrow for their sins and to have confidence in their sovereign Lord, who freely chose to suffer and die out of love for them, his friends. This account of Christ's triumph over death and his passing over to the Father would have given hope to dying persons that they would be forgiven and that they also would be lifted up in death.

Passion Prayer

After the readings from John's gospel, the rubrics suggest that the dying person (or some other person for him) should say the prayer to "our Lord Jesus Christ about each article of his passion." The translated text reads:

V. We adore you, O Christ, and we bless you.
R. Because by the holy Cross you have redeemed the world.
O God, you did will, in order to redeem the world, to be born, to be circumcised, to be rejected by the Jews, to be betrayed with a kiss by the traitor Judas, to be bound in chains, to be led to the

slaughter as an innocent lamb, to be offered indecently as a spectacle to Annas, Caiaphas, Pilate, and Herod, to be accused by false witnesses, to be tortured by scourging and mockery, to be spat upon with spit, to be crowned with thorns, to be whipped, to be struck with a reed, to be blindfolded, to be stripped of your clothes, to be nailed to the cross, to be lifted up on the cross, to be counted among criminals, to be given drink with vinegar and gall, and to be pierced with a lance: you, Lord, through your sacred sufferings, which I am unworthy to call to mind, and through your holy cross and death, deliver me (or if another person says the prayer for the dying person: deliver your servant) from the pains of hell/underworld, and lead me to the place where you led the good thief who was crucified with you. You who live and reign with the Father and the holy Spirit for all eternity. Amen.[17]

While there is mention of Jesus' birth and circumcision, the prayer focuses on detailed aspects of his suffering and death. Since the dying persons would devoutly recite each article of Christ's passion, they would be led to articulate and further internalize the account of the passion that was just read to them. This prayer becomes the dying persons' opportunity to acknowledge each act of suffering that Christ endured. Aware of their own unworthiness and fearful of the pains or punishments of hell, the dying persons would recognize that it is through Christ's "sacred sufferings" and through Christ's "holy cross and death" that they would find their own deliverance as death approaches. While the memory of Christ's sufferings would inspire any repentance that was lacking, these same sufferings of Christ also served as the means to free the dying persons from the fear of the pains or punishments of hell and to inspire hope that they, like the good thief, would join Christ in his passing to glory.[18]

This mention of the good thief is the first reference to Luke 23:42-43 that we have seen in the 1614 *RR*'s rite of the commendation of the soul. The image of paradise is one of the themes that Bernard Botte judges to derive from the earliest stratum of the tradition of prayers for the dead. Botte suggests that paradise is the symbol of perfect happiness that human beings, created in the image of God, enjoyed in the "garden of delights" (Gen. 2:8), and from which they were exiled because of sin.[19] The good thief, crucified with Christ, availed himself of the opportunity of opening himself to Christ's forgiveness and love. So, now, the dying persons, remembering each of Christ's sufferings, pray with confidence that like the good thief they also will be delivered from the pains or punishments of hell (which they deserve, unworthy as they are) and be led by Christ into paradise.

David Power insightfully shows how the two Johannine readings and the passion prayer complement one another so that these three elements can be seen as a liturgical subunit. The reading from John 17:1-26, Jesus' sacerdotal prayer in which he makes an offering of himself on behalf of humankind, is followed by John's passion account, which relates Jesus' sacerdotal act. The reading of the John's passion is then followed by the passion prayer, which accentuates each of Jesus' sufferings. With this prayer, the dying persons, unworthy as they are, appeal to Jesus' sufferings as the means by which they will be delivered from the pains or punishments of hell. Through this exercise the dying persons are relieved of their fears and can approach their death with confidence and hope that they will join Christ in paradise. As Power notes, hope for release from the punishment for sin by reason of the merits of Christ's passion and confidence in a peaceful transition in communion with Christ are thus combined.[20]

Recitation of Psalms 117[118] and 118[119]

After the lections from John's gospel are read by the priest and the passion prayer is recited by the dying person, the rubrics suggest that Psalm 117[118], *Confitemini Domino*, and the first thirty-two verses of Psalm 118[119], *Beati immaculati*, may be recited.

The first psalm, *Confitemini Domino*, has a long history in the funeral rites, most commonly in combination with the antiphon *Aperite mihi*, where five of the eight Roman *ordines* report its use and over eighty manuscripts witness to its later presence. Some witnesses specify the use of this antiphon-psalm combination during the procession to the place of burial, others cite it as being sung during the station at the cemetery, and several witnesses do not state explicitly when it is sung. The majority of the Roman *ordines*, however, specify its use while the body is being placed into the tomb.[21]

Psalm 117[118] and Psalm 118[119] are designated as the two

psalms to be said after the commendation prayers in the *Pontifical of the Roman Curia* of the thirteenth century.[22] The *FRB* includes Psalm 119[120] with these same two psalms,[23] Castellano's *LS* includes only Psalm 117[118] and Psalm 118[119],[24] and Santori's *RSR* specifies the use of Psalm 117[118] and Psalm 118[119], but also instructs that the Gradual Psalms (119-133[120-134]) may be used if there is still time.[25]

Power suggests that the note of repentance and trust that the preceding liturgical unit inspired is carried over into the recitation of these psalms.[26] The first of the two psalms, *Confitemini Domino*, proclaims in thanksgiving and with confidence that the Lord is the dying persons' help. Aligning themselves with the psalmist, the dying persons cry out in the midst of their own distress, while continually proclaiming the steadfast love of God. In particular, through the psalmist, the dying persons maintain: "I shall not die, but live" (v. 17, DV). They also plead with God, "Open ye to me the gates of justice: I will go in to them, and give praise to the Lord" (v. 19, DV).

The second psalm, *Beati immaculati*, the longest in the psalter, is a meditation on the gift of God's law in the life of the psalmist. This same law provides the dying persons, moved to repentance by the memory of Christ's passion, with a means by which to judge their adherence and transgression.[27] Through a conversion that has been inspired in various ways throughout the rite (the pastor's encouragement to confess their sins, the commendation prayers' concern for the forgiveness of sins, the meditation on Christ's passion and death), their conformity to the law has become a comfort for the dying persons and the motivation with which to pray: "My soul hath slumbered through heaviness: strengthen thou me in thy words" (v. 28, DV). Through the psalmist's voice, the dying persons look forward to being lifted up from this sojourn to be able to follow the Lord's precepts more perfectly. Faithful to God's law, the dying persons cry: "I have stuck to thy testimonies, O Lord: put me not to shame" (v. 31, DV).

Selection and Function of Biblical Texts within the Post-Conciliar Commendation Rites

Among the new texts in the 1972 *OUI* and the 1983 *PCS*, the post-conciliar commendation rite has included short biblical formulae, which are listed in Table 4.

Table 4. Short Biblical Formulae

—Who will separate us from the love of Christ? (Rom. 8:35).

—Whether we live or whether we die, we are the Lord's (Rom. 14:8).

—We have an eternal home in heaven (2 Cor. 5:1).

—We will be with the Lord forever (1 Thess. 4:17).

—We will see God as he is (1 John 3:2).

—We have passed from death to life because we have loved one another (the brothers) (1 John 3:14).

—To you, O Lord, I lifted up my soul (Ps. 24[25]:1).

—The Lord is my light and my salvation (Ps. 26[27]:1).

—I believe that I will see the goodness of the Lord in the land of the living (Ps. 26[27]:13).

—My soul has thirsted for the living God (Ps. 41[42]:3).

—Though I walk in the valley of the shadow of death, I will fear no evil because you are with me (Ps. 22[23]:4).

—Come, blessed by my Father, said the Lord Jesus, inherit the kingdom prepared for you (Matt. 25:34).

—Amen I say to you: Today you will be with me in paradise, said the Lord Jesus (Luke 23:43).

—There are many rooms in my Father's house, said the Lord Jesus (John 14:2).

—The Lord Jesus said: I go to prepare a place for you, and I will take you to myself (John 14:2-3).

—I desire that where I am, they also will be with me, said the Lord Jesus (John 17:24).

—Everyone who believes in the Son has eternal life (John 6:40).

—Into your hands, O Lord, I commend my spirit (Ps. 30[31]:6a).

—Lord Jesus, receive my spirit (Acts 7:59).

—Holy Mary, pray for me.

—Saint Joseph, pray for me.

—Jesus, Mary, and Joseph, assist me in my last agony.

According to the introductory paragraphs, these texts are to be recited slowly, repeating the same one softly two or three times, with periods of silence interjected. Of the twenty-two texts supplied, nineteen are scriptural texts (drawn from the Vulgate in the 1972 *OUI* and from translations from original texts in the 1983 *PCS*). These texts embody hope and confidence in God's love and faithfulness, encouraging the dying persons to focus on an everlasting future filled with God's presence, heaven (paradise/kingdom), salvation, and eternal life. Having yearned for God throughout life, the dying persons are encouraged through these many short texts to trust in God, giving themselves over to God in these last moments of life. The last three texts call upon Jesus, Mary, and Joseph for their assistance in this struggle.

The post-conciliar rites have included numerous biblical readings (twenty-five readings in the *OUI* and twenty-one readings in the *PCS*), but they have also omitted certain readings from the 1614 *RR's* commendation rite: John 17, the passion from John, as well as Psalms 117[118] and 118[119]. Marked by the emphasis on trust in the Lord's promise of eternal life and of resurrection that characterizes the rites of the dying (*PCS*, no. 161), the post-conciliar commendation rite is permeated with references in these biblical texts that encourage the dying persons to accept death in the hope of eternal life and of resurrection, and to encourage imitation of Christ's patient suffering and dying. Table 5 lists the selection of texts in the 1972 *OUI* and in the 1983 *PCS*.

Table 5. Selection of Biblical Texts

1972 *OUI*[28]	1983 *PCS*[29]
[Strengthen the feeble hands.]	*Isa. 35:1-10
Job 19:23-27a [I know that my redeemer lives.]	Job 19:23-27
Ps. 22[23] [The Lord is my Shepherd.] Ps. 24[25]:1, 4b-11 [To you I lift up my soul.] Ps. 90[91] [You who dwell in the shelter of the Most High.] Ps. 113[114]:1-8 [When Israel went out from Egypt.] Ps. 114[116]:3-5 [I called on the name of the Lord.]	Ps. 23 Ps. 25:1, 4-11 Ps. 91

Ps. 120[121]:1-4 [I lift up my eyes to the hills.] Ps. 122[123] [To you I lift up my eyes.]	Ps. 121:1-5, 7-8 *Ps. 123
1 Cor. 15:1-4 [I handed on to you . . . that Christ died for our sins.] *1 Cor. 15:12-20 [If there is no resurrection of the dead, then neither is Christ risen.] *2 Cor. 5:1, 6-10 [We have an everlasting home in heaven.] 1 John 4:16 [God is love.] Rev. 21:1-5a, 6-7 [God our Father is the God of newness and life.] *Rev. 22:17, 20-21 [Come, Lord Jesus.]	*1 Cor. 15:1-4 *1 Cor. 15:12-20 *2 Cor. 5:1, 6-10 1 John 4:16 Rev. 21:1-5a, 6-7 *Rev. 22:17, 20-21
Matt. 25:1-13 [Jesus bids us be prepared for our ultimate destiny, which is eternal life.] Mark 15:33-37 [My God, my God, why have you forsaken me?] Mark 16:1-8 [And very early on the first day of the week . . . they went to the tomb.] Luke 22:39-46 [Father, if it is your will, take this cup from me.] Luke 23:42-43 [Today you will be with me in paradise.]	Matt. 25:1-13 Luke 22:39-46
    Luke 24:1-8 [Why do you search for the living among the dead?] *John 6:35-40 [It is the will of my Father that I will not lose what he has given me.] John 6:37-40 [No one who comes will I ever reject.] *John 6:54-59 [Whoever eats this bread has eternal life.] John 14:1-6, 23, 27 [Do not let your hearts be troubled.]	Luke 23:44-49 [Father, into your hands I commend my spirit.] Luke 24:1-8 *John 6:35-40 John 6:37-40 *John 6:53-58 John 14:1-6, 23, 27

The excerpts from the passion narrative in the 1972 *OUI* and the 1983 *PCS* are significant alterations to the 1614 *RR*'s *Ordo commendationis animae*, which includes the full passion narrative from John, preceded by Jesus' sacerdotal prayer from John 17 and followed by the passion prayer, which lists the individual sufferings and indignities endured by Christ. As we have seen, in this context the reading of the passion serves to move the dying persons to a deeper personal contrition for sins and at the same time allows the dying persons to appeal to Christ as the sufficient reason to release them from the pains and punishments of hell, thus freeing them from fear and inspiring hope and confidence that they will join Christ in paradise.

As excerpts of the passion narrative, the texts in the commendation rite of the 1972 *OUI* and the 1983 *PCS* function differently. Instead of anxiety and fear concerning the pains and punishments of the afterlife, the concern of the contemporary Christian is the fear and anxiety of death itself, something which is innate in all human beings (*PCS*, no. 215). The pericopes selected from the passion narrative in the 1983 *PCS* (Luke 22:39-46 and Luke 23:44-49) and in the 1972 *OUI* (Mark 15:33-37, Luke 22:39-46, 23:42-43) are meant to assist the dying Christians in their anguish through the example of Christ who accepts his death and surrenders with trust into the Father's hands.

Two passion excerpts, one from Mark and one from Luke, illustrate this point. In its starkness the Marcan account of Christ's death (Mark 15:33-37) indicates that Jesus spent six hours of agony on the cross. His last words ("My God, my God, why hast thou forsaken me?" [v. 34, DV]) and death are the ultimate act of self-giving and trust in the face of total abandonment. As for the Lucan narrative, only its account of the agony in the garden (Luke 22:39-46) depicts Jesus' agony as causing his sweat to become as drops of blood. Meeting this anguish with prayer ("And being in an agony, he prayed the longer" [v. 43, DV]), Jesus commits himself in love and obedience to the Father. These two passages assist dying persons to overcome their own anxiety about death, for the dying persons can now rely upon Christ, who in trust and obedience has suffered and died, thus overcoming death itself. Further the dying persons, with hope placed in the power of Christ's death, have before them an example of the patient suffering and dying of Christ, which they are called to imitate. Through these pericopes, the dying Christians are called to imitate this example but also to be united or configured with Christ in their suffering, so that "linked with the paschal mystery and patterned on the dying Christ, they will hasten forward to resurrection in the strength which comes from hope."[30]

Hence, while there may be less emphasis or worry about sin and the punishment due to sin—a prime concern of the Johannine passion reading in the 1614 *RR*—contemporary Christians continue to experience great anxiety and fear about death itself, and the excerpts of the passion narrative assist the dying persons to overcome this anguish in the power of Christ's death. The gospel excerpts used in the post-conciliar commendation rites point to a change in pastoral care that a contemporary Christian approach to death summons.

Further Alterations by ICEL

In the 1983 *PCS* ICEL has by and large followed the order of the 1972 *OUI*. However, by drawing on the revisions of several Roman liturgies published over a number of years after Vatican II, ICEL has constituted a *ritus continuus* which joins into one *ordo* initiation, penance, anointing of the sick, visits to the sick, viaticum, commendation of the dying, and prayers immediately following death.

The principal changes in content and meaning have to do with the particular selection of prayers and biblical texts and with their translation from the Latin originals, which give rise to some problems of meaning. Each of these changes in the biblical texts has an effect on the attitude to dying and the afterlife.

The Selection of Biblical Texts

ICEL has made some significant changes to the 1972 *OUI*'s *Ordo commendationis morientium* in its selection of biblical texts. The 1972 *OUI* and the 1983 *PCS* have twenty-one readings in common for use in the commendation rite. However, the 1983 *PCS* has omitted five readings and has added one other reading to those included in the 1972 *OUI*. Two of the psalms, Psalms 113[114]:1-8 and 114[116]:3-5, are omitted from the 1983 *PCS*'s commendation rite but are included in the *Order of Christian Funerals*. Perhaps ICEL thought them more suitable to funerals than to prayers for the dying. The other omissions include two excerpts from the passion narratives, Mark 15:33-37 and Luke 23:42-43, and the resurrection account in Mark 16:1-8. The reading of Luke 23:42 appears as a Short Text, although its rich history in the commendation rites with the pertinent themes for the dying (forgiveness, trust, hope) calls for its inclusion as a biblical reading. The 1983 *PCS*'s addition of Luke 23:44-49 indicates a preference for the Lucan account of the death of Jesus over the Marcan. The omission of Mark 15:33-37 (and Mark 16:1-8), in an attempt to eliminate "discomforting" readings, may prevent the very acceptance of the anxiety of death that the rite intends to support. The elimination of certain verses of pericopes in the 1983 *PCS*, such as in Psalm 122[123],[31] would come under the same criticism.

The Translation of the Biblical Texts

In addition to the change in the selection of biblical texts, there are some differences of meaning that arise between the shared biblical texts of the 1972 *OUI* and the 1983 *PCS*. This change of meaning results from the different translations used by each ritual. While the 1972 *OUI* works with the Vulgate, ICEL gives translations of biblical texts from the original languages. Thus Isaiah 35:7b in its contemporary translation does not mention "the dens where the dragons dwelt." The new translation, "the abode where the jackals lurk," is less likely to encourage the dying person to think of the dangers of the afterlife alluded to in this verse in its Vulgate version.[32]

Another passage, Job 19:23-27 (Job 19:23-27a is specified in the 1972 *OUI*), is retained in the 1983 *PCS*, but it suggests a strikingly different understanding of the afterlife in the Vulgate text, upon which the 1972 *OUI* relies, than in the New American Bible translation, upon which the 1983 *PCS* relies. The verses from the Vulgate in their translation in the Douay Rheims Version read:

> (23) Who will grant me that my words may be written? Who will grant me that they may be marked down in a book?
> (24) With an iron pen and in a plate of lead, or else be graven with an instrument in flint stone?
> (25) For I know that my Redeemer liveth, and in the last day I shall rise out of the earth.
> (26) And I shall be clothed again with my skin, and in my flesh I shall see my God.
> (27a) Whom I myself shall see, and my eyes shall behold, and not another. (DV)[33]

In the NAB these same verses read:

> (23) Oh, would that my words were written down! Would that they were inscribed in a record:
>
> (24) That with an iron chisel and with lead they were cut in the rock forever!
>
> (25) But as for me, I know that my Vindicator lives, and that he will at last stand forth upon the dust;
>
> (27) Whom I myself shall see: my own eyes, not another's, shall behold him,
>
> (26) And from my flesh I shall see God; my inmost being is consumed with longing.

A note in *The Catholic Study Bible* edition of the NAB indicates that the meaning of this passage is obscure because the original text has been poorly preserved and the ancient versions do not agree among themselves. It is certain that Job expresses his belief in a future vindication by God, but the time and manner of this vindication are undefined. In the Vulgate text Job indicates a belief in physical resurrection after death ("and in the last day I shall rise out of the earth. And I shall be clothed again with my skin, and in my flesh I shall see my God"), while the Hebrew and the other ancient versions are less specific.[34] In addition, the Vulgate's use of the name "redeemer" suggests a christological source for redemption,[35] something which the NAB translation leaves more ambivalent.

The Vulgate text is in conformity with the earliest Christian understanding of the afterlife, whereby the faithful departed were believed to rest in peace and await the Day of the Lord in the hope of the resurrection. But this text and others from Job lend themselves to a later reinterpretation in the Middle Ages that connected the complaints, fears, and hopes expressed in the words of Job no longer with immediate physical death, but with the sufferings of the souls in the afterlife before the Second Coming of Christ.[36] Read from either of these two perspectives, as it is rendered in the Vulgate, Job 19:23-27 would serve to reinforce the hope of the dying person to be raised up from rest or suffering on the Day of the Lord, to enjoy forever the vision of God. In its NAB translation, however, this reading gives voice to the dying person who is assured and gives testimony that at the end of the passage from death, he/she will enjoy forever the vision of God. However, in the contemporary translation of these verses the belief in the resurrection is no longer affirmed.

Hence, from our few selected examples, we can see that the perils of the afterlife are muted in the NAB translation, and in the case of Job 19 belief in the resurrection is no longer affirmed as it is in the Vulgate text. These two examples indicate that ICEL's translation of biblical texts from the original languages does give rise, in a few instances, to some problems of meaning.

Conclusion

Changing attitudes toward death and the afterlife require changes in the assistance that is provided for the dying. The 1972 Vatican reform of the commendation of the dying involves a changed ritual context, a changed ritual, and changed texts that reflect these changing attitudes to death and the afterlife. No longer so concerned about the need for forgiveness of sins and deliverance from the pains and punishment of hell, the 1972 *Ordo commendationis morientium* invites the dying person to share in the paschal mystery, completing what has begun in baptism, and to share in the hope of eternal communion with God and the resurrection of the body. In order to accomplish this goal, the readings (and prayers) of the commendation rite attempt to assist the dying person to overcome the anxiety and fear of death in the power of Christ, who in dying destroyed death, encouraging him/her to imitate Christ in his suffering and death and to accept his/her own fear and anxiety about death in the hope of heavenly life and of resurrection. For its part, the 1983 ICEL translations of biblical (and euchological texts) reflect further theological complexities, such as the changed meaning of some biblical texts in their translation from original languages.[37]

Whatever shortcomings one may find in the commendation rite of the 1983 *PCS*, there is a richness of prayers, litanies, aspirations, psalms, and readings for use by the minister and the members of the family who are present. Undoubtedly, even in the absence of a priest or deacon, other members of the community should be prepared to carry out this ministry, for their presence shows more clearly that this Christian dies in the communion of the church (*OUI*, no. 142; *PCS*, no. 213). In all its richness, this rite is offered by the church to strengthen and comfort a dying Christian in passage from this life, to help him/her to "embrace death in mysterious union with the crucified and risen Lord, who awaits them in the fullness of life" (*PCS*, no. 163).

Notes

[1]*Pastoral Care of the Sick: Rites of Anointing and Viaticum*, the Roman Ritual Revised by Decree of the Second Vatican Ecumenical Council and Published by Authority of Pope Paul VI, Approved for Use in the Dioceses of the United States of America by the National Conference of Catholic Bishops and Confirmed by the Apostolic See, Prepared by the International Commission on English in the Liturgy: A Joint Commission of Catholic Bishops' Conferences (New York: Catholic Book Publishing, 1983). This rite is hereafter referred to as *PCS*.

[2]*Ordo Unctionis infirmorum eorumque pastoralis curae*, Rituale Romanum ex decreto sacrosancti oecumenici Concilii Vaticani II instauratum auctoritate Pauli PP. VI promulgatum, editio typica (Rome: Typis Polyglottis Vaticanis, 1972). This rite is hereafter referred to as *OUI*.

[3]*Ritvale Romanvm Pavli V. Pont. Max. ivssv editvm* (Romae: Ex Typographia Reuerendae Camerae Apostolicae, 1614; Paris: CIPOL [Centre international de publications oecuméniques des liturgies], Documents en microfiches, 1973). This ritual is hereafter referred to as *RR*. There are no title or chapter numbers in this edition of the 1614 *RR*; they were introduced in the nineteenth century. As new material is included in the 1614 *RR* in the form of either a new title (such as Title III, Confirmation, in the 1952 edition) or a new chapter (such as chapter six, Apostolic Blessing, in the 1752 edition), the numbering of titles and chapters continues to change. In the 1614 edition of the *RR*, the *Ordo commendationis animae* appears in what would be the sixth chapter of Title V, *De sacramento extremae unctionis*.

[4]The Latin text, found in *RR*, 55, reads: "*Accipe frater, vel soror, Viaticum Corporis Domini nostri IESV Christi, qui te custodiat ab hoste maligno, et perducat in vitam aeternam.*"

[5]The Latin text, found in *Decrees of the Ecumenical Councils*, vol. 2, ed. Norman P. Tanner, trans. Edward Yarnold (Washington, D.C.: Georgetown University Press, 1990), 834, reads: "*Praeter ritus seiunctos unctionis infirmorum et viatici, conficiatur ordo continuus secundum quem unctio aegroto conferatur post confessionem et ante receptionem viatici.*" The English translation, found in the same work (p. 834), reads: "To supplement the separate rites of the anointing of the sick and communion for the dying, a continuous rite is to be drawn up, in which a sick person will be anointed after making a confession and before receiving communion."

[6]*Ordo Romanus XLIX* provides an early witness to a different context and meaning for viaticum. One of the various *ordines* that penetrated Gallican territory during the period of 700 to 750, *OR XLIX* is totally focused on the resurrection on

the last day. Communion given as the person approaches the point of departure is given as the defense and help against death and for assurance of resurrection. The passions of the Lord, read after communion has been received until the soul departs the body, serve to provide hope and confidence for the dying person that, united with the Lord, he/she too will pass from this world to eternal life. As late as the thirteenth century, we find holy communion administered in close proximity to the commendation of the dying person. In time, however, viaticum became separated from the moment of death by the rites of extreme unction and the commendation of the soul. The *Franciscan Regula Breviary* of 1260 served to spread and perpetuate the separation of viaticum from the hour of death. Two important sixteenth-century liturgical rituals, Alberto Castellano's *Liber Sacerdotalis* (1523) and Julius Santori's *Rituale Sacramentorum Romanum* (1584-1602), give witness to this entrenched practice, which was taken up and continued in the 1614 *RR*.

[7]Michel Andrieu believes that *OR XLIX* is authentically Roman, although there are some internal indications of a monastic influence, such as the organized rank and service that one would expect to find in a monastery. See Michel Andrieu, *Ordo XLIX, in Les textes: Ordines XXXV-XLIX*, vol. 4 of *Les Ordines romani du haut moyen âge*, Spicilegium Sacrum Lovaniense, no. 28 (Louvain: Université Catholique de Louvain, 1956), 523-525.

[8]The Latin text, found in Andrieu, *OR XLIX*, vol. 4, 529, reads: "*Post communionem percepta, legenda sunt passionis dominice ante corpus infirmi seu presbiteri seu diaconi, quousque egrediatur anima de corpore.*" See David N. Power, "Commendation of the Dying and the Reading of the Passion," in *Rule of Prayer, Rule of Faith: Essays in Honor of Aidan Kavanagh, O.S.B.*, ed. Nathan Mitchell and John F. Baldovin (Collegeville, Minnesota: The Liturgical Press, 1996), 285.

[9]*Liber Sacramentorum Augustodunensis*, ed. O. Heiming, CCSL, vol. 159B (Turnholti: Typographi Brepols Editores Pontificii, 1984), 241-242, no. 1914. See Power, "Commendation of the Dying and the Reading of the Passion," 283.

[10]Andrieu, *OR XLIX*, vol 4, 523-525. See Power, "Commendation of the Dying and the Reading of the Passion," 284-285.

[11]The *Franciscan Regula Breviary* of 1260 was issued with a three-part Ritual for the Last Sacraments, entitled *Ordo fratrum minorum secundum consuetudinem Romane ecclesie*. A critical edition has been made available in English in "The Ritual for the Last Sacraments (1260)," in *The Ordinals by Haymo of Faversham and Related Documents (1243-1307)*, ed. S. J. P. van Dijk, *Sources of the Modern Liturgy*, vol. 2 (Leiden: Brill, 1963), 385-408. This ritual is hereafter referred to as the *FRB*. See Power, "Commendation of the Dying and the Reading of the Passion," 286.

[12]Alberto Castellano, *Liber Sacerdotalis nuperrime ex libris s[an]c[t]e romane eccl[es]ie et q[ua]rundum aliarum ecclesiarum: et ex antiq[ui]s codicibus apostolice: et ex iuriu[m] sanctionibus et ex doctorum ecclesiasticorum scriptis ad revere[n]dorum patrum sacerdotu[m] parrochialium et a[n]i[m]arum cura[m] habentiu[m] com[m]odum collectus atq[u]e compositus: ac auctoritate Sanctissime*

D. D[omi]ni n[ost]ri Leonis decimi approbatus. In q[uo] continentur et officia o[mn]ium sacr[ament]orum et resolut[i]o[n]es o[mn]ium dubiorum ad ea pertine[n]tium: Et o[mn]ia alia q[uae] a sacerdotibus fieri possunt: q[uae] q[ua]m sint pulchra et utilia ex i[n]dice collige (Venice: M. Sessam and P. De Ravanis, 1523; Paris: CIPOL [Centre international de publications oecuméniques des liturgies], Documents en microfiches, 1973). This ritual is hereafter referred to as the *LS*.

[13]Julius Antonius Cardinal Santori, *Ritvale Sacramentorvm Romanvm Gregorii Papae XIII Pont. Max. ivssv editvm* (Rome: 1584-1602; Paris: CIPOL [Centre international de publications oecuméniques des liturgies], Documents en microfiches, 1973). This ritual is hereafter referred to as the *RSR*.

[14]In order to keep closer to the original Latin meaning of the biblical texts as they appear in the 1614 *RR*, translations from the Douay Rheims Version (DV) will be used. See *The Holy Bible: Douay Rheims Version*, rev. Bishop Richard Challoner, 1749-1752 (Baltimore: John Murray Company, 1899; reprint, Rockford, Ill.: Tan Books and Publishers, Inc., 1989).

[15]James McPolin, *John*, New Testament Message Series, vol. 6 (Wilmington, Del.: Michael Glazier, 1979), 190.

[16]Power, "Commendation of the Dying and the Reading of the Passion," 290.

[17]The Latin text, found in *RR*, 96, reads:

"V. *Adoramus te, Christe, et benedicimus tibi.*

R. *Quia per sanctam Crucem tuam redemisti mundum.*

*Deus, qui pro redemptione mundi voluisti nasci, circumcidi, a Iudaeis reprobari, a Iuda traditore osculo tradi, vinculis alligari; sicut agnus innocens ad victimam duci, atque conspectibus Annae, Caiphae, Pilati, & Herodis indecenter offerri; a falsis testibus accusari, flagellis, et opprobriis vexari, sputis conspui, spinis coronari, colaphis caedi, arundine percuti, facie velari, vestibus exui, cruci clauis affigi, in cruce leuari, inter latrones deputari, felle et aceto potari, et lancea vulnerari: Tu Domine per has sanctissimas poenas tuas, quas ego indignus recolo, et per sanctam crucem et mortem tuam libera me (**vel si alius dicit pro eo,** libera famulum tuum **N.**) a poenis inferni, et perducere digneris, quo perduxisti latronem tecum crucifixum. Qui cum Patre, et Spiritu sancto viuis, et regnas in secula seculorom. Amen.*"

[18]Power, "Commendation of the Dying and the Reading of the Passion," 290-291.

[19]Bernard Botte, "The Earliest Formulas of Prayer for the Dead," in *Temple of the Holy Spirit: Sickness and Death of the Christian in the Liturgy*, trans. Matthew J. O'Connell (New York: Pueblo Publishing Company, 1983), 19.

[20]Power, "Commendation of the Dying and the Reading of the Passion," 290-291.

[21]Damien Sicard, *La Liturgie de la mort dans l'église latine des origines à la réforme carolingienne*, Liturgiewissenschaftliche Quellen und Forschungen, vol. 63 (Münster: Aschendorff, 1978), 224-226.

²²*Le pontifical de la curie romaine au XIIIe siècle*, 2:501, in *Le pontifical romain au moyen-âge*, ed. Michel Andrieu, Studie e Testi, vols. 86, 87, 88, 99 (Vatican City, 1937, 1940, 1940, 1941).

²³*FRB*, 392.

²⁴*LS*, 135r-138v.

²⁵*RSR*, 345-352.

²⁶Power, "Commendation of the Dying and the Reading of the Passion," 291.

²⁷Ibid.

²⁸In no. 144, the 1972 *OUI* lists a number of readings to be used from the Old Testament, the Psalms, the New Testament, and the Gospels. Among the various additional texts used in the rites for the sick, found in Chapter VII, there are several for the dying. These texts will be designated with an asterisk.

²⁹In addition to the biblical selections listed, the 1983 *PCS*, no. 218, allows for a selection from "Part III: Readings, Responses, and Verses from Sacred Scripture," where some of the 1972 *OUI* texts are included. These texts will be designated with an asterisk.

³⁰*Gaudium et spes (The Pastoral Constitution of the Church in the Modern World)*, art. 22, in *The Documents of Vatican II*, ed. Walter M. Abbott (New York: Guild Press, 1966), 221.

³¹Although this psalm aptly captures the distress of the dying person who hopes for the Lord ("so our eyes on the Lord, our God, till he have pity on us" [v. 2c, NAB]), ICEL has omitted verses 3 and 4 of this psalm. Perhaps ICEL wanted to avoid verses that it thought would be discomforting to the dying: "we are more than sated with contempt; our souls are more than sated with the mockery of the arrogant, with the contempt of the proud" (vv. 3b-4, NAB). However, the attempt to "comfort" the dying persons may actually discomfort them by suppressing the true anxiety of death that is captured in this psalm, as well as in Psalm 114[116].

³²The omission of terms that refer to suffering in the afterlife and to eternal death and damnation is in keeping with the 1969 *Ordo Exsequiarum* and is more apparent in the prayer texts.

³³The Latin text, taken from *Biblia sacra iuxta vulgatam clementinam nova editio* (Vatican City: Typis Polyglottis Vaticanis, 1951), reads: "*Quis mihi tribuat ut scribantur sermones mei? Quis mihi det ut exarentur in libro stilo ferreo, et plumbi lamina vel celte sculpantur in silice? Scio enim quod redemptor meus vivit, et in novissimo die de terra surrecturus sum. Et rursum circumdabor pelle mea et in carne mea videbo Deum meum. Quem visurus sum ego ipse, et oculi mei conspecturi sunt, et non alius.*"

³⁴*New American Bible*, Including the Revised Psalms and the Revised New Testament, Translated from the Original Languages with Critical Use of All the Ancient Sources, in *The Catholic Study Bible*, ed. Donald Senior et al. (New York: Oxford University Press, 1990), 626.

³⁵Knud Ottosen (*The Responsories and Versicles of the Latin Office of the Dead* [Aarhus, Denmark: Aarhus University Press, 1993], 59) comments: "Whatever the correct meaning of the Hebrew word (*Goel*) in the biblical text may be, the

Latin translation, *redemptor*, has always, since Gregory the Great, been interpreted as identical with the Son of God, who, by his own death, has paid the ransom for the liberation of man."

[36]Ibid., 47.

[37]A study of the prayer texts also would reveal translation problems resulting in euchological texts that are narrow in meaning, prosaic, and conceptual, rather than poetic and richly imaginative.

BROADENING HORIZONS: SCRIPTURE AND COMPARATIVE THEOLOGY

Theology and Sacred Scripture Reconsidered in the Light of a Hindu Text

Francis X. Clooney

One way to explore the theme of "Theology and Sacred Scripture" from a comparative perspective, with special attention to India, would be to attempt a summation and overview of the history of ritual, mytho-logical, and contemplative holy texts in traditional India, the development of categories and theologies of scripture, revelation and inspiration, and the rise of vernacular literatures and the consequent expansion of canons beyond Sanskrit-language sources. This approach would be important and instructive; by it we would gain an overview of how "sacred scripture" and "theology" are understood and problematized in a tradition other than our own Catholic tradition. But so massive a project, however worthwhile, is best pursued in a more leisurely context that would allow for a comprehensive exposition of all the detailed information involved.[1]

This descriptive project is also secondary, because at a fundamental level we need to think about how Christians should encounter and learn from the sacred scriptures and theologies of other traditions, and to connect such learning to our already developed understandings of the Bible and what we learn from it. Comparative reflection of this sort can only occur to a limited extent on a general level; it is best pursued in terms of specific examples. I have therefore chosen to reflect on a single Hindu text and its reception in a Hindu tradition, so as to open up some new avenues for reflection on theology in relation to sacred scripture. First, then, let us consider the text that will be the subject of our reflection.

A Hindu Text and Context

1 He has exalted me for all time,
day after day he has made me himself
and by me he now sings himself in sweet Tamil
my Lord, my first one, my abiding light—what shall I sing of
him?

2 What shall I sing of him?
become one with my sweet life
he makes me sing sweet songs in my own words,
by his own words,
my marvelous one now praises himself
first among the three forms, singing ahead of me.

3 Ahead of me, it was clear,
he came and entered my tongue, he was there from the first
and to his first pure devotees sang himself in good sweet songs;
he is first in my mouth—can I ever forget my father?

4 Can I ever forget my father?
he has become me and he himself faultlessly sings himself in
    these songs;
he exalts me, he keeps on mending this doer of unequaled evil
I have seen his excellence.

5 I have seen his excellence and was mended,
but even then I lacked the excellence to sing proper sweet songs,
until he made unlovely me himself,
the highest one whom all the earth praises
for the sweet songs he sings by me.

6 It is not by the sweet songs of the best singers
that he sings his song about himself
but now he has come near, he makes me one with himself,
by me he sings fine songs about himself, my Lord of Vaikunta.[2]

7 My Lord of Vaikunta completely destroys my strong deeds,
he is wielder of the pike, making me himself and by me

singing melodious sweet songs in praise of himself as Vaikunta's
  Lord;
he is my helper, will I ever have pondered him enough?

8 Will I ever have enough of praising
the Lord whose lovely hand holds the discus,
will I ever have enough if earth and sky and water should all melt
together and I should drink them up?
he made unlovely me himself, he gained excellence for himself
through me, such is his nature.

9 Would I have enough of him
if I should drink for all times past and future
the excellence of Shri's Lord[3]
who has the ability to do everything well?
he made me himself and now I cannot forget how
I sing many sweet songs suitable to his excellence because he
  helps me.

10 He helps me, so I thought I would give my life to him in return,
but then I reconsidered, since that too is totally his;
this father sings himself in sweet songs by me,
there is nothing at all I can do for him, neither here nor there.

11 "Neither here nor there can anything exist without the Holy
  Lord."
Shatakopan from glorious Kuruhur[4] was the sort to see this, and so
he sang in this way these ten verses from his thousand, and so
however you sing them, their fruit is bliss.[5]

This song is one of a hundred of eleven verses each, which together comprise a work entitled *Tiruvaymoli*, meaning the "Word (*moli*)
of the Holy (*tiru*) Mouth (*vay*)" or "the Holy (*tiru*) Word (*moli*) of
Mouth (*vay*)." *Tiruvaymoli* is composed in the south Indian Tamil
language, probably in the ninth century during a major flourishing of
devotional writing in south India where Vaishnava saints (known as
alvars, "those immersed in God"), and Shaiva saints (known as
nayanmars, "the masters"), praised respectively Vishnu and Shiva as
supreme universal Lords.[6] The themes of the songs in *Tiruvaymoli* are

varied, but in one way or another all of them are Vaishnava, meaning focused on Vishnu, who, along with his consort Shri Lakshmi, is honored as the source and lord of the universe, liberator of all conscious beings, the personal and most attractive object of the desire and love of all individual persons.[7] *Tiruvaymoli* is attributed to Shatakopan, a south Indian Hindu devotee of Vishnu—Narayana, Krishna, Rama— who is revered as the foremost of the alvars and who by tradition was a member of the fourth, *shudra* caste.

The song cited above is the ninth song in the seventh decade of songs (and so, from now on, we will designate it simply as 7.9). Although it seems to be a programmatic song, it is not given any privileged place in the whole, since it only appears approximately two-thirds of the way through the whole and is not marked in any special way. Yet it does have interesting features: it is one of just four songs in the hundred that speak to the topic of the alvar's own self-understanding as a poet and, unlike many of the songs in *Tiruvaymoli* that are local in reference and distinguished by specific Hindu themes, this song has little by the way of geographical or mythic reference. Shatakopan seems deliberately to focus on his own internal state and God's action within himself, perhaps with the intent of speaking as universally as possible. I have chosen the song because it is beautiful, because its style and content make it seem all the more welcoming of our consideration and response, and, as is appropriate to this volume's theme, because it focuses on inspiration, sacred speech, tradition, revelation, and the interconnection of divine and human words. I hope to show what we can learn from this lovely song and, more important, how reflecting on it illuminates how we go about learning from scripture and doing theology in a theological comparative context.

First of all, before any elaborate speculation, it is important to stay with the text, becoming familiar with it and learning to read it and perhaps even recite it. Ideally, this should be done in Tamil, but in my opinion reading it in English will also be beneficial. Much can be achieved simply by reading it again and again until we have learned it, made its words and themes our own simply by hearing them over and over. In this way we will be able to appropriate its rhythms, images, and meanings as resources for our own spiritual and theological reflection. Were we to move too quickly to themes and issues of methodology, we would miss the opportunity actually to hear the song and take it to heart. It is also central to the Shrivaishnava tradition that songs like this be memorized, recited, or sung, and featured as a part of the regular life of the community, with the aim of infusing it into the lives of devotees, insuring its living heritage in people whose lives are shaped by it.[8] Similarly, in some small way, our repeating the song as often as we can is an excellent starting point for beginning to learn from it as well, and I recommend that readers try this.

In addition to being recited, the song has also been thought about and carefully investigated in the Hindu tradition, treated with the deepest intellectual respect and assumed to be instructive in its every word. It has generated a long tradition of commentary, during which the community cumulatively fashioned a definite perspective on the song and its meaning, by itself and as part of *Tiruvaymoli*. Most famously, great teachers—in the twelfth century Pillan, and in the thirteenth century Nanjiyar, Nampillai, Periyavacchan Pillai, Tiru Koneri Dasai (all of them in a tradition that looks to the theologian Ramanuja, who wrote in Sanskrit, as their founder)—expounded the songs and their meanings, in detailed expositions that have been preserved and come down to us in the form of commentaries.[9]

After we have begun to master the song itself, a second step is to begin to read and ponder it along with these great teachers. How does one use commentaries?[10] Ideally, here too, one might first learn Tamil and Sanskrit (since Sanskrit texts are frequently cited) so as to be able to read the verses with the commentaries, sitting patiently with each verse and each word of each verse, noting how the various commentators tease out meanings line by line, word by word. Here I will simply illustrate this rather arduous endeavor by highlighting some of the insights and themes that come to the fore as the commentators interpreted interesting and key words and lines in 7.9.[11]

In introducing the entire song and commenting in a preliminary way on the claim that "He has made me Himself" (verse 1), Nampillai takes seriously the creative power at work here as the Lord makes the alvar a new being. He refers to the ancient Sanskrit-language *Taittiriya Upanishad* 2.5, "Whoever thinks that Brahman does not exist becomes non-existent; whoever thinks that Brahman does exist, people know that person to exist truly." Equating Brahman, the Ultimate Reality, with God, Nampillai then sees this Upanishadic verse as illustrating perfectly what it means to say that God makes the alvar Himself: one does not truly exist unless one knows God; to know God is to be conformed to God, taken over and made anew by God; if God thus graciously transforms a person, then that person begins to exist.

By me he now sings himself in sweet Tamil, my Lord, my first one, my abiding light (verse 1): Nampillai again cites the Taittiriya, but this time to highlight a contrast. The Taittiriya points out the limitations of language as words fail to express what Brahman is, "Whence words turn back, along with mind," (2.4, 2.9); likewise, the Kena Upanishad 2.3 says, "To whom it is unknown, it is truly known; whoever knows it, that person does not know it." Brahman, the Self, the highest realities are all beyond the grasp of words and mind. By contrast, and without the benefit of Sanskrit erudition, Shatakopan speaks powerfully expressive words that inform us of God's mystery, because it is God who speaks in the alvar's words. The words "my abiding light," Nampillai adds, indicate that the Lord is like a light, always shining, always revealing His beauty. Seeing God's beauty is at the heart of inspiration and revelation, even before ideas and words are heard or enunciated.

[H]e makes me sing sweet songs in my own words (verse 2): The Lord and the alvar become one, and then, although the Lord is the original source of the songs, they become famous as the alvar's words and not as the Lord's. Were it only original thoughts or authoritative words that mattered, then the Lord alone might be praised, not the alvar. But here, by the Lord's choice, the alvar is rightly praised, for the song comes forth from his experience in his human words. The situation is like that of the Bhagavad Gita: Krishna revealed himself to Arjuna and inspired him, but it was Arjuna who gained fame for winning the war by his deeds. God speaks perfectly, but does not worry about who gets the credit.

[H]e came and entered my tongue, he was there from the first, and to his first pure devotees he sang himself (verse 3): There is an unbroken tradition of those who teach after they have been taught, in a lineage reaching from our time back to the alvar and to the Lord who is the first teacher. *Tiruvaymoli* is new and unheard of, but it is deeply connected with a tradition that stretches out before and after it. At the words "Can I ever forget my father?" Nampillai reflects on the unusual phenomenon that although time passes, the alvar is nonetheless increasingly unable to forget what has occurred; the event is so extraordinary that instead of gradually forgetting it as time passes, the alvar remembers all the more clearly what God has done. Time's flow is reversed.

[H]e has become me and he himself faultlessly sings himself in these songs (verse 4): Alavandar—a teacher the generation before Ramanuja—is remembered as teaching that the fact that the Lord can compose through an imperfect human being shows us that God can do anything. But Ramanuja focused on a different nuance: it is easy for a human to err, and easy for God to be perfect, but what is truly marvelous here is that God works so perfectly through an imperfect human person.

[I]t is not by the sweet songs of the best singers that he sings his song about himself (verse 6): Here Nampillai elaborately cites an earlier alvar in order to indicate how Shatakopan is the supreme poet. In the eighth century Bhut Alvar composed one hundred verses in honor of Vishnu. Nampillai refers us to a pair of his verses to elucidate by a kind of prophecy how the Lord has achieved something new with Shatakopan. In verse 74 Bhut Alvar confesses his own spiritual prowess and hard work as a devout poet:

> I have done penances over seven births and always,
> I have these penances, Lord,
> I have composed fine garlands of Tamil for your feet,
> I am great in Tamil, great. (74)

But then, curiously, Bhut Alvar's next verse describes elephants on Venkatam, Vishnu's holy mountain:

> Ichor dripping down, the male elephant stands before the female
> holding out to her some jointed bamboo with honey dripping
>   from it—
> see, it happens on Venkatam,
> the mountain of the Lord whose color mingles with sky. (75)

In Nampillai's view, the unexpected juxtaposition of the two verses compels us to ponder their connection, since it is not possible that they be arbitrarily juxtaposed. To resolve the apparent disjunction one must move toward a deeper insight, which reveals a convincing connection. The prowess of Bhut Alvar announced in verse 74 is not disputed, yet his unusual and sensuous symbolism in verse 75 is taken as pointing to a deeper kind of intimacy with God that goes beyond what Bhut Alvar himself had achieved through his earnest penances. The further and graced moment occurs only in the union of the Lord and Shatakopan. Like elephants in heat, they mingle in a delight beyond the comprehension of the earlier alvars who, though great in poetic skill, still speak of God from a distance. Such poets compose intelligently, but Shatakopan speaks from the force of intimate inner experience where his life and God's, his words and God's, mix inseparably.

[M]y Lord of Vaikunta (verse 7): Periyavacchan Pillai says that although Vishnu is Lord of Vaikunta (or heaven), he becomes involved in the world and experiences suffering and need. This is what occurred in the Ramayana epic, where lord Rama allowed himself to be in difficult situations, especially when his wife Sita was kidnapped. Rama even allowed himself to come to need the help of the monkey king Sugriva in his search to recover Sita. Tiru Koneri Dasai rereads the first line of the verse as if it is the Lord who is saying, "This man is the lord of my Vaikunta," my heaven and bliss. The Lord so identifies with the alvar that the alvar's suffering, bliss, and poetic accomplishment are now his too, the focus of the divine life. God and Shatakopan have a shared experience, which is the story of both of them, and both sing from shared experience, not just the alvar.

[H]e made unlovely me himself (verse 8): Nampillai observes that the alvar is saying he is unlovely for a second time. When this was said first in verse 5—"until he made unlovely me himself"—it referred to the alvar's lack of understanding and desire for God; here in verse 8 it must mean something more, since mere repetition is not likely. Here it must mean that the alvar would not even prepare to awaken a desire for God, unless the Lord instigates him to move in this direction. Nothing happens except by divine initiative; nothing is lovely in itself, but all is lovely when infused by God.

[N]ow I cannot forget how I sing many sweet songs suitable to his excellence (verse 9): According to Pillan, although the Vedas could not speak properly of God, the alvar succeeds in singing many fine and suitable songs about God. Nanjiyar confirms that the alvar is singing again and better what the Vedas had proclaimed earlier; *Tiruvaymoli* succeeds in accomplishing what the Vedas merely attempted.

[T]here is nothing at all I can do for him, neither here nor there (verse 10): Periyavacchan Pillai observes that since the Lord and the alvar have already mingled, the Lord has already become the alvar's "I," and indeed had become so even before the alvar realized this. When the alvar sees this, he also sees that while it would be appropriate to give the Lord everything, in fact there is nothing to be given,

since all belongs to the Lord already. All the alvar or anyone in that position can do is surrender and allow the Lord to act in accord with how he has already acted. Nampillai points to the verse as evidence of the new and liminal situation in the life of the alvar: "I want to give something, yet there is nothing to give." It is persons on the edge of liberation who think this way, Nampillai says, since they are still enough "on this side" to want to give something to God, but they are also sufficiently "on the other side" so as to realize that God is all and all is God's, so that there is nothing that might still be given.

Insights of this sort could be multiplied, but I hope these few examples will illustrate the kind of reflective reading the commentators bring to bear in interpreting *Tiruvaymoli*. Readers might well wish to add the insights they have drawn from reading the verses. Like scriptural commentators everywhere, these Shrivaishnava commentators firmly believe that scripture is inexhaustibly rich in meanings. They continue to delve more deeply into the texts, probing each word for nuances and meanings that become evident only to those who are patient and willing to learn. At this stage, the commentarial insights are often disconnected, momentary, and unsystematized, but key themes successfully come to the fore: divine initiative and creative power, the alvar's sense of unworthiness and yet also acceptance of the divine action, the overflow of mutual delight in words that emerge from both mouths at once. Such examples also tell us about how the Shrivaishnava commentators generated theological and spiritual insights from scripture. We can begin to understand their theology-from-scripture in a way that could never be replicated merely by accepting their conclusions or by comparing them with similar conclusions drawn in the Christian tradition. We must rather read their scripture with them and think through the development of their theology, as if it were our scripture, our tradition, and our theology.

In addition to the elaboration of meaning through word by word commentary, the Shrivaishnava theologians collaborated over several generations in imagining a proper context for the songs of *Tiruvaymoli*, a narrative that could map the development of the alvar's spiritual life in relation to the sequence of one hundred songs.[12] For instance, Periyavacchan Pillai spells out the context for song 7.9 by way of a dialogical back-and-forth that fills in the divine intentions and words presumed to have inspired the human intentions and words: "Before this song the alvar had cried out many times, 'I cannot bear this world; apart from You there is no way to survive it, You alone are my way.

So please break my bond to material nature, since it is an obstacle to my gaining You!'"

The alvar thus presents a desire for liberation and purification that is equated with liberation from the body; this is a standard theme throughout the narrative portions of the commentaries on *Tiruvaymoli*. But it is an equally constant insight that the Lord has other ideas which he patiently intends to teach the alvar:

> The Lord does not immediately make clear His intentions to the alvar. Instead He reveals just a particle of His qualities to him and so brings about in him a total attachment to that small particle. But since the alvar still does not understand the Lord's intention he asks, "If you can give yourself unimpeded and without any obstacle to a few people, what is this idea of keeping me alive, yet without giving Yourself totally to me?"

It turns out that the songs are both the expression of the alvar's anguish and the reason why he is made to continue dwelling in the body:

> The Lord then makes His intention clear by responding, "[During the Mahabharata war] I placed [the dying] Bhishma on a bed of arrows and gave him clarity of vision [so that before dying he could give a final discourse on righteousness]. In the same way I am making you stay in this world until you complete your cycle of songs—for it is that which helps Me and My people survive."

The alvar reacts to the divine initiative in wonder, and the specific result is song 7.9:

> The Lord is the consort of the goddess Shri, has all His desires satisfied, and is the highest of all persons. Nonetheless, He is lacking in one way, i.e., He has not heard all of the alvar's songs, and He wants to complete His perfection by hearing them. The alvar realizes this and is immensely delighted. But he also sees that the Lord is thus putting aside the Vedas, the Ramayana composed by lord Valmiki, the Vishnu Purana composed by lord Parashara, poems by other seers, and even the songs composed by the first alvars "who sang in pure Tamil."[13] Instead, the Lord has taken hold of him and made him compose these songs. He thinks about this great gift and sees that there is no way to give

something in return. He is astounded, and so he sings: "He has exalted me for all time, day after day. . . ."[14]

As the alvar recognizes the gifts he has received—the Lord's attention, and the inspiration to compose songs—he also recognizes with amazement that this creative process is to God's own benefit; the human composition of powerful, lovely songs gives God pleasure that he would not otherwise have. The act of inspiring the alvar contributes to the overall divine plan, for the sake of the world and even for the sake of the Lord's own fulfillment.

Beyond commentary there is more explicit theological development. It is not possible in this brief presentation to explore the further and more systematic development of Shrivaishnava theology in relation to the song, but it is important to note that Shrivaishnava thinkers did explore further levels of rational reflection about the meaning and truth of the song and the array of commentarial insights (even if, as might be expected, it did not develop according to the standards of European Christian systematic theology). I will give two brief examples.

In the fourteenth century Vedanta Deshika argued that the songs of *Tiruvaymoli* explain the attributes of God. In his Dramida Upanisad Tatparya Ratnavali,[15] he links each of *Tiruvaymoli*'s 1102 verses with a particular claim about God. The reader may wish to puzzle through the more and less obvious correlations Deshika makes of divine attributes with the ten primary verses of 7.9: 1) Vishnu is lord, 2) His deeds are marvelous, 3) He makes words blossom forth, 4) He uplifts his people, 5) He is the lord of Vaikunta, 6) He has the power to achieve the impossible, 7) His self is pure, 8) He possesses the discus as His weapon,[16] 9)He is beloved of the daughter of the waters, 10) He is father—and so "He draws together His people in praise of Himself to whom one can give nothing in return." In other works, Deshika will then proceed to defend such claims about God, putting forward his reasons why it makes sense to think of God in this way.[17]

Second, about twenty-five years ago the respected Shrivaishnava commentator Uttamur Viraraghavacharya included in his comment on 7.9.2 a more systematic explanation of the process of inspiration. It occurs in relation to a reflection on the cosmic creative and destructive process wherein gods like Brahma and Shiva create and destroy by the Lord's power, although they think of themselves as acting on their own:

The alvar thinks as follows. Just as Vishnu acts by entering within the deities Brahma and Shiva and working through them, here too my singing is His. He is the inner ruler of all beings, but more than that He enters specially into Brahma and Shiva; so too, He enters into me. Words come flowering forth from my mouth, but I am not their author. The Lord speaks first, I speak after Him. He enters within me and speaks within my heart. I reflect on that inner word by the power of my knowing and then I speak it with my mouth.

In some places He speaks right inside my mouth, and then I speak immediately. He sings repeatedly, and then I sing. It is like when Valmiki spoke the words "Hunter, may you never attain the unchanging state, for you have killed one love-struck Krauncha bird of a pair . . ." as his own words, even though, without his knowledge, it was really Brahma speaking within him.[18] Since I am immersed in the sweet taste of experiencing the Lord, in such instances there is no chance for me to set my mind on speaking.

All the songs are the result of the flow of experience.[19]

Viraraghavacharya's interpretation ably correlates cosmic creation by way of deities, and the composition of *Tiruvaymoli* via Shatakopan; he elegantly sorts out several modes of inspiration, one requiring the alvar's reflection on the inner word, and the other more immediate and intuitive. His reference to Valmiki indicates again the Shrivaishnava concern to link the songs to the tradition, here by finding analogies for the way in which Shatakopan was inspired; he emphasizes the flow of sweet experience out of which the songs arise. We can appreciate this theology of inspiration, even while seeing how it reaches beyond the data of the song, elaborating structures at best implicit in the alvar's own words. Sacred scripture has here provided inspiration for theology, yet has also yielded to it.

This further reflection, of course, goes beyond what the song or even the oldest commentaries have to say, and we need to remain attentive to differences and changes over time. But the theological reception of sacred scripture is of great interest in the comparative context, just as it is in our own tradition, and the comparative project would be incomplete were we to focus solely on scriptural or commentarial texts. By exploring Hindu theological developments, we appreciate better the power of the original and core texts and also create still more possibilities for making intelligent connections between our tradition and the Hindu tradition.

A Christian Context

I have thus far introduced (though only to a limited extent) a Hindu scriptural text and (to a still lesser extent) its reception in its Hindu tradition. In the second part of this reflection I now turn to the question of what Catholic theologians can learn from this particular Hindu tradition of text and commentary.[20] On one level, the practical demands are very similar and straightforward: comparative study is no easier, nor radically different from, other forms of theological reflection. Learning from Hindu scripture and theology is similar to how we might learn from scripture and theology in the Christian tradition. To do comparative work, we need to understand how Catholic theologians have learned from scripture, from pre-modern theology, and from the interplay of scripture and theological reasoning in our own tradition. Indeed, comparative study can help us to raise and review basic questions about how we have used Christian resources in the past, and thus enable us to use them more intelligently today.

On a practical level, I suggest that it is possible to learn from texts like 7.9 by an analogy of scripture, treating the text according to practices deemed appropriate to the reception of Christian scripture, at least as if *Tiruvaymoli* is sacred scripture, whether or not one is willing to accept *Tiruvaymoli* as in fact God's Word. By analogy at least, one can receive and think through scriptural, commentarial, and theological texts from the Hindu and Christian traditions together.

It is worth noting at the start that it is perfectly reasonable for us to be concerned about how to relate 7.9 to the Christian tradition, lest we dilute the value of our own scriptural tradition by a hasty relativism. There are good religious reasons for privileging our own tradition, while respect for our own sacred scripture as God's Word is a respect we share with the Shrivaishnavas. As we have seen, they too labored to figure out how to situate new sacred texts, such as *Tiruvaymoli*, in relation to earlier texts of the orthodox tradition. With them we share a sense that God is one, that God has spoken to us graciously and powerfully in words that are perfect and efficacious. With them, we also share a respect for earlier authors in our tradition whom we do not wish to push aside. At various points both traditions have felt it necessary to make room for new words of God, but nonetheless both have always been concerned to do this in a way that leaves room for the old and continues to respect it. Struggling to make sense of new sacred texts is a concern we and these Hindus share, so it is neither a Christian fixation nor a special sign of Christian distinctiveness that we have this concern. Nonetheless, the concern remains perfectly legitimate.

If we are to become more conscious of the links of 7.9 with the Christian tradition, here too there is a need for patient and careful reflection, attention to what makes sense and what does not, notice of what is similar and what is different. As a starting point, we need to appropriate 7.9 yet again and in a different way, this time by reading it along with some text(s) from the Christian scriptural and theological tradition. For example—by chance, a quite appropriate example—take the psalm reading for Pentecost, from Psalm 104:[21]

> [28]When you give to them, they gather it up;
>   when you open your hand, they are filled
>   with good things.
> [29]When you hide your face, they are dismayed;
>   when you take away their breath, they die
>   and return to their dust.
> [30]When you send forth your spirit, they are created;
>   and you renew the face of the earth.
>
> [31]May the glory of the LORD endure for ever,
>   may the LORD rejoice in his works,
> [32]who looks on the earth and it trembles,
>   who touches the mountains and they smoke!
> [33]I will sing to the LORD as long as I live;
>   I will sing praise to my God while I have being.
> [34]May my discourse be pleasing to him,
>   for I rejoice in the Lord.[22]

It is of course well worth our time to reflect on the psalm passage, and the whole psalm, simply as a treasure of our own scriptural tradition. We can sort out its meaning in the original Hebrew-language context, its interpretation in the Rabbinic tradition, and likewise its role in Christian prayer and worship. We can also reflect on how it appears to us in relation to 7.9, reading back and forth between the traditions as might be exemplified in this pattern:

[28]When you give to them, they gather it up; when you open your hand, they are filled with good things.
[29]When you hide your face, they are dismayed; when you take away their breath, they die and return to their dust.
[30]When you send forth your Spirit, they are created; and you renew the face of the earth.
[31]May the glory of the Lord endure for ever, may the Lord rejoice in his works,
[32]who looks on the earth and it trembles, who touches the mountains and they smoke!
[33]I will sing to the Lord as long as I live; I will sing praise to my God while I have being.
[34]May my discourse be pleasing to him, for I rejoice in the Lord.

[1]He has exalted me for all time, day after day he has made me himself
and by me he now sings himself in sweet Tamil
my Lord, my first one, my abiding light—what shall I sing of him?
[8]Will I ever have enough of praising
the Lord whose lovely hand holds the discus,
will I ever have enough if earth and sky and water should all melt together
and I should drink them up?
he made unlovely me himself, he gained excellence for himself through me,
such is his nature.
[10]He helps me, so I thought I would give my life to him in return,
but then I reconsidered, since that too is totally his;
this father sings himself in sweet songs by me,
there is nothing at all I can do for him, neither here nor there.
[11]"Neither here nor there can anything exist without the Holy Lord."
Shatakopan from glorious Kuruhur
was the sort to see this, and so he sang in this way these ten verses from his thousand, and so however you sing them, their fruit is bliss.

Just as the columns are difficult to read together and demand that the eye move back and forth in varying patterns, so too in comparative reflection we must find strategies for reading two texts from two traditions without confusing them entirely. By comparative reading we introduce 7.9 into the context of reflection on a biblical text, deepen our reading of the Hindu song in that context, and yet see the psalm differently as well. This complex reading illumines both texts by taking advantage of the creative tension between them. Their remarkable assonance need not be spoiled, however, if we also notice interesting and important differences between the two texts. But I must leave this comparative exercise to my readers.[23]

Similarly, learning from sacred scripture can lead to learning from Hindu and Christian commentarial and theological texts read together. We can re-read relevant texts from the Christian tradition, first for their own sake, and then in relation to the commentaries on *Tiruvaymoli*. As an easily available instance, I recommend St. Augustine's commentary on Psalm 104. While space does not allow extensive quotation from his commentary, here, for example, is what Augustine has to say on several of the psalm verses.[24] At verse 30, he contrasts the (material and spiritual) poverty of God's people, as actors and speakers who have nothing of their own to do or say, except to allow God's power to operate in their lives:

> When you send forth your Spirit, they are created. You shall take away their spirit, and send forth Your own: You shall take away their spirit: they shall have no spirit of their own. Are they then forsaken? Blessed are the poor in spirit; but they are not forsaken, for theirs is the Kingdom of God. (Matthew 5.3) They refused to have a spirit of their own: they shall have the Spirit of God. Such were our Lord's words to the future martyrs: When they take you and deliver you up, take no thought how or what you shall speak. For it is not you that speak, but the Spirit of your Father which speaks in you. (Matthew 10.19-20) Attribute not your courage to yourselves. If it is yours, He says, and not Mine, it is obstinacy, not courage. For we are His workmanship, says the Apostle, created unto good works. (Ephesians 2.10) From His Spirit we have received grace, that we may live unto righteousness: for it is He that justifies the ungodly.

Unsurprisingly, Augustine emphasizes the infusion of spirit/Spirit, which effects a new creation even in the face of intensely felt human failure and inadequacy:

> When you take away their breath, they die and return to their dust. When you send forth your Spirit, they are created; and you renew the face of the earth. That is, with new men, confessing themselves to have been justified, not righteous of their own power, so that the grace of God is in them. . . . What then? When He has taken away our spirit, we shall be turned again into dust, to our edification beholding our weakness, that when we receive His Spirit we may be refreshed.

At verse 31 Augustine turns to the results of this divine initiative, pointing to the psalmist's new identity, re-created toward seeing the world from God's point of view; all action and speech are the work and word of God:

> May the glory of the Lord endure for ever. Not yours, not mine, not his, nor hers; not for a season. May the glory be the Lord's, not for a season, but for ever. May the Lord rejoice in His works. Not in yours, as if they were yours: because if your works are evil, it is through your iniquity; if good, it is through the grace of God.

At verse 34 Augustine observes how the psalmist is enabled to respond to God in words of joy and praise that reflect God's speaking in and through him by God's own word/Word:

> May my discourse be pleasing to him, for I rejoice in the Lord. What is it to discourse with God other than the confession of sins? . . . Unfold yourself to Him who knows you, that He may unfold Himself to you who know not Him. Let my discourse be pleasing to Him. Behold, it is your discourse that pleases the Lord; the offering of your humility, the tribulation of your heart, the holocaust of your life, this pleases God. But what is pleasing to yourself? I rejoice in the Lord. This is that discourse which I meant, of God and yourself: show yourself to Him who knows you, and He shows Himself unto you who know not him.

Human words and the divine Word merge into one act of confession, which is both humble admission and selfless praise: "Pleasing unto Him is your confession: sweet unto you is His grace. He has spoken Himself unto you. How? By the Word. What Word? Christ."

In commenting on the psalm, Augustine highlights themes similar to those we found in the Hindu commentarial readings of 7.9: the necessary complete surrender to God; the simultaneous realization of one's unworthiness and the enablement to speak freely in God's name; the deepening of self-awareness that bears fruition in continuous praise of God. Whatever the differences in traditions, similar sacred texts generate similar theological reflections. Neither tradition has a monopoly on scriptural testimony to inspiration or on a theology of inspiration. But, again, such insights ought not to be put forward glibly, without the patient study and acquired skill they demand. To appropriate more deeply 7.9 and Psalm 104 and the traditions of commentary on both, we must again be willing to re-read Augustine and the Hindu texts in light of one another, moving back and forth between the scriptural and commentarial texts, and examining both together:

When you send forth your Spirit, they are created. You shall take away their spirit, and send forth Your own: You shall take away their spirit: they shall have no spirit of their own. Are they then forsaken? Blessed are the poor in spirit; but they are not forsaken, for theirs is the Kingdom of God. (Matthew 5.3) They refused to have a spirit of their own: they shall have the Spirit of God. Such were our Lord's words to the future martyrs: When they take you and deliver you up, take no thought how or what you shall speak. For it is not you that speak, but the Spirit of your Father which speaks in you.

He helps me so I thought I would give my life to him in return but then I reconsidered since that too is totally his: the substance of the self is eternal, defined by knowledge and bliss, and worthy of praise. So what does it mean to give this to another? The alvar has explained this fundamentally earlier when he said, Who possesses the highest, unsurpassable good? that One.[25] Previously, he gave his self, and during his time of error it seemed as if it was he who was surrendering it. But when he recognized the Lord's help for him, and then sought out what he could give in return, he

(Matthew 10.19-20) Attribute not your courage to yourselves. If it is yours, He says, and not Mine, it is obstinacy, not courage. For we are His workmanship, says the Apostle, created unto good works. (Ephesians 2.10) From His Spirit we have received grace, that we may live unto righteousness: for it is He that justifies the ungodly.

When you take away their breath, they die and return to their dust. When you send forth your Spirit, they are created; and you renew the face of the earth. That is, with new men, confessing themselves to have been justified, not righteous of their own power, so that the grace of God is in them. . . . What then? When He has taken away our spirit, we shall be turned again into dust, to our edification beholding our weakness, that when we receive His Spirit we may be refreshed.

May the glory of the Lord endure for ever. Not yours, not mine, not his, nor hers; not for a season. May the glory be the Lord's, not for a season, but for ever. May the Lord rejoice in His works. Not in yours, as if they were yours: because if your works are evil, it is through your iniquity; if good, it is through the grace of God. (Augustine on Psalm 104)

became confused. He saw that it was during his time of error that he could [think of] giving his self. Once things became clear, he could no longer say, "I have given my very being to Him. From time without beginning he has seized my self." Once this becomes clear, to say that "I have given the substance of my self" is simply to act in accord with that ancient seizure.

. . . It was only as long as there seemed to be evident excellence in his heart that he could speak of his own being as his own. As it says, [My self] was surrendered by me . . . but what is it that I could surrender?[26] As the alvar himself says, I ended up giving my own self—but who is my self, who am I?[27]

. . . He is totally dependent on the Lord, since neither his surrender of his self nor his remembrance of what the Lord did is his own achievement. (Nampillai at verse 10)

Just as one reads back and forth between Psalm 104 and *Tiruvaymoli* 7.9, one also reads back and forth between theological reflections on those scriptural texts, perhaps with close attention to the ideas and methods by which theological insights are derived from the scriptural texts. Our examination of this example of a psalm and its reception by Augustine, re-read in a comparative context, obviously requires of us an equally slow and patient process of remembering the Christian tradition of theologizing from commentary on scripture and then using it anew. This slow process is necessary, since it is on this basis that one can properly begin to read together the Christian and Hindu traditions of sacred scripture and theology based on that scripture. One can then become alert to what is new and different but also to what is (perhaps only implicitly at first) familiar in that other, when the other tradition may be a tradition of scripture and theology very much like our own. With patient reflection we learn to see similar appreciations of divine initative, human dependence on God, the entering of God into the human, and the composition of texts that are both human words and divine speech. A new theological foundation has been laid.

A New Context

Once we have engaged patiently in familiarizing ourselves with Hindu scripture, commentary, and theology, and become accustomed to the process of reading back and forth between these resources and comparable texts of the Christian tradition, we become ready to begin drawing our own Christian theological conclusions. This consequent theologizing remains an experimental process in which we theologize only experimentally, noticing provisional theological conclusions that may or may not work, and, if possible, understanding why this is so. We learn to look more deeply into our own tradition, and then across boundaries into the other, and so are educated theologically in a new and richly complicated sense.

In the final section of this essay, I identify a few theological insights we should be able to accept at least as viable bases for further reflection and experimentation.[28] In each of the following paragraphs I draw theological insights that I have gathered primarily from reading 7.9 and its tradition along with the psalm and St. Augustine, but I deliberately speak only in general terms—referring explicitly to neither the Hindu nor the Christian texts—with the expectation that the insights I offer will make some sense at least in both the Catholic and Shrivaishnava traditions, perhaps for different reasons and with different nuances. If it appears that there is nothing dramatically new in what I have to say, that in itself should not be a major problem. After all, something merely novel may not be worth our attention, and rarely are theological claims, even within the Christian tradition, actually new. If my reflections, composed as it were on the edge between the traditions, affirm what we already in some way know from the Christian tradition, even this fact may re-create our own theology and encourage us to think differently about what we are doing when we theologize.

Inspiration surely has strong cognitive, volitional, and linguistic elements that are richly defined by various contextual possibilities requiring close analysis. But the event of inspiration and the composition of sacred texts are first of all acts of God, who chooses graciously to enter into only some individuals, to be sure, but for the sake of all. God enters such persons and takes possession of them, their limitations and resistances notwithstanding. Although this occurs in a way that leaves the person's identity and freedom intact, the divine entering is a deeply significant event that transforms the person and effects a new creation. Whatever the precedents in tradition that endure, the initiative of God is original and creative, a gracious event that makes the recipient a new being, as it were summoned forth from nowhere and returned to the community, to the surprise of all. God becomes deeply engaged in the life and experience of the newly inspired and newly created person; there is an intimate mingling of persons in which God shows forth beauty and evokes wonder in the face of the divinely beautiful.

The intense divine involvement, manifestation of divine beauty, and mingling of selves deeply affects the human recipient, who speaks freshly and differently. The person into whom God has entered is filled with intense feelings of unworthiness: he or she is not divine, not ready for the encounter with God, and his or her word is definitely not the divine word. At the same time, though, recognition of unexpected inspiration fosters an increase of marvel, a sense of being entered by God, and one becomes a voice for God even if still speaking merely with a human voice. This admission intensifies memory, as one hearkens back ever more constantly to the starting point where and when God entered one's life. Time passes, but we remember more and more of what God has done, not less. If tradition is a kind of communal remembering, the new experience of God also makes possible a deeper and richer sense of tradition, a more complete grasp of it than had previously been possible. Opened to God's creative power, we have a more vivid and grateful sense of the history we share with God; we remember it more vividly than could those who have gone before us.

The result of all this is a paradoxical cooperation of two tongues, divine and human, both involved in proclaiming inspired words that are both divine and human compositions. These words are heard twice and simultaneously, as it were, as neither voice is drowned out by the other. Because inspired words remain the composition of a human singer, they are thoroughly human words that need to be interpreted as such; yet they are God's words, which need to be received without reservation. The trick in interpretation then is to hear-twice and read-twice, assimilating the full force of the text's double claim that it is in a way addressed to God while yet being God's word to the community.

Because the words spoken by the person entered and re-created by God are the product of divine speech, always and everywhere resonant with divine presence, they are endlessly revelatory of God, and not just when something novel is said or when a name or names of God are explicitly mentioned. A path of discovery is opened up that urges close reading and close engagement, if God is to be found in every word of everything that is said in sacred scripture. This pervasive presence is more instructive and illuminating, and vastly more powerful, than the cautious notion that God plays a role behind the text or stands simply as the text's topic. The events of inspiration and internal transformation result in inspired/inspiring compositions that everywhere offer particular insights into the nature of God and into how God is now to be thought of. God is everywhere in the text, seemingly imperfectly and unevenly there, yet always liable to be revealed and heard. The speaking itself is a divine act. God speaks in human words that are suddenly not just ours, human words that are suddenly also strange, divine words. When received and interiorized, they speak God powerfully and replicate in the experience of the hearer the same experience that occurs in the speaker(s).

In the mingling of the divine and human, God entrusts God's own self into human hands. Although God speaks and is spoken about by every word, God also remains hidden in human words, permitting humans to speak for God. God freely chooses to be self-forgetful, to become "lost" in and behind human words, not seeking credit. God may choose to remain anonymous and unheard, hidden in all the things that people say, inside and outside one's own tradition. For while it may be of importance to ask whose words are most important, which scriptural texts are more immediate and perfect expressions of the divine self, and who—and which community—is to get the credit for communicating most clearly the divine speech, God may be less concerned about these questions than we are.

Finally, one can acknowledge the promise offered to the wider community by the experience and speech of persons graciously inspired by God. The inspiration and resultant speech are for the sake of the community that receives the word, hears and enjoys it, but then too learns to reproduce it, celebrate it by further performance, and pass it along to new generations. The divine speech in human speech forms and nourishes a community of believers. Sacred scriptures trace out a way to God that members of the community can follow as they advance spiritually: "however you sing them, their fruit is bliss."

However You Sing Them, Their Fruit Is Bliss

While I have not attempted to describe thoroughly the range of Hindu views of sacred scripture and theology, and likewise have not attempted to state decisively what Christians are to learn from 7.9 and its commentaries, I do hope to have clarified how we might go about this learning and how we might subsequently engage in Christian theologizing on the basis of that learning. The sum total of these points may prompt us to a new-yet-old recognition of how God's word is yet also a human word, how one can imagine God—who speaks to us specifically and perfectly (as both Christians and Shrivaishnavas would agree)—and who also speaks to other people in words they can understand (as both Christians and Shrivaishnavas would agree), and how we can find ourselves addressed by what God has said to those other people in words meant for them but also then for us. God speaks to us perfectly well in our own tradition, but we may also listen in on God speaking to us through other mouths.

If the ideas I have been suggesting have some worth, 7.9 would then become part of Christian theological reflection, analogously our own sacred scripture, in other words, Shatakopan voicing God to us.

If all of this is true enough to merit theological attention and further discussion among the theologians who have patiently learned to learn even from outside their own tradition, then the further work of stating again the nature of the scripture-theology relationship can begin. But that too will be a long process, rooted in re-reading the old and the new and in further small experiments in comparative study.

It should also be obvious that however rich and interesting my examples have been, they are all drawn from just one Hindu text understood in its traditional commentarial context. Hindu India, India more broadly, and then other traditions large and small around the world, are likewise filled with innumerable other examples. The process exemplified here merely indicates a tiny portion of the project to be undertaken. While it is perfectly possible to discuss sacred scripture and theology without reference to India at all, in the end it would be foolhardy to proceed as if we can understand even our own faith on our own, as if God has nothing to teach us in other traditions, in human voices from other places. In case God is speaking, should we not listen?

Notes

[1] For aspects of scripture and its theological reception in India, see, for instance, Jeffrey Timm, ed., *Texts in Context: Traditional Hermeneutics in South Asia* (Albany: State University of New York Press, 1992). On the Hindu understanding of the theological issues related to canon formation, see Francis X. Clooney, *Hindu God, Christian God: How Reason Helps Break Down the Boundaries between Religions* (New York: Oxford University Press, 2001), chapter 5.

[2] Heaven, the place of divine glory.

[3] Shri, Lakshmi, is the eternal consort of Vishnu.

[4] Shatakopan's birthplace, also known as Alvartirunagari.

[5] All translations from the Tamil here and throughout are my own.

[6] The Vaishnavas and Shaivas are devoted respectively to Lord Vishnu and Lord Shiva as the supreme deities.

[7] For a fuller exposition of the themes and styles of *Tiruvaymoli*, see Francis X. Clooney, *Seeing through Texts: Doing Theology among the Srivaisnavas of South India* (Albany: State University of New York Press, 1996), chapter 2.

[8] On the use of *Tiruvaymoli* in the Shrivaishnava community, see Vasudha Narayanan, *The Vernacular Veda: Revelation, Recitation, and Ritual* (Columbia, South Carolina: University of South Carolina Press, 1994).

[9] Needless to say, there were also oral expositions, mentioned in the commentaries, that were not written down and have not directly survived. On the commentarial tradition, see Clooney, *Seeing through Texts;* Narayanan, *The Ver-*

nacular Veda; and also Vasudha Naryanan and John Carman, *The Tamil Veda: Pillan's Interpretation of the Tiruvaymoli* (Chicago: University of Chicago Press, 1989).

[10]An informative recent resource on the tradition of commentary is Paul Griffiths's *Religious Reading: The Place of Reading in the Practice of Religion* (New York: Oxford University Press, 1999).

[11]In what follows I most commonly, except where noted, am using Nampillai's rather comprehensive commentary.

[12]See Clooney, *Seeing through Texts*, chapter 3.

[13]This praise of the earliest alvars is from Tirumankai Alvar's *Periya Tirumoli* 2.8.2.

[14]Manavala Mamuni (fourteenth century) puts it this way: "'Why did you put me here?' I asked, and the Lord said, 'So that you will sing beautifully and give pleasure to me and my devotees.' There is pleasure for everyone in the singing of Maran (the alvar) who could give nothing in return."

[15]"Necklace of Meanings in the Southern Upanishad," meaning in *Tiruvaymoli*.

[16]The discus traditionally signifies divine power.

[17]For an example of how Deshika makes these further arguments in defense of Shrivaishnava claims about God, see Francis X. Clooney, "Vedanta Desika's 'Definition of the Lord' (Isvarapariccheda) and the Hindu Argument about Ultimate Reality," *Ultimate Realities*, ed. Robert Neville (Albany: State University of New York Press, 2000), 95-123.

[18]In a famous paradigm of inspiration, Valmiki, though not previously a poet, began to compose instinctively when he saw a hunter kill one of a pair of love birds. Once he discovered his ability to compose, he went on to compose the entire epic Ramayana.

[19]See Uttamur Viraraghavacharya, *Prabandha Raksha*, vol. 4 (Chennai: The Vishistadvaita Pracharini Sabha, 1975), the section on 7.9.2.

[20]I concede, of course, that everything I have written thus far in this essay has been filtered through my own Catholic sensibilities.

[21]This presentation occurred on May 31; June 3, 2001; the last day of the meeting was Pentecost Sunday.

[22]I have used the New Revised Standard Version translation, with several modifications.

[23]On this method of comparison, see Clooney, *Seeing through Texts*, chapter 5.

[24]Since it is available on the web in the Christian Classics Ethereal Library (http://www.ccel.org), I have used the 1854 translation of Augustine's commentary, though making small adaptations in the style of English used: *Expositions on the Book of Psalms by St. Augustine*, six volumes, trans. H. M. Wilkins (Oxford: John Henry Parker, 1853). Psalm 104 is found in volume 5 of the *Expositions*, which in turn is volume 37 in the entire series, A Library of Fathers of the Holy Catholic Church. (Oxford: John Henry Parker, 1853).

[25]*Tiruvaymoli* 1.1.1.

[26]Alavandar's *Stotraratna*, verses 52-53. My translation from the Sanskrit.

[27]*Tiruvaymoli* 2.3.4.

[28]It is important to note that the approach I am suggesting is intentionally differ-ent from—even if complementary to—the a priori Christian reflection on what other religions might mean for Christians, which occupies the theology of reli-gions discipline. Rather than beginning with a search for Christian resources that would make possible and give permission for learning from a non-Christian tradi-tion, I begin with the learning. But I invite theologians of religions to assess from their perspective what one accomplishes by the approach I take.

Contributors

Regina A. Boisclair is Associate Professor of Religious Studies and Cardinal Newman Chair of Catholic Theology at Alaska Pacific University, Anchorage, Alaska. Her current research interest focuses on hermeneutical aspects of the three-year lectionary.

Jason Bourgeois serves on the faculty at St. Mary's University of Minnesota. His doctoral dissertation at Marquette University was devoted to "The Aesthetic Hermeneutics of Hans-Georg Gadamer and Hans Urs von Balthasar: A Comparative Analysis."

Russell A. Butkus received his Ph.D. from Boston College and is Associate Professor of Theology at the University of Portland, Oregon, where he is the current chair of the Department of Theology and associate director of the Environmental Studies Program. He has recently contributed to the volume *All Creation Is Groaning: An Interdisciplinary Vision for Life in a Sacred Universe*, which he co-edited with Carol J. Dempsey, OP.

Francis X. Clooney, SJ, Professor of Theology at Boston College, did his doctoral work at the University of Chicago. His pioneering work in comparative theology has yielded eight books, among them the prize-winning *Seeing Through Texts: Doing Theology Among the Srivaishnas of South India* (SUNY Press, 1996). He was founding president of the Society for Hindu-Christian Studies.

Carol J. Dempsey, OP, Associate Professor of Theology at the University of Portland, Oregon, received her Ph.D. in Biblical Studies from The Catholic University of America. She is the author of two books, *Hope Amid the Ruins: The Ethics of Israel's Prophets* and *The Prophets: A Liberation Critical Reading*, and is a contributor to and co-editor of *All Creation Is Groaning: An Interdisciplinary*

Vision for Life in a Sacred Universe, and an associate editor of the *Catholic Biblical Quarterly*. She is currently working on a manuscript on biblical justice, and a commentary on *Isaiah 1-39*.

James M. Donohue, CR, holds a doctorate from The Catholic University of America and teaches at Mount St. Mary's College, Emmitsburg, Maryland. His recent articles on the Rite of the Commendation of the Dying have appeared in the *Proceedings of the North American Academy of Liturgy* and in *Liturgical Ministry*.

Diana L. Hayes is Associate Professor of Systematic Theology at Georgetown University, where she specializes in liberation theologies in the United States. She holds a Juris Doctor degree as well as a Ph.D. in Religious Studies and the Doctor of Sacred Theology degree, both from the Catholic University of Louvain (Belgium). She is the author of five books and was recently awarded the U.S. Catholic 2001 Award for furthering the role of women in the church.

William P. Loewe, whose Ph.D. is from Marquette University, is author of *The College Student's Introduction to Christology*. Current president of the College Theology Society, he teaches at The Catholic University of America and writes on christology, soteriology, and Lonergan studies.

Amy-Jill Levine is E. Rhodes and Leona B. Carpenter Professor of New Testament Studies and Director of the Carpenter Program in Religion, Gender, and Sexuality at Vanderbilt University Divinity School. Her current projects include the editing of the twelve-volume series, *The Feminist Companions to the New Testament and Early Christian Literature* and the completion of a volume on images of women in the Old Testament Apocrypha.

Patricia McDonald, SHCJ, is Associate Professor of Theology at Mount Saint Mary's College, Emmitsburg, Maryland. She received her Ph.D. in biblical studies from The Catholic University of America. She has published articles on a variety of New Testament topics, and her current book project is titled *The Peaceable Bible*.

Kathleen M. O'Connor is Professor of Old Testament Language, Literature, and Exegesis at Columbia Theological Seminary in Decatur, Georgia. She has just published a book titled *Lamentations and the Tears of the World*. She is also the author of *The*

Wisdom Literature, and *The Confessions of Jeremiah* and co-editor of *Troubling Jeremiah*. Dr. O'Connor holds a Ph.D. from Princeton Theological Seminary and is an editor for the Abingdon Old Testament Commentary Series.

Maria Pascuzzi is Assistant Professor of Theology at the University of San Diego, where she has taught for the past two years. She obtained her Licentiate in Sacred Scripture at the Pontifical Biblical Institute and her doctorate at the Gregorian University in 1997. Dr. Pascuzzi's area of specialization is the Pauline Corpus. She is currently writing a commentary on 1-2 Corinthians for the Collegeville Bible Commentary Series.

Terrence W. Tilley, Ph.D. from the Graduate Theological Union at Berkeley, is Chair and Professor in the Department of Religious Studies at the University of Dayton. Past president of the College Theology Society and recipient of several awards for teaching and scholarship, he is the author of six books and numerous articles. His most recent book is *Inventing Catholic Tradition.*

John Topel, SJ, is Professor of Biblical Theology at Seattle University. He holds master's degrees in Philosophy, Systematic Theology, and Biblical Exegesis and a Ph.D. in Religious Studies. Professor Topel is the author of *Children of a Compassionate God: A Theological Exegesis of Luke's Sermon on the Plain* and *The Way to Peace.*

Daniel Van Slyke, who received his doctorate in historical theology from St. Louis University, teaches in the Department of Theology and Philosophy at Caldwell College in Caldwell, New Jersey.